THE DAILY STUDY BIBLE

THE LETTERS OF JAMES AND PETER

REVISED EDITION

THE LETTERS OF
JAMES
AND
PETER

REVISED EDITION

WILLIAM BARCLAY

THE SAINT ANDREW PRESS
EDINBURGH

TO
J.M.
ON WHOSE STAFF
IT WAS MY PRIVILEGE TO SERVE
IN GRATITUDE FOR HELP AND GUIDANCE
SO OFTEN AND SO GRACIOUSLY GIVEN

Published by
THE SAINT ANDREW PRESS
121 George Street, Edinburgh

©William Barclay 1976
First Edition 1958
Revised Edition 1976
Reprinted 1979, 1981, 1983, 1986, 1987, 1990

For copyright reasons not for sale in the USA or Canada

ISBN 0 7152 0283 9

Printed in Great Britain by Bell and Bain Ltd., Glasgow

GENERAL INTRODUCTION

The Daily Study Bible series has always had one aim—to convey the results of scholarship to the ordinary reader. A. S. Peake delighted in the saying that he was a "theological middleman", and I would be happy if the same could be said of me in regard to these volumes. And yet the primary aim of the series has never been academic. It could be summed up in the famous words of Richard of Chichester's prayer—to enable men and women "to know Jesus Christ more clearly, to love him more dearly, and to follow him more nearly".

It is all of twenty years since the first volume of *The Daily Study Bible* was published. The series was the brain-child of the late Rev. Andrew McCosh, M.A., S.T.M., the then Secretary and Manager of the Committee on Publications of the Church of Scotland, and of the late Rev. R. G. Macdonald, O.B.E., M.A., D.D., its Convener.

It is a great joy to me to know that all through the years *The Daily Study Bible* has been used at home and abroad, by minister, by missionary, by student and by layman, and that it has been translated into many different languages. Now, after so many printings, it has become necessary to renew the printer's type and the opportunity has been taken to restyle the books, to correct some errors in the text and to remove some references which have become outdated. At the same time, the Biblical quotations within the text have been changed to use the Revised Standard Version, but my own original translation of the New Testament passages has been retained at the beginning of each daily section.

There is one debt which I would be sadly lacking in courtesy if I did not acknowledge. The work of revision and correction has been done entirely by the Rev. James Martin, M.A., B.D., minister of High Carntyne Church, Glasgow. Had it not been for him this task would never have been undertaken, and it is

impossible for me to thank him enough for the selfless toil he
has put into the revision of these books.

It is my prayer that God may continue to use *The Daily
Study Bible* to enable men better to understand His word.

Glasgow   **WILLIAM BARCLAY**

CONTENTS

CONTENTS

THE LETTER OF JAMES

INTRODUCTION TO THE
LETTER OF JAMES

James is one of the books which had a very hard fight to get
into the New Testament. Even when it did come to be regarded
as Scripture, it was spoken of with a certain reserve and
suspicion, and even as late as the sixteenth century Luther
would gladly have banished it from the New Testament
altogether.

THE DOUBTS OF THE FATHERS

In the Latin-speaking part of the Church it is not until the
middle of the fourth century that *James* emerges in the writings
of the fathers. The first list of New Testament books ever to
be compiled is the Muratorian Canon, which dates to about
A.D. 170, and *James* is absent from it. Tertullian, writing in
the middle of the third century, is an immense quoter of
Scripture; he has 7,258 quotations from the New Testament,
but never one from *James*. The first appearance of *James* in
Latin is in a Latin manuscript called the Codex Corbeiensis,
which dates to about A.D. 350. This manuscript attributes the
authorship of the book to James the son of Zebedee; and
includes it, not with the universally acknowledged New Testament books, but with a collection of religious tracts written by
the early fathers. *James* has now emerged, but it is accepted
with a certain reservation. The first Latin writer to quote James
verbatim is Hilary of Poitiers in a work *On the Trinity,* written
about A.D. 357.

If, then, *James* was so late in emerging in the Latin Church
and if, when it did emerge, it was still regarded with some
uncertainty, how did it become integrated into the New
Testament? The moving influence was that of Jerome, for he
unhesitatingly included *James* in his Vulgate version of the
New Testament. But even then there is an accent of doubt. In
his book *On Famous Men,* Jerome writes, "James, who is called
the brother of the Lord . . . wrote only one epistle, which is
one of the seven catholic epistles, and which, some people say,

was issued by someone else under James's name." Jerome fully accepted the letter as Scripture, but he felt that there was some doubt as to who the writer was. The doubt was finally set at rest by the fact that Augustine fully accepted *James,* and was not in doubt that the James in question was the brother of our Lord.

James was late in emerging in the Latin Church; for long there was a kind of question mark against it; but Jerome's inclusion of it in the Vulgate and Augustine's full acceptance of it, brought it in the end, albeit after a struggle, full recognition.

THE SYRIAN CHURCH

One would have thought that the Syrian Church would have been the first to accept *James,* if it was really written in Palestine and was really the work of the brother of our Lord; but in the Syrian Church there was the same oscillation. The official New Testament of the Syrian Church is called the Peshitto. This was to the Syrian Church what the Vulgate was to the Latin Church. It was made by Rabbula, the Bishop of Edessa, about A.D. 412 and in it for the first time *James* was translated into Syriac. Up to that time there was no Syriac version of the book, and up to A.D. 451 there is no trace of *James* in Syriac religious literature. After that *James* was widely enough accepted, but as late as A.D. 545 Paul of Nisibis was still questioning its right to be in the New Testament. It was not, in fact, until midway through the eighth century that the great authority of John of Damascus did for *James* in the Syrian Church what Augustine had done for it in the Latin.

THE GREEK CHURCH

Although *James* emerged sooner in the Greek-speaking Church than it did in the Latin and Syrian, it was none the less late in making a definite appearance. The first writer to quote it by name is Origen, head of the school of Alexandria. Writing almost midway through the third century, he says,

"If faith is called faith, but exists apart from works, such a faith is dead, as we read in the letter which is currently reported to be by James." It is true that in other works he quotes it as being without doubt by James and shows that he believes James to be the brother of our Lord; but once again there is the accent of doubt. Eusebius, the great scholar of Caesarea, investigated the position of the various books in the New Testament or on its fringe midway through the fourth century. He classes *James* amongst the books which are "disputed"; and he writes of it: "The first of the epistles called Catholic is said to be his (James's); but it must be noted that some regard it as spurious; and it is certainly true that very few of the ancient writers mention it." Here again is the accent of doubt. Eusebius himself accepted *James* but he was well aware that there were those who did not. The turning-point in the Greek-speaking Church came in A.D. 367. In that year Athanasius issued his famous Easter Letter in Egypt. Its purpose was to inform his people what books were Scripture and what were not, because apparently their reading had become too wide, or at least, too many books were being regarded as Holy Writ. In that Letter *James* was included without qualification; and its position was thenceforth safe.

So, then, in the early church no one really questioned the value of *James*; but in every branch of it it was late in emerging and had to go through a period when its right to be considered a New Testament book was under dispute.

In fact the history of *James* is still to be seen in its position in the Roman Catholic Church. In 1546 the Council of Trent once and for all laid down the Roman Catholic Bible. A list of books was given to which none could be added and from which none could be subtracted, and which had to be read in the Vulgate Version and in no other. The books were divided into two classes; those which were *proto-canonical,* that is to say, those which had been unquestioningly accepted from the beginning; and those which were *deutero-canonical,* that is to say, those which only gradually won their way into the New Testament. Although the Roman Catholic

Church never had any doubts about *James,* it is none the less in the second class that it is included.

LUTHER AND JAMES

In our own day it is true to say that *James,* at least for most people, does not occupy a position in the forefront of the New Testament. Few would mention it in the same breath as *John* or *Romans,* or *Luke* or *Galatians.* There is still for many a kind of reservation about it. Why should that be? It cannot have to do with the doubt about *James* in the early church, for the history of the New Testament books in these distant days is not known to many people in the modern Church. The reason lies in this. In the Roman Catholic Church the position of *James* was finally settled by the Edict of the Council of Trent; but in the Protestant Church its history continued to be troubled, and indeed, became even more troubled, because Luther attacked it and would have ejected it from the New Testament altogether. In his printing of the German New Testament Luther had a contents page with the books set out and numbered. At the end of the list there was a little group, separate from the others and with no numbers assigned to them. That group comprised *James, Jude, Hebrews* and *Revelation.* These were books which he held to be secondary.

Luther was specially severe on *James,* and the adverse judgment of a great man on any book can be a millstone round its neck for ever. It is in the concluding paragraph of his *Preface to the New Testament* that there stands Luther's famous verdict on James:

In sum: the gospel and the first epistle of St. John, St. Paul's epistles, especially those to the Romans, Galatians and Ephesians; and St. Peter's first epistle, are the books which show Christ to you. They teach everything you need to know for your salvation, even if you were never to see or hear any other book or hear any other teaching. In comparison with these the epistle of James is an *epistle full of straw,* because it contains nothing evangelical. But more about this in other prefaces.

As he promised, Luther developed this verdict in the *Preface to the Epistles of St. James and St. Jude*. He begins: "I think highly of the epistle of *James,* and regard it as valuable although it was rejected in early days. It does not expound human doctrines, but lays much emphasis on God's law. Yet to give my own opinion, without prejudice to that of anyone else, I do not hold it to be of apostolic authorship." He then goes on to give his reasons for this rejection.

First, in direct opposition to Paul and the rest of the Bible, it ascribes justification to works, quoting Abraham wrongly as one who was justified by his works. This in itself proves that the epistle cannot be of apostolic origin.

Second, not once does it give to Christians any instruction or reminder of the Passion, Resurrection, or Spirit of Christ. It mentions Christ only twice. Then Luther goes on to state his own principle for testing any book: "The true touchstone for testing any book is to discover whether it emphasises the prominence of Christ or not. . . . What does not teach Christ is not apostolic, not even if taught by Peter or Paul. On the other hand what does preach Christ is apostolic, even if Judas, Annas, Pilate, or Herod does it." On that test *James* fails. So Luther goes on: "The epistle of *James* however only drives you to the law and its works. He mixes one thing to another to such an extent that I suspect some good and pious man assembled a few things said by disciples of the apostles, and put them down in black and white; or perhaps the epistle was written by someone else who made notes of a sermon of his. He calls the law a law of freedom (*James* 1: 25; 2: 12), although St. Paul calls it a law of slavery, wrath, death, and sin" (*Galatians* 3: 23 f.; *Romans* 4: 15; 7: 10 f.).

So Luther comes to his conclusion: "In sum: he wishes to guard against those who depended on faith without going on to works, but he had neither the spirit, nor the thought, nor the eloquence equal to the task. He does violence to Scripture, and so contradicts Paul and all Scripture. He tries to accomplish by emphasising law what the apostles bring about by attracting man to love. I therefore refuse him a place among the writers of the true canon of my Bible; but I would not prevent anyone else placing him or raising him where he likes, for the epistle contains many excellent passages. One man does not count as a man even in the eyes of the world; how then shall this single and isolated writer count against Paul and all the rest of the Bible?"

Luther does not spare *James*; and it may be that once we have studied the book we may think that for once he allowed personal prejudice to injure sound judgment.

Such, then, is the troubled history of *James*. Now we must try to answer the questions it poses regarding authorship and date.

THE IDENTITY OF JAMES

The author of this letter gives us practically no information about himself. He calls himself simply: "James, a servant of God and of the Lord Jesus Christ" (*James* 1:1). Who then is he? In the New Testament there are apparently at least five people who bear that name.

(i) There is the James who was the father of the member of the Twelve called Judas, not Iscariot (*Luke* 6:16). He is no more than a name and cannot have had any connection with this letter.

(ii) There is James, the son of Alphaeus, who was a member of the Twelve (*Matthew* 10:3; *Mark* 3:18; *Luke* 6:15; *Acts* 1:13). A comparison of *Matthew* 9:9 with *Mark* 2:14 makes it certain that Matthew and Levi were one and the same person. Levi was also a son of Alphaeus, and therefore Matthew and this James must have been brothers. But of James, the son of Alphaeus, nothing else is known; and he also can have had no connection with this letter.

(iii) There is the James who is called *James the Younger* and is mentioned in *Mark* 15:40 (cp. *Matthew* 27:56; *John* 19:25). Again nothing is known of him, and he cannot have had any connection with this letter.

(iv) There is James, the brother of John, and the son of Zebedee, a member of the Twelve (*Matthew* 10:2; *Mark* 3:17;

Luke 6:14; *Acts* 1:13). In the gospel story James never appears independently of his brother John (*Matthew* 4:21; 17:1; *Mark* 1:19, 29; 5:37; 9:2; 10:35, 41; 13:3; 14:33; *Luke* 5:10; 8:51; 9:28, 54). He was the first of the apostolic band to be martyred, for he was beheaded on the orders of Herod Agrippa the First in the year A.D. 44. He has been connected with the letter. The fourth century Latin Codex Corbeiensis at the end of the epistle, has a note quite definitely ascribing it to James the son of Zebedee. The only place where this ascription of authorship was taken seriously was in the Spanish Church, in which, down to the end of the seventeenth century, he was often held to be the author. This was due to the fact that St. James of Compostella, the patron saint of Spain, is identified with James the son of Zebedee; and it was natural that the Spanish Church should be predisposed to wish that their country's patron saint should be the author of a New Testament letter. But the martyrdom of James came too early for him to have written the letter, and in any event there is nothing beyond the Codex Corbeiensis to connect him with it.

(v) Finally, there is James, who is called the brother of Jesus. Although the first definite connection of him with this letter does not emerge until Origen in the first half of the third century, it is to him that it has always been traditionally ascribed. The Roman Catholic Church agrees with this ascription, for in 1546 the Council of Trent laid it down that *James* is canonical and is written by an apostle.

Let us then collect the evidence about this James. From the New Testament we learn that he was one of the brothers of Jesus (*Mark* 6:3; *Matthew* 13:55). We shall later discuss in what sense the word brother is to be taken. During Jesus's ministry it is clear that his family did not understand or sympathize with him and would have wished to restrain him (*Matthew* 12:46–50; *Mark* 3:21, 31–35; *John* 7:3–9). John says bluntly, "For even his brothers did not believe in him" (*John* 7:5). So, then, during Jesus's earthly ministry James was numbered amongst his opponents.

With *Acts* there comes a sudden and unexplained change.

When *Acts* opens, Jesus's mother and his brothers are there with the little group of Christians (*Acts* 1: 14). From there onwards it becomes clear that James has become the leader of the Jerusalem Church although how that came about is never explained. It is to James that Peter sends the news of his escape from prison (*Acts* 12: 17). James presides over the Council of Jerusalem which agreed to the entry of the Gentiles into the Christian Church (*Acts* 15). It is James and Peter whom Paul meets when he first goes to Jerusalem; and it is with Peter, James and John, the pillars of the Church, that he discusses and settles his sphere of work (*Galatians* 1: 19; 2: 9). It is to James that Paul comes with his collection from the Gentile Churches on the visit to Jerusalem which is destined to be his last and which leads to his imprisonment (*Acts* 21: 18–25). This last episode is important, for it shows James very sympathetic to the Jews who still observe the Jewish law, and so eager that their scruples should not be offended, that he actually persuades Paul to demonstrate his loyalty to the law by assuming responsibility for the expenses of certain Jews who are fulfilling a Nazirite vow.

Plainly, then, James was the leader of the Jerusalem Church. As might be expected, this was something which tradition greatly developed. Hegesippus, the early historian, says that James was the first bishop of the Church at Jerusalem. Clement of Alexandria goes further and says that he was chosen for that office by Peter and John. Jerome in his book, *On Famous Men,* says, "After the Passion of the Lord, James was immediately ordained bishop of Jerusalem by the apostles. . . . He ruled the Church of Jerusalem for thirty years, that is, until the seventh year of the reign of Nero." *The Clementine Recognitions* take the final step in the development of the legend, for they say that James was ordained Bishop of Jerusalem by none other than Jesus himself. Clement of Alexandria relates a strange tradition: "To James the Just, and John and Peter, after the Resurrection, the Lord committed knowledge; they committed it to the other apostles; and the other apostles to the seventy." The later developments are not to be accepted but the basic fact remains that James was the undisputed head of the Church at Jerusalem.

JAMES AND JESUS

Such a change must have some explanation. It may well be that we have it in a brief sentence in the New Testament itself. In 1 *Corinthians* 15 Paul gives us a list of the Resurrection appearances of Jesus and includes the words: "Then he appeared to James" (1 *Corinthians* 15: 7). It so happens that there is a strange reference to James in the *Gospel according to the Hebrews,* which was one of the early gospels which did not gain admittance to the New Testament but which, to judge from its surviving fragments, had much of value in it. The following passage from it is handed down by Jerome:

> Now the Lord, when he had given the linen cloth unto the servant of the High Priest, went unto James and appeared to him (for James had sworn that he would not eat bread from that hour, wherein he had drunk the Lord's cup, until he should see him risen again from among them that sleep). And again after a little, "Bring ye," saith the Lord, "a table and bread," and immediately it is added: "He took bread and blessed and brake it and gave it unto James the Just and said unto him, 'My brother, eat thy bread, for the Son of Man is risen from among them that sleep.'"

That passage is not without its difficulties. The beginning seems to mean that Jesus, when he rose from the dead and emerged from the tomb, handed the linen shroud, which he had been wearing in death, to the servant of the High Priest and went to meet his brother James. It also seems to imply that James was present at the Last Supper. But although the passage has its obscurities, one thing is clear. Something about Jesus in the last days and hours had fastened on James's heart and he had vowed that he would not eat until Jesus had risen again; and so Jesus came to him and gave him the assurance for which he waited. That there was a meeting of James and the Risen Christ is certain. What passed at that moment we shall never know. But we do know this, that after it the James who had been hostile and unsympathetic to Jesus became his servant for life and his martyr in death.

That James died a martyr's death is the consistent statement of early tradition. The accounts of the circumstances vary, but the fact that he was martyred remains constant. Josephus's account is very brief (*Antiquities* 20: 9.1):

> So Ananus, being that kind of man, and thinking that he had got a good opportunity because Festus was dead and Albinus not yet arrived, holds a judicial council; and he brought before it the brother of Jesus, who was called Christ—James was his name—and some others, and on the charge of violating the Law he gave them over to be stoned.

Ananus was a Jewish High Priest; Festus and Albinus were procurators of Palestine, holding the same position as Pilate had held. The point of the story is that Ananus took advantage of the interregnum between the death of one procurator and the arrival of his successor to eliminate James and other leaders of the Christian Church. This, in fact, well fits the character of Ananus as it is known to us and would mean that James was martyred in A.D. 62.

A much longer account is given in the history of Hegesippus. Hegesippus's history is itself lost, but his account of the death of James has been preserved in full by Eusebius (*Ecclesiastical History* 2: 23). It is lengthy, but it is of such interest that it must be quoted in its entirety.

> To the government of the Church in conjunction with the apostles succeeded the Lord's brother, James, he whom all from the time of the Lord to our own day call the Just, as there were many named James. And he was holy from his mother's womb; wine and strong drink he drank not, nor did he eat flesh; no razor touched his head, he anointed himself not with oil, and used not the bath. To him alone was it permitted to enter the Holy Place, for neither did he wear wool, but linen clothes. And alone he would enter the Temple, and be found prostrate on his knees beseeching pardon for the people, so that his knees were callous like a camel's in

consequence of his continual kneeling in prayer to God and beseeching pardon for the people. Because of his exceeding righteousness he was called the Just, and Oblias, which is in Greek Bulwark of the People, and Righteousness, as the prophets declare concerning him.

Therefore, certain of the seven sects among the people, already mentioned by me in the *Memoirs,* asked him: "What is the door of Jesus?" and he said that He was the Saviour—of whom some accepted the faith that Jesus is the Christ. Now the aforesaid sects were not believers either in a Resurrection or in One who should come to render to every man according to his deeds; but as many as believed did so because of James. So, since many of the rulers, too, were believers, there was a tumult of the Jews and Scribes and Pharisees, for they said there was danger that all the people would expect Jesus the Christ. Accordingly they said, when they had met together with James: "We entreat thee restrain the people since it has gone astray unto Jesus, holding him to be the Christ. We entreat thee to persuade concerning Jesus all those who come to the day of the Passover, for we all listen to thee. For we and all the people testify to thee that thou art just and that thou respectest not persons. So thou, therefore, persuade the people concerning Jesus, not to go astray, for all the people and all of us listen to thee. Take thy stand, therefore, on the pinnacle of the Temple, that up there thou mayest be well seen, and thy words audible to all the people. For because of the Passover all the tribes have come together and the gentiles also."

So the aforesaid Scribes and Pharisees set James on the pinnacle of the Temple and called to him: "O thou, the Just, to whom we all ought to listen, since the people is going astray after Jesus the crucified, tell us what is the door of Jesus?" And with a loud voice he answered: "Why do you ask me concerning the Son of Man? He sitteth himself in heaven on the right hand of the great Power, and shall come on the clouds of heaven." And when many were convinced and gave glory for the witness of James, and said, "Hosanna to the Son of David," then again the same Scribes and Pharisees said to one another, "We were wrong to permit such a testimony to Jesus; but let us go up and cast him (James) down, that through fear they may not believe him." And they cried out saying, "Ho, Ho! even the Just has gone astray," and they fulfilled the Scriptures written in *Isaiah*: "Let us away with the Just, because he is troublesome to us; therefore they shall eat the fruits of their doings."

Accordingly they went up and cast the Just down. And they said to one another, "Let us stone James the Just," and they began to stone him, since he was not killed by the fall, but he turned and knelt down saying, "I beseech thee, Lord God Father, forgive them, for they know not what they do." And so, as they were stoning him, one of the Priests of the sons of Rechab, the son of Rechabim. mentioned by Jeremiah the prophet, cried out saying, "Stop! what are ye doing? The Just prays for you." And a certain one of them, one of the fullers, taking the club with which he pounds clothes, brought it down on the head of the Just; and so he suffered martyrdom.

And they buried him there on the spot, near the Temple. A true witness has he become both to Jews and Greeks that Jesus is Christ. And immediately Vespasian besieges them.

The last sentence shows that Hegesippus had a different date for the death of James. Josephus makes it A.D. 62; but, if this happened just before the siege of Vespasian, the date is perhaps about A.D. 66.

Much in the story of Hegesippus may well be legendary but from it two things emerge. First, it is again evidence that James died a martyr's death. Second, it is evidence that, even after James became a Christian, he remained in complete loyalty to the orthodox Jewish Law, so loyal that the Jews regarded him as one of themselves. This would fit well with what we have already noted of James's attitude to Paul when he came to Jerusalem with the collection for the Jerusalem Church (*Acts* 21: 18–25).

THE BROTHER OF OUR LORD

There is one other question about the person of James which we must try to solve. In *Galatians* 1: 19 Paul speaks of him as *the Lord's brother*. In *Matthew* 13: 55 and in *Mark* 6: 3 he is named among the brothers of Jesus; and in *Acts* 1: 14, although no names are given, the brothers of Jesus are said to be amongst his followers in the earliest Church. The question of the meaning of *brother* is one which must be faced, for the Roman Catholic Church attaches a great deal of importance to the answer, as does the Anglo-Catholic section of the Anglican Church. Ever since the time of Jerome there has been continuous argument in the Church on this question. There are three theories of the relationship of these "brothers" to Jesus; and we shall consider them one by one.

THE HIERONYMIAN THEORY

The Hieronymian Theory takes its name from Jerome, who in Greek is Hieronymos. It was he who worked out the theory which declares that the "brothers" of Jesus were in fact his *cousins*; and this is the settled belief of the Roman Catholic Church, for which it is an article of faith. It was put forward by Jerome in A.D. 383 and we shall best grasp his complicated argument by setting it out in a series of steps.

(i) James the brother of our Lord is included among the apostles. Paul writes: "But I saw none of the other apostles except James the Lord's brother" (*Galatians* 1: 19).

(ii) Jerome insists that the word *apostle* can be used only of the Twelve. If that be so, we must look for James among them. He cannot be identified with James, brother of John and son of Zebedee, who apart from anything else was martyred by the time of *Galatians* 1: 19, as *Acts* 12: 2 plainly tells us. Therefore he must be identified with the only other James among the Twelve, James the son of Alphaeus.

(iii) Jerome proceeds to make another identification. In *Mark* 6: 3 we read: "Is not this the carpenter, the son of Mary, brother of James and Joseph?"; and in *Mark* 15: 40 we find beside the Cross Mary the mother of James the Younger and of Joses. Since James the Younger is the brother of Joses and the son of Mary, he must therefore be the same person as the James of *Mark* 6: 3, who is the brother of our Lord. Therefore, according to Jerome, James the brother of the Lord, James the son of Alphaeus and James the Younger are the same person under different descriptions.

(iv) Jerome bases the next and final step of his argument on a deduction made from the lists of the women who were there when Jesus was crucified. Let us set down that list as given by the three gospel writers.

In *Mark* 15: 40 it is:

> Mary Magdalene, Mary the mother of James and Joseph, and Salome.

In *Matthew* 27: 56 it is:

> Mary Magdalene, Mary the mother of James the Younger and of Joses, and the mother of the sons of Zebedee.

In *John* 19: 25 it is:

> Jesus's mother, his mother's sister, Mary the wife of Cleopas, and Mary Magdalene.

Now let us analyse these lists. In each of them Mary Magdalene appears by name. It is safe to identify Salome and the mother of the sons of Zebedee. But the real problem is *how many women are there in John's list?* Is the list to be read like this:

  (i) Jesus's mother;
  (ii) Jesus's mother's sister;
 (iii) Mary the wife of Cleopas;
 (iv) Mary Magdalene.

Or is the list to be read like this:

  (i) Jesus's mother;
  (ii) Jesus's mother's sister, Mary the wife of Cleopas;
 (iii) Mary Magdalene.

Jerome insists that the second way is correct and that Jesus's mother's sister and Mary, the wife of Cleopas, are one and the same person. If that be so, she must also be the Mary who in the other lists is the mother of James and Joses. This James who is her son is the man who is variously known as James the Younger and as James the son of Alphaeus and as James the apostle who is known as the brother of our Lord. This means that James is the son of Mary's sister and therefore is Jesus's cousin.

There, then, is Jerome's argument. Against it at least four criticisms can be levelled.

(i) Again and again James is called the *brother* of Jesus or is numbered amongst the *brothers* of Jesus. The word used in each case is *adelphos,* the normal word for brother. True, it can describe people who belong to a common fellowship, just as the Christians called each other *brother*. True, it can be used as a term of endearment and we may call someone with whom we enjoy personal intimacy a *brother*. But when it is used of those who are kin, it is, to say the least of it, very doubtful that it can mean *cousin*. If James was the *cousin* of Jesus, it is extremely unlikely—perhaps impossible—that he would be called the *adelphos* of Jesus.

(ii) Jerome was quite wrong in assuming that the term *apostle* could be used only of the Twelve. Paul was an apostle (*Romans* 1:1; *1 Corinthians* 1:1; *2 Corinthians* 1:1; *Galatians* 1:1). Barnabas was an apostle (*Acts* 14:14; *1 Corinthians* 9:6). Silas was an apostle (*Acts* 15:22). Andronicus and Junia were apostles (*Romans* 16:7). It is impossible to limit the word *apostle* to the Twelve; since, therefore, it is not necessary to look for James the Lord's brother among the Twelve, the whole argument of Jerome collapses.

(iii) It is on the face of it much more likely that *John* 19:25 is a list of four women, not three, for, if Mary the wife of Cleopas were the sister of Mary, Jesus's mother, it would mean that there were two sisters in the same family both called Mary, which is extremely unlikely.

(iv) It must be remembered that the Church knew nothing of this theory until A.D. 383 when Jerome produced it; and it is quite certain that it was produced for no other reason than to conserve the doctrine of the perpetual virginity of Mary.

The theory that those called Jesus's brothers were, in fact, his cousins must be dismissed as rendered quite untenable by the facts of the case.

THE EPIPHANIAN THEORY

The second of the great theories concerning the relationship of Jesus and his "brothers" holds that these "brothers" were, in fact, his half-brothers, sons of Joseph by a previous marriage. This is called the Epiphanian Theory after Epiphanius who strongly affirmed it about A.D. 370. He did not construct it. It existed long before this and may indeed be said to be the most usual opinion in the early church.

The substance of it already appears in an apocryphal book called the *Book of James* or the *Protevangelium* which dates back to the middle of the second century. That book tells how there was a devout husband and wife called Joachim and Anna. Their great grief was that they had no child. To their great joy in their old age a child was born to them, and this too, apparently, was regarded as a virgin birth. The child, a girl, was called Mary and was to be the mother of Jesus. Joachim and Anna vowed their child to the Lord; and when she reached the age of three they took her to the Temple and left her there in the charge of the priests. She grew up in the Temple; and when she reached the age of twelve the priests took thought for her marriage. They called together the widowers of the people, telling each man to bring his rod with him. Among them came Joseph the carpenter. The High Priest took the rods, and Joseph's was last. To the other rods nothing happened; but from the rod of Joseph there flew a dove which came and settled on Joseph's head. In this way it was revealed that Joseph was to take Mary to wife. Joseph at first was very unwilling. "I have sons," he said, "and I am an old man, but she is a girl: lest I become a laughing-stock to the children of Israel" (*Protevangelium* 9: 1). But in the end he took her in obedience to the will of God, and in due time Jesus was born. The material of the *Protevangelium* is, of course, legendary; but it shows that by the middle of the second century the theory which was one day to bear the name of Epiphanius was widely held.

There is no direct evidence for this theory whatsoever and all the support adduced in its favour is of an indirect character.

(i) It is asked: would Jesus have committed his mother to the care of John, if she had other sons besides himself? (*John* 19: 26, 27). The answer is that, so far as we know, Jesus's family were quite out of sympathy with him and it would hardly have been possible to commit his mother to their care.

(ii) It is argued that the behaviour of Jesus's "brothers" to him is that of elder brothers to a younger brother. They questioned his sanity and wished to take him home (*Mark* 3: 21, 31–35); they were actively hostile to him (*John* 7: 1–5). But it could just as well be argued that their conduct was due to the simple fact that they found him an embarrassment to the family in a way that had nothing to do with age.

(iii) It is argued that Joseph must have been older than Mary because he vanishes completely from the gospel story and, therefore, probably had died before Jesus's public ministry began. The mother of Jesus was at the wedding feast at Cana of Galilee, but there is no mention of Joseph (*John* 2: 1). Jesus is called, at least sometimes, the son of Mary, and the implication is that Joseph was dead and Mary was a widow (*Mark* 6: 3; but cp. *Matthew* 13: 55). Further, Jesus's long stay in Nazareth until he was thirty years of age (*Luke* 3: 23), is most easily explained by the assumption that Joseph had died and that Jesus had become responsible for the support of the household. But the fact that Joseph was older than Mary does not by any means prove that he had no other children by her; and the fact that Jesus stayed in Nazareth as the village carpenter in order to support the family would much more naturally indicate that he was the eldest, and not the youngest, son.

To these arguments Lightfoot would add two more of a general nature.

First, he says that this is the theory of Christian tradition; and, second, he claims that anything else is "abhorrent to Christian sentiment."

But basically this theory springs from the same origin as the Hieronymian theory. Its aim is to conserve the perpetual virginity of Mary. There is no direct evidence whatsoever for it; and no one would ever have thought of it had it not been for the desire to think that Mary never ceased to be a virgin.

THE HELVIDIAN THEORY

The third theory is called the Helvidian Theory. It states quite simply that the brothers and sisters of Jesus were in the full sense of the term his brothers and sisters, that, to use the technical term, they were his uterine brothers and sisters. Nothing whatever is known of the Helvidius with whose name this theory is connected except that he wrote a treatise to support it which Jerome strongly opposed. What then may be said in favour of it?

(i) No one reading the New Testament story without theological presuppositions would ever think of anything else. On the face of it that story does not think of Jesus's brothers and sisters as anything else but his brothers and sisters in the full sense of the term.

(ii) The birth narratives both in *Matthew* and *Luke* presuppose that Mary had other children. Matthew writes: "When Joseph woke from sleep, he did as the angel of the Lord commanded him: he took his wife, but knew her not till she had borne a son" (*Matthew* 1: 24, 25). The clear implication is that Joseph entered into normal married relationships with Mary after the birth of Jesus. Tertullian, in fact, uses this passage to prove that both virginity and the married state are consecrated in Christ by the fact that Mary was first a virgin and then a wife in the full sense of the term. Luke in writing of the birth of Jesus says: "She gave birth to her *first-born* son" (*Luke* 2: 7). To call Jesus a first-born son is plainly to indicate that other children followed.

(iii) As we have already said, the fact that Jesus remained in Nazareth as the village carpenter until the age of thirty is at least an indication that he was the eldest son and had to take upon himself the responsibility of the support of the family after the death of Joseph.

We believe that the brothers and sisters of Jesus were in truth his brothers and sisters. Any other theory ultimately springs from the glorification of asceticism and from a wish to regard Mary as for ever a virgin. It is surely a far more lovely thing to believe in the sanctity of the home than to insist that celibacy is a higher thing than married love.

So, then, we believe that James, called the Lord's brother, was in every sense the brother of Jesus.

Can we then say that this James was also the author of this letter? Let us collect the evidence in favour of that view.

(i) If James wrote a letter at all, it would most naturally be a general epistle, as this is. James was not, like Paul, a traveller and a man of many congregations. He was the leader of the Jewish section of the Church; and the kind of letter we would expect him to write would be a general epistle directed to all Jewish Christians.

(ii) There is scarcely anything in the letter that a good Jew could not accept. So much so that there are those who think that it is actually a Jewish ethical tract which has found its way into the New Testament. A. H. McNeile has pointed out that in instance after instance there are phrases in *James* which can be read equally well in a Christian or a Jewish sense. The Twelve Tribes of the Dispersion (1: 1) could be taken either of the exiled Jews scattered all over the world or of the Christian Church, the new Israel of God. "The Lord" can again and again in this letter be understood equally well of Jesus or of God (1: 7; 4: 10, 15; 5: 7, 8, 10, 11, 14, 15). Our bringing forth by God by the word of his truth to be the first fruits of his creation (1: 18) can equally well be understood of God's first act of creation or of his re-creation of men in Jesus Christ. The perfect law and the royal law (1: 25; 2: 8), can equally well be understood of the ethical law of the Ten Commandments or of the new law of Christ. The elders of the Church, the *ekklēsia* (5: 14), can equally well be understood as meaning the elders of the Christian Church or the Jewish elders, for in the *Septuagint ekklēsia* is the title of the chosen nation of God. In 2: 2 "your *assembly*" is spoken of. The word there used for *assembly* is *sunagōgē*, which can mean the *synagogue* even more readily than it can mean *the Christian congregation*. The habit of addressing its readers as *brothers* is thoroughly Christian, but it is equally thoroughly Jewish. The coming of the Lord and the picture of the Judge standing at the door (5: 7, 9) are just as common in Jewish thought as in Christian thought. The accusation that they have murdered the righteous man (5: 6) is a phrase which occurs again and again in the prophets, but a Christian could read it as a statement of the Crucifixion of Christ. There is nothing in this letter which an orthodox Jew could not heartily accept, if he read it in his own terms.

It could be argued that all this perfectly suits James. He was the leader of what might be called Jewish Christianity; he was the head of that part of the Church which remained centred in Jerusalem. There must have been a time when the Church was very close to Judaism and it was more a reformed Judaism than anything else. There was a kind of Christianity which had not the width or the universality which the mind of Paul put into it. Paul himself said that the sphere of the Gentiles had been allocated to him and the sphere of the Jews to Peter, James and John (*Galatians* 2: 9). The letter of James may well represent a kind of Christianity which had remained in its earliest form. This would explain two things.

First, it would explain the frequency with which *James* repeats the teaching of the Sermon on the Mount. We may, out of many instances, compare *James* 2: 12, 13 and *Matthew* 6: 14, 15; *James* 3: 11–13 and *Matthew* 7: 16–20; *James* 5: 12 and *Matthew* 5: 34–37. Any Jewish Christian would be supremely interested in the ethical teaching of the Christian faith.

Second, it would help to explain the relationship of this letter to the teaching of Paul. At a first reading *James* 2: 14–26 reads like a direct attack on Paulinism. "A man is justified by works and not by faith alone" (*James* 2: 24) seems a flat contradiction of the Pauline doctrine of justification by faith. But what *James* is attacking is a so-called faith which has no ethical results and one thing is quite clear—anyone who charges Paul with preaching such a faith cannot possibly have read his letters. They are full of ethical demands, as, for instance, a chapter like *Romans* 12 illustrates. Now James died in A.D. 62 and, therefore, could not have read Paul's letters which did not become the common property of the Church until at least A.D. 90. Therefore what *James* is attacking is either a misunderstanding of what Paul said or a perversion of it; and nowhere was such a misunderstanding or perversion more likely to arise than in Jerusalem, where Paul's stress on faith and grace and his attack on the law were likely to be regarded with more suspicion than anywhere else.

(iii) It has been pointed out that *James* and the letter of the Council of Jerusalem to the Gentile Churches have at least two rather curious resemblances. Both begin with the word *Greeting* (*James* 1: 1; *Acts* 15: 23). The Greek is *chairein*. This was the normal Greek beginning to a letter, but nowhere else in all the New Testament is it found other than in the letter of Claudius Lysias, the military officer, to the governor of the province quoted in *Acts* 23: 26–30. Second, *Acts* 15: 17 has a phrase in the letter of the Council of Jerusalem in which it speaks of the Gentiles *who are called by my name*. This phrase occurs nowhere else in the New Testament other than in *James* 2: 7 where it is translated *the name by which you are called*. Although the Revised Standard Version translations differ slightly, the Greek is exactly the same. It is curious that the letter of the Council of Jerusalem presents us with two unusual phrases which recur only in *James*, when we remember that the letter of the Council of Jerusalem must have been drafted by James.

There is then evidence which lends colour to the belief that *James* was the work of James, the Lord's brother and head of the Jerusalem Church.

On the other hand there are facts which make us a little doubtful if he was, after all, the author.

(i) If the writer was the brother of our Lord, we would have expected him to make some reference to that fact. All he calls himself is "a servant of God and of the Lord Jesus Christ" (1: 1). Such a reference would not have been in any sense for his own personal glory, but simply to lend authority to his letter. And such authority would have been specially useful outside Palestine, in countries where James could hardly have been known. If the author was indeed the Lord's brother, it is surprising that he makes no reference, direct or indirect, to that fact.

(ii) Failing a reference to his relationship to Jesus, we would have expected a reference to the fact that he was an apostle. It was Paul's regular custom to begin his letters with a reference to his apostleship. Again it is not a question of personal prestige but simply a guarantee of the authority by which he writes. If this James was indeed the Lord's brother and the head of the Jerusalem Church, we should have expected some reference at the beginning of the letter to his apostolic status.

(iii) The most surprising fact of all is that which made Luther question the right of this letter to a place in the New Testament—the almost complete absence of any references to Jesus Christ. Only twice in the whole letter is his name mentioned and these mentions are almost incidental (1:1; 2:1).

There is no reference at all to his Resurrection. We know well that the early church was built on faith in the Risen Christ. If this letter is the work of James, it is contemporary with the events of *Acts* in which the Resurrection is mentioned no fewer than twenty-five times. What makes it still more surprising is that James had a personal reason for writing about the appearance of Jesus which may well have been what changed the direction of his life. It is surprising that anyone writing at such a time in the Church's history should write without reference to the Resurrection of Jesus; and it is doubly surprising if the writer should be James the brother of our Lord.

Further, there is no reference to Jesus as Messiah. If James, the leader of the Jewish Church, was writing to Jewish Christians in these very early days, one would have thought his main aim would have been to present Jesus as Messiah or that at least he would have made his belief in that fact plain; but the letter does not mention it.

(iv) It is plain that the writer of this letter is steeped in the Old Testament; it is also plain that he is intimately acquainted with the Wisdom Literature; and that in James is only to be expected. There are in his letter twenty-three apparent quotations from the Sermon on the Mount; that too is easy to understand, because from the very beginning, long before the gospels were written, compendiums of Jesus's teaching must have circulated. It is argued by some that he must have known Paul's letters to the Romans and to the Galatians in order to write as he does about faith and works, and it is argued rightly that a Jew who had never been outside Palestine and who died in A.D. 62 could not have known these letters. As we have seen, this argument will not stand, because the criticism of Paul's doctrine in *James* is criticism which could have been offered only by someone who had not read the letters of Paul at first hand and who is dealing with a misunderstanding or a perversion of Pauline doctrine. But the phrase in 1: 17: "Every good endowment and every perfect gift," is an hexametre line and clearly a quotation from some Greek poet; and the phrase in 3: 6: "the cycle of nature" may be an Orphic phrase from the mystery religions. How could James of Palestine pick up quotations like these?

There are things which are difficult to account for on the assumption that James, the brother of our Lord, was the author of this letter.

The evidence for and against James's authorship of this letter is extraordinarily evenly balanced. For the moment we must leave the matter in suspense and turn to certain other questions.

THE DATE OF THE LETTER

When we turn to the evidence for the date of the letter we find this same even balance. It is possible to argue that it is very early, and equally possible to argue that it is rather late.

(i) When James was writing, it is clear that the hope of the Second Coming of Jesus Christ was still very real (5: 7–9). Now the expectation of the Second Coming never left the Christian Church, but it did to some extent fade from the foreground of its thought as it was unexpectedly long delayed. This would suggest an early date.

(ii) In the early chapters of *Acts* and in the letters of Paul, there is a continuous background of Jewish controversy against the accepting of the Gentiles into the Church on the basis of faith alone. Wherever Paul went the Judaizers followed him, and the acceptance of the Gentiles was not a battle which was readily won. In *James* there is not even a hint of this Jewish-Gentile controversy, a fact which is doubly surprising when we remember that James, the Lord's brother, took a leading part in settling it at the Council of Jerusalem. That being so, this letter could be either very early and written before that controversy emerged; or, it could be late and written after the last echo of the controversy had died away. The fact that there is no mention of the Jewish-Gentile controversy can be used as an argument either way.

(iii) The evidence from the Church order reflected in the letter is equally conflicting. The meeting place of the Church is still called the *sunagōgē* (2: 2). That points to an early date; later an assembly of Christians would definitely be called the *ekklēsia,* for the Jewish term was soon dropped. The elders of the Church are mentioned (5: 14), but there is no mention of either deacons or bishops. This again indicates an early date, and possibly a Jewish connection, for the eldership was a Jewish institution before it was a Christian one. James is worried about the existence of *many teachers* (3: 1). This could well indicate a very early situation, before the Church had systematized its ministry and introduced some kind of order; or, it could indicate a late date, when many false teachers had arisen to plague the Church.

There are two general facts which seem on the whole to indicate that *James* is late. First, as we have seen there is hardly any mention of Jesus at all. The subject of the letter is, in fact, the inadequacies and the imperfections, the sins and the mistakes of the members of the Church. This seems to point to a fairly late date. The early preaching was ablaze with the grace and the glory of the Risen Christ; later preaching became, as it so often is today, a tirade against the imperfections of the members of the Church. The second general fact is the condemnation of the rich (2: 1–3; 5: 1–6). The flattery of the rich and the arrogance of the rich seem to have been real problems when this letter was written. Now in the very early church there were few, if any, rich men (1 *Corinthians* 1: 26, 27). *James* seems to indicate a later time when the once poor Church was being threatened with a spirit of worldliness in its members.

THE PREACHERS OF THE ANCIENT WORLD

It will help us to date this so-called letter of James and may also help us to identify its author, if we place it in its context in the ancient world.

The sermon is identified with the Christian Church, but it was by no means its invention. It had roots in both the Hellenistic and the Jewish world; and when we set *James* beside the Hellenistic and the Jewish sermons we cannot fail to be struck by the resemblances.

1. Let us look first at the Greek preachers and their sermons. The wandering philosopher was a common figure in the ancient world. Sometimes he was a Stoic; far more often he was a Cynic. Wherever men were gathered together you would find him there calling them to virtue. You would find him at the street corner and in the city squares; you would find him at the vast concourses which gathered for the games; you would even find him at the gladiatorial games, sometimes even directly addressing the emperor, rebuking him for luxury and tyranny, and calling him to virtue and justice. The ancient preacher, the philosopher-missionary, was a regular figure in the ancient world. There was a time when philosophy had been the business of the schools, but now its voice and its ethical demands were to be heard daily in the public places.

These ancient sermons had certain characteristics. The method was always the same; and that method had deeply influenced Paul's presentation of the gospel, and James was in the same line of descent. We list some of the tricks of the trade of these ancient preachers, noting how they occur in *James* and bearing in mind the way in which Paul writes to his Churches. The main aim of these ancient preachers, it must be remembered, was not to investigate new truth; it was to awaken sinners to the error of their ways and compel them to look at truths, which they knew but were deliberately neglecting or had forgotten. Their aim was to confront men with the good life in the midst of the looseness of their living and their forgetfulness of the gods.

(i) They frequently carried on imaginary conversations with imaginary opponents, speaking in what has been called a kind of "truncated dialogue." James also uses that method in 2: 18f. and 5: 13f.

(ii) They habitually effected their transition from one part of the sermon to another, by way of a question which introduced the new subject. Again James does that in 2: 14 and 4: 1.

(iii) They were very fond of imperatives in which they commanded their hearers to right action and to the abandoning of their errors. In *James's* 108 verses there are almost 60 imperatives.

(iv) They were very fond of the rhetorical question flung out at their audience. James frequently employs such questions (cp. *James* 2: 4, 5; 2: 14–16; 3: 11, 12; 4: 4).

(v) They frequently dealt in apostrophes, vivid direct addresses to particular sections of the audience. So James apostrophizes the merchants out for gain and the arrogant rich (4: 13; 5: 6).

(vi) They were fond of personifying virtues and vices, sins and graces. So James personifies sin (1: 15); mercy (2: 13); rust (5: 3).

(vii) They sought to awaken the interest of their audience by pictures and figures from everyday life. The figure of the bridle, the rudder and the forest fire are standard figures in the ancient sermons (cp. *James* 3: 3–6). Amongst many others James vividly uses the picture of the farmer and his patience (5: 7).

(viii) They frequently used the example of famous men and women to point their moral. So James uses the examples of Abraham (2: 21–23); Rahab (2: 25); Job (5: 11); Elijah (5: 17).

(ix) It was the custom of the ancient preachers to begin their sermon with a paradox which would arrest the attention of their hearers. James does that by telling a man to think it all joy when he is involved in trials (1: 2). In the same way the ancient preachers often pointed out how true goodness meant the reversal of all popular verdicts on life. So James insists that the happiness of the rich lies in their being brought low (1: 10). They used the weapon of irony as James does (2: 14–19; 5: 1–6).

(x) The ancient preachers could speak with harshness and with sternness. So James addresses his reader as: "Foolish fellow!" and calls those who listen to him unfaithful creatures (2: 20; 4: 4). The ancient preachers used the lash and so does James.

(xi) The ancient preachers had certain standard ways of constructing their sermons.

(*a*) They often concluded a section with a vivid antithesis, setting the right beside the wrong way. James follows the same custom (cp. 2: 13; 2: 26).

(*b*) They often made their point by means of a searching question fired at the hearer; and so does James (4: 12).

(*c*) They often used quotations in their preaching. This also James does (5: 20; 1: 11, 17; 4: 6; 5: 11).

It is true that we do not find in James the bitterness, the scolding, the frivolous and often broad humour that the Greek preachers used; but it is plain to see that he uses all the other methods which the wandering Hellenistic preachers used to win their way into the minds and hearts of men.

2. The Jewish world also had its tradition of preaching. That preaching was done mainly by the Rabbis at the services of

the synagogue. It had many of the characteristics of the preaching of the Greek wandering philosophers. It had its rhetorical questions and its imperatives and its pictures taken from life, and its quotations and its citations of the heroes of the faith. But Jewish preaching had one curious characteristic. It was deliberately disconnected. The Jewish masters instructed their pupils never to linger for any length of time on any one subject, but to move quickly from one subject to another in order to maintain the interest of the listener. Hence one of the names for preaching was *charaz*, which literally means *stringing beads*. The Jewish sermon was frequently a string of moral truths and exhortations coming one after another. This is exactly what *James* is. It is difficult, if not impossible, to extract from it a continuous and coherent plan. Its sections follow each other with a certain disconnectedness. Goodspeed writes: "The work has been compared to a chain, each link related to the one before and the one after it. Others have compared its contents to beads on a string. . . . And, perhaps, *James* is not so much a chain of thoughts or beads as it is a handful of pearls dropped one by one into the hearer's mind."

James, whether looked at from the Hellenistic or from the Jewish point of view, is a good example of an ancient sermon. And here is, perhaps, the clue we need to its authorship. With all this in mind, let us now turn to ask who the author is.

THE AUTHOR OF JAMES

There are five possibilities.

(i) We begin with a theory worked out in detail by Meyer more than half a century ago and revived by Easton in the new *Interpreter's Bible*. One of the commonest things in the ancient world was for books to be published in the name of some great figure of the past. Jewish literature between the Testaments is full of writings like that, ascribed to Moses, the Twelve Patriarchs, Baruch, Enoch, Isaiah, and people of like standing in order that the added authority might give greater encouragement to their readers. This was an accepted practice. One of the best-known books in the Apocrypha is the *Wisdom of Solomon,* in which the later Sage attributes new wisdom to the wisest of the kings.

Let us remember three things about *James.* (*a*) There is nothing in it which an orthodox Jew could not accept, if the two references to Jesus in 1: 1 and 2: 1 are removed, as they easily may be. (*b*) The Greek for James is in fact *Iakōbos* which of course is the Old Testament *Jacob.* (*c*) The book is addressed to "the twelve tribes who are scattered abroad." This theory holds that *James* is nothing other than a Jewish writing, written under the name of Jacob and meant for the Jews who were scattered throughout the world to encourage them in faith and belief amidst the trials through which they might be passing in Gentile lands.

This theory is further elaborated in this way. In *Genesis* 49 we have Jacob's last address to his sons. The address consists of a series of short descriptions in which each son is in turn characterized. Meyer professed to be able to find in *James* allusions to the descriptions of each of the patriarchs and, therefore, of each of the twelve tribes, in Jacob's address. Here are some of his identifications.

Asher is the wordly rich man; *James* 1: 9–11; *Genesis* 49: 20.

Issachar is the doer of good deeds; *James* 1: 12; *Genesis* 49: 14, 15.

Reuben is the first fruits; *James* 1: 18; *Genesis* 49: 3.

Simeon stands for anger; *James* 1: 19, 20; *Genesis* 49: 5–7.

Levi is the tribe which is specially connected with religion and is alluded to in *James* 1: 26, 27.

Naphtali is characterized by peace; *James* 3: 18; *Genesis* 49: 21.

Gad stands for wars and fightings; *James* 4: 1, 2; *Genesis* 49: 19.

Dan represents waiting for salvation; *James* 5: 7; *Genesis* 49: 18.

Joseph represents prayer; *James* 5: 13–18; *Genesis* 49: 22–26.

Benjamin stands for birth and death; *James* 5: 20; *Genesis* 49: 27.

That is a most ingenious theory. No one can either finally prove it or disprove it; and it certainly would explain in the most natural way the reference in 1: 1 to the twelve tribes scattered abroad. It would hold that some Christian came upon this Jewish tract, written under the name of Jacob to all the exiled Jews, and was so impressed with its moral worth, that he made certain adjustments and additions to it and issued it as a Christian book. There is no doubt that this is an attractive theory—but it is possible for a theory to be too ingenious.

(ii) Just as the Jews did, the Christians also wrote many books under the names of the great figures of the Christian faith. There are gospels issued under the name of Peter and Thomas and James himself; there is a letter under the name of Barnabas; there are gospels of Nicodemus and Bartholomew; and there are Acts of John, Paul, Andrew, Peter, Thomas, Philip and others. The technical title for these books is *pseudonymous*, that is, written under a *false name*.

It has been suggested that *James* was a letter written by someone else under the name of the Lord's brother. That is apparently what Jerome thought when he said that this letter "was issued by someone under James's name." But, whatever else this work is, it cannot be that because, when anyone wrote such a book, he was careful to make quite clear who was supposed to have written it. If this had been pseudonymous no possible doubt would have been left that the author was supposed to be James *the brother of our Lord*; but this fact is not mentioned at all.

(iii) Moffatt inclined to the theory that the writer was not the brother of our Lord, or any other well-known James, but simply a teacher called James of whose life and story we have no information whatever. That is by no means impossible for the name James was just as common then as it is now; but it would be rather difficult to understand how such a book gained entry into the New Testament, and how it came to be connected with the name of the Lord's brother.

(iv) The traditional view is that the book was written by James, the Lord's brother. We have already seen that it seems strange that such a book should have only two incidental references to Jesus, and none at all to the Resurrection or to Jesus as the Messiah. A further and most serious difficulty is this. The book is written in good Greek. Ropes says that Greek must have been the mother tongue of the man who wrote it; and Mayor, himself one of the greatest of Greek scholars, says, "I should be inclined to rate the Greek of this epistle as approaching more nearly to the standard of classical purity than that of any other book in the New Testament with the exception perhaps of the Epistle to the Hebrews." Quite certainly James's mother tongue was Aramaic and not Greek; and quite certainly he would not be a master of classical Greek. His orthodox Jewish upbringing would make him despise and avoid it, as a Gentile and accursed tongue. It is next to impossible to think of James actually penning this letter.

(v) So we come to the fifth possibility. Let us remember how closely *James* resembles a sermon. It is possible that this is, in substance, a sermon preached by James, taken down by someone else, translated into Greek, added to and decorated a little and then issued to the Church at large so that all men should benefit from it. That explains its form and how it came to be attached to the name of James. It even explains the scarcity of the references to Jesus, to the Resurrection, and to the Messiahship of Jesus; for in one single sermon James could not go through the whole gamut of orthodoxy and is, in fact, pressing moral duty upon men, and not talking about theology. It seems to us that this is the one theory which explains the facts.

One thing is certain—we may approach this little letter feeling that it is one of the lesser books of the New Testament; but if we study it faithfully, we will lay it down thanking God that it was preserved for our edification and inspiration.

JAMES

GREETINGS

James 1: 1

> James, the slave of God and of the Lord Jesus Christ, sends greetings to the twelve tribes who are scattered throughout the world.

AT the very beginning of his letter James describes himself by the title wherein lies his only honour and his only glory, *the slave of God and of the Lord Jesus Christ*. With the exception of Jude he is the only New Testament writer to describe himself by that term (*doulos*) without any qualification. Paul describes himself as the slave of Jesus Christ and his apostle (*Romans* 1: 1; *Philippians* 1: 1). But James will go no further than to call himself the slave of God and of the Lord Jesus Christ. There are at least four implications in this title.

(i) It implies *absolute obedience*. The slave knows no law but his master's word; he has no rights of his own; he is the absolute possession of his master; and he is bound to give his master unquestioning obedience.

(ii) It implies *absolute humility*. It is the word of a man who thinks not of his privileges but of his duties, not of his rights but of his obligations. It is the word of the man who has lost himself in the service of God.

(iii) It implies *absolute loyalty*. It is the word of the man who has no interests of his own, because what he does, he does for God. His own profit and his own preference do not enter into his calculations; his loyalty is to him.

(iv) Yet, at the back of it, this word implies a certain *pride*. So far from being a title of dishonour it was the title by which the greatest ones of the Old Testament were known. Moses was the *doulos* of God (1 *Kings* 8: 53; *Daniel* 9: 11; *Malachi* 4: 4); so were Joshua and Caleb (*Joshua* 24: 29; *Numbers* 14: 24); so were the great patriarchs, Abraham, Isaac and Jacob (*Deuteronomy* 9: 27); so was Job (*Job* 1: 8); so was

Isaiah (*Isaiah* 20: 3); and *doulos* is distinctively the title by which the prophets were known (*Amos* 3: 7; *Zechariah* 1: 6; *Jeremiah* 7: 25). By taking the title *doulos* James sets himself in the great succession of those who found their freedom and their peace and their glory in perfect submission to the will of God. The only greatness to which the Christian can ever aspire is that of being the slave of God.

There is one unusual thing about this opening salutation. James sends greetings to his readers; using the word *chairein* which is the regular opening word of salutation in secular Greek letters. Paul never uses it. He always uses the distinctively Christian greeting, "Grace and peace" (*Romans* 1: 7; 1 *Corinthians* 1: 3; 2 *Corinthians* 1: 2; *Galatians* 1: 3; *Ephesians* 1: 2; *Philippians* 1: 2; *Colossians* 1: 2; 1 *Thessalonians* 1: 1; 2 *Thessalonians* 1: 2; *Philemon* 3). This secular greeting occurs only twice in the rest of the New Testament, in the letter which Claudius Lysias, the Roman officer, wrote to Felix to ensure the safe journeying of Paul (*Acts* 23: 26), and in the general letter issued after the decision of the Council of Jerusalem to allow the Gentiles into the Church (*Acts* 15: 23). This is interesting, because it was James who presided over that Council (*Acts* 15: 13). It may be that he used the most general greeting that he could find because his letter was going out to the widest public.

THE JEWS THROUGHOUT THE WORLD

James 1: 1 (*continued*)

THE letter is addressed to *the twelve tribes who are scattered abroad*. Literally the greeting is to the twelve tribes in the *Diaspora,* the technical word for the Jews who lived outside Palestine. All the millions of Jews who were, for one reason or another, outside the Promised Land were the *Diaspora*. This dispersal of the Jews throughout the world was of the very greatest importance for the spread of Christianity, because it meant that all over the world there were synagogues, from which the Christian preachers could take their start; and it meant that all over the world there were groups of men and women who themselves already knew the Old Testament, and who had persuaded others among the Gentiles, at least to be interested in their faith. Let us see how this dispersal took place.

Sometimes—and the process began in this way—the Jews were forcibly taken out of their own land and compelled to live as exiles in foreign lands. There were three such great movements.

(1) The first compulsory removal came when the people of the Northern Kingdom, who had their capital in Samaria, were conquered by the Assyrians and were carried away into captivity in Assyria (2 *Kings* 17: 23; 1 *Chronicles* 5: 26). These are the lost ten tribes who never returned. The Jews themselves believed that at the end of all things all Jews would be gathered together in Jerusalem, but until the end of the world these ten tribes, they believed, would never return. They founded this belief on a rather fanciful interpretation of an Old Testament text. The Rabbis argued like this: "The ten tribes never return for it is said of them, 'He will cast them into another land, as at this day' (*Deuteronomy* 29: 28). As then this day departs and never returns, so too are they to depart and never return. As this day becomes dark, and then again light, so too will it one day be light again for the ten tribes for whom it was dark."

(ii) The second compulsory removal was about 580 B.C. At that time the Babylonians conquered the Southern Kingdom whose capital was at Jerusalem, and carried the best of the people away to Babylon (2 *Kings* 24: 14–16; *Psalm* 137). In Babylon the Jews behaved very differently; they stubbornly refused to be assimilated and to lose their nationality. They were said to be congregated mainly in the cities of Nehardea and Nisibis. It was actually in Babylon that Jewish scholarship reached its finest flower; and there was produced the Babylonian *Talmud,* the immense sixty-volume exposition of the Jewish law. When Josephus wrote his *Wars of the Jews,* the first edition was not in Greek but in Aramaic, and was designed for the scholarly Jews in Babylon. He tells us that the Jews rose to such power there that at one time the province of Mesopotamia was under Jewish rule. Its two Jewish rulers were Asidaeus and Anilaeus; and on the death of Anilaeus it was said that no fewer than 50,000 Jews were massacred.

(iii) The third compulsory transplantation took place much later. When Pompey conquered the Jews and took Jerusalem in 63 B.C., he took back to Rome many Jews as slaves. Their rigid adherence to their own ceremonial law and their stubborn observance of the Sabbath made them difficult slaves; and most of them were freed. They took up residence in a kind of quarter of their own on the far side of the Tiber. Before long they were to be found flourishing all over the city. Dio Cassius says of them, "They were often suppressed, but they nevertheless mightily increased, so that they achieved even the free exercise of their customs." Julius Caesar was their great protector and we read of them mourning all night long at his bier. We read of them present in large numbers when Cicero was defending Flaccus. In A.D. 19 the whole Jewish community was banished from Rome on the charge that they had robbed a wealthy female proselyte on pretence of sending the money to the Temple and at that time 4,000 of them were conscripted to fight against the brigands in Sardinia; but they were soon received back. When the Jews of Palestine sent their deputation to Rome to complain of the rule of Archelaus, we read that the deputation was joined by 8,000 Jews resident in the city. Roman literature is full of contemptuous references to the Jews, for anti-Semitism is no new thing; and the very number of the references is proof of the part that the Jews played in the life of the city.

Compulsory transplantation took the Jews by the thousand to Babylon and to Rome. But far greater numbers left Palestine of their own free-will for more comfortable and more profitable lands. Two lands in particular received thousands of Jews. Palestine was sandwiched between the two great powers, Syria and Egypt and was, therefore, liable at any time to become a battleground. For that reason many Jews left it to take up residence either in Egypt or in Syria.

During the time of Nebuchadnezzar there was a voluntary exodus of many Jews to Egypt (2 *Kings* 25: 26). As far back as 650 B.C. the Egyptian king Psammetichus was said to have had Jewish mercenaries in his armies. When Alexander the Great founded Alexandria special privileges were offered to settlers there and the Jews came in large numbers. Alexandria was divided into five administrative sections; and two of them were inhabited by Jews. In Alexandria alone there were more than 1,000,000 Jews. The settlement of the Jews in Egypt went so far that about 50 B.C. a temple, modelled on the Jerusalem one, was built at Leontopolis for the Egyptian Jews.

The Jews also went to Syria. The highest concentration was in Antioch, where the gospel was first preached to the Gentiles and where the followers of Jesus were first called Christians. In Damascus we read of 10,000 of them being massacred at one time.

So, then, Egypt and Syria had very large Jewish populations. But they had spread far beyond that. In Cyrene in North Africa we read that the population was divided into citizens, agriculturists, resident aliens and Jews. Mommsen, the Roman historian, writes: "The inhabitants of Palestine were only a portion, and not the most important portion, of the Jews; the Jewish communities of Babylonia, Syria, Asia Minor and Egypt were far superior to those of Palestine." That mention of Asia Minor leads us to another sphere in which the Jews were numerous. When Alexander's empire broke up on his death, Egypt fell to the Ptolemies, and Syria and the surrounding districts fell to Seleucus and his successors, known as the Seleucids. The Seleucids had two great characteristics. They followed a deliberate policy of the fusion of populations hoping to gain security by banishing nationalism. And they were inveterate founders of cities. These cities needed citizens, and special attractions and privileges were offered to those who would settle in them. The Jews accepted citizenship of these cities by the thousand. All over Asia Minor, in the great cities of the Mediterranean sea coast, in the great commercial centres, Jews were numerous and prosperous. Even there there

were compulsory transplantations. Antiochus the Great took
2,000 Jewish families from Babylon and settled them in Lydia
and Phrygia. In fact, so great was the drift from Palestine that
the Palestine Jews complained against their brethren who left
the austerities of Palestine for the baths and feasts of Asia and
Phrygia; and Aristotle tells of meeting a Jew in Asia Minor
who was "not only Greek in his language but in his very soul."

It is quite clear that everywhere in the world there were Jews.
Strabo, the Greek geographer, writes: "It is hard to find a spot
in the whole world which is not occupied and dominated by
Jews." Josephus, the Jewish historian writes: "There is no city,
no tribe, whether Greek or barbarian, in which Jewish law and
Jewish customs have not taken root." The Sibylline Oracles,
written about 140 B.C., say that every land and every sea is
filled with the Jews. There is a letter, said to be from Agrippa
to Caligula, which Philo quotes. In it he says that Jerusalem is
the capital not only of Judaea but of most countries by reason
of the colonies it has sent out on fitting occasions into the
neighbouring lands of Egypt, Phoenicia, Syria, Coelesyria, and
the still more remote Pamphylia and Cilicia, into most parts of
Asia as far as Bithynia, and into the most distant corners of
Pontus; also to Europe, Thessaly, Boeotia, Macedonia,
Aetolia, Attica, Argos, Corinth, and the most and best parts of
the Peloponnese. And not only is the continent full of Jewish
settlements, but also the more important islands—Euboea,
Cyprus, Crete—to say nothing of the lands beyond the
Euphrates, for all have Jewish inhabitants.

The Jewish Diaspora was coextensive with the world; and
there was no greater factor in the spread of Christianity.

THE RECIPIENTS OF THE LETTER

James 1: 1 (*continued*)

JAMES writes to the *twelve tribes in the Diaspora*. Who has he
in his mind's eye as he writes? *The twelve tribes in the Diaspora*
could equally well mean any of three things.

(i) It could stand for all the Jews outside of Palestine. We have seen that they were numbered by the million. There were actually far more Jews scattered throughout Syria and Egypt and Greece and Rome and Asia Minor and all the Mediterranean lands and far off Babylon than there were in Palestine. Under the conditions of the ancient world it would be quite impossible to send out a message to such a huge and scattered constituency.

(ii) It could mean Christian Jews outside Palestine. In this instance, it would mean the Jews in the lands closely surrounding Palestine, perhaps particularly those in Syria and in Babylon. Certainly if anyone was going to write a letter to these Jews, it would be James, for he was the acknowledged leader of Jewish Christianity.

(iii) The phrase could have a third meaning. To the Christians, the Christian Church was the real Israel. At the end of *Galatians* Paul sends his blessing to the *Israel of God* (*Galatians* 6: 16). The nation Israel had been the specially chosen people of God; but they had refused to accept their place and their responsibility and their task. When the Son of God came they had rejected him. Therefore all the privileges which had once belonged to them passed over to the Christian Church, for it was in truth the chosen people of God. Paul (cp. *Romans* 9: 7, 8) had fully worked out the idea. It was his conviction that the true descendants of Abraham were not those who could trace their physical descent from him but those who had made the same venture of faith as he had made. The true Israel was composed not of any particular nation or race but of those who accepted Jesus Christ in faith. So, then, this phrase may well mean *the Christian Church at large*.

We may choose between the second and the third meanings, each of which gives excellent sense. James may be writing to the Christian Jews scattered amidst the surrounding nations; or he may be writing to the new Israel, the Christian Church.

TESTED AND TRIUMPHANT

James 1: 2–4

My brothers, reckon it all joy whenever you become involved in all
kinds of testings, for you are well aware that the testing of your faith
produces unswerving constancy. And let constancy go on to work
out its perfect work that you may be perfect and complete, deficient
in nothing.

JAMES never suggested to his readers that Christianity would
be for them an easy way. He warns them that they would find
themselves involved in what the Authorized Version calls
divers temptations. The word translated temptations is
peirasmos, whose meaning we must fully understand, if we are
to see the very essence of the Christian life.

Peirasmos is not *temptation* in our sense of the term; it is
testing (*trial* in the Revised Standard Version). *Peirasmos* is
trial or testing *directed towards an end,* and the end is that he
who is tested should emerge stronger and purer from the
testing. The corresponding verb *peirazein,* which the
Authorized Version usually translates *to tempt,* has the same
meaning. The idea is not that of seduction into sin but of
strengthening and purifying. For instance, a young bird is said
to test (*peirazein*) its wings. The Queen of Sheba was said to
come to test (*peirazein*) the wisdom of Solomon. God was said
to test (*peirazein*) Abraham, when he appeared to be
demanding the sacrifice of Isaac (*Genesis* 22: 1). When Israel
came into the Promised Land, God did not remove the people
who were already there. He left them so that Israel might be
tested (*peirazein*) in the struggle against them (*Judges* 2: 22;
3: 1, 4). The experiences in Israel were tests which went to the
making of the people of Israel (*Deuteronomy* 4: 34; 7: 19).

Here is a great and uplifting thought. Hort writes: "The
Christian must expect to be jostled by trials on the Christian
way." All kinds of experiences will come to us. There will be
the test of the sorrows and the disappointments which seek to
take our faith away. There will be the test of the seductions

which seek to lure us from the right way. There will be the tests of the dangers, the sacrifices, the unpopularity which the Christian way must so often involve. But they are not meant to make us fall; they are meant to make us soar. They are not meant to defeat us; they are meant to be defeated. They are not meant to make us weaker; they are meant to make us stronger. Therefore we should not bemoan them; we should rejoice in them. The Christian is like the athlete. The heavier the course of training he undergoes, the more he is glad, because he knows that it is fitting him all the better for victorious effort. As Browning said, we must "welcome each rebuff that turns earth's smoothness rough," for every hard thing is another step on the upward way.

THE RESULT OF TESTING

James 1: 2–4 (*continued*)

JAMES describes this process of testing by the word *dokimion*. It is an interesting word. It is the word for *sterling coinage,* for money which is genuine and unalloyed. The aim of testing is to purge us of all impurity.

If we meet this testing in the right way, it will produce *unswerving constancy* (or *steadfastness* as the Revised Standard Version translates it). The word is *hupomonē*, which the Authorized Version translates as *patience*; but patience is far too passive. *Hupomonē* is not simply the ability to bear things; it is the ability to turn them to greatness and to glory. The thing which amazed the heathen in the centuries of persecution was that the martyrs did not die grimly, they died singing. One smiled in the flames; they asked him what he found to smile at there. "I saw the glory of God," he said, "and was glad." *Hupomonē* is the quality which makes a man able, not simply to suffer things, but to vanquish them. The effect of testing rightly borne is strength to bear still more and to conquer in still harder battles.

This unswerving constancy in the end makes a man three things.

(i) It makes him *perfect*. The Greek is *teleios* which usually has the meaning of *perfection towards a given end*. A sacrificial animal is *teleios* if it is fit to offer to God. A scholar is *teleios* if he is mature. A person is *teleios* if he is full grown. This constancy born of testing well met makes a man *teleios* in the sense of being fit for the task he was sent into the world to do. Here is a great thought. By the way in which we meet every experience in life we are either fitting or unfitting ourselves for the task which God meant us to do.

(ii) It makes him *complete*. The Greek is *holokleros* which means *entire, perfect in every part*. It is used of the animal which is fit to be offered to God and of the priest who is fit to serve him. It means that the animal or the person has no disfiguring and disqualifying blemishes. Gradually this unswerving constancy removes the weaknesses and the imperfections from a man's character. Daily it enables him to conquer old sins, to shed old blemishes and to gain new virtues, until in the end he becomes entirely fit for the service of God and of his fellow-men.

(iii) It makes him *deficient in nothing*. The Greek is *leipesthai* and it is used of the defeat of an army, of the giving up of a struggle, of the failure to reach a standard that should have been reached. If a man meets his testing in the right way, if day by day he develops this unswerving constancy, day by day he will live more victoriously and reach nearer to the standard of Jesus Christ himself.

GOD'S GIVING AND MAN'S ASKING

James 1: 5-8

If any of you is deficient in wisdom, let him ask it from God, who gives generously to all men and never casts up the gift, and it will be given to him. Let him ask in faith, with no doubts in his mind; for he who oscillates between doubts is like a surge of the sea,

wind-driven and blown hither and thither. Let not that man think
that he will receive anything from the Lord, a man with a divided
mind, inconstant in all his ways.

THERE is a close connection between this passage and what
has gone before. James has just told his readers that, if they
use all the testing experiences of life in the right way, they will
emerge from them with that unswerving constancy which is
the basis of all the virtues. But immediately the question arises,
"Where can I find the wisdom and the understanding to use
these testing experiences in the right way?" James's answer is,
"If a man feels that he has not the wisdom to use aright the
experiences of this life—and no man in himself possesses that
wisdom—let him ask it from God."

One thing stands out. For James, the Christian teacher with
the Jewish background, wisdom is a practical thing. It is not
philosophic speculation and intellectual knowledge; it is concerned with the business of living. The Stoics defined wisdom
as "knowledge of things human and divine." But Ropes defines
this Christian wisdom as "the supreme and divine quality of
the soul whereby man knows and practises righteousness."
Hort defines it as "that endowment of heart and mind which
is needed for the right conduct of life." In the Christian
wisdom there is, of course, knowledge of the deep things of
God; but it is essentially practical; it is such knowledge turned
into action in the decisions and personal relationships of
everyday life. When a man asks God for that wisdom, he must
remember two things.

(i) He must remember *how God gives*. He gives generously
and never casts up the gift. "All wisdom," said Jesus the son
of Sirach, "cometh from the Lord and is with him for ever"
(*Ecclesiasticus* 1: 1). But the Jewish wise men were well aware
how the best gift in the world could be spoiled by the manner
of the giving. They have much to say about how the fool gives.
"My son, blemish not thy good deeds, neither use uncom-
fortable words when thou givest anything . . . Lo, is not a word
better than a gift? But both are with a gracious man. A fool

will upbraid churlishly, and a gift of the envious consumeth the eyes" (i.e., "brings tears") (*Ecclesiasticus* 18: 15–18). "The gift of a fool shall do thee no good when thou hast it; neither yet of the envious for his necessity; for he looketh to receive many things for one. He giveth little, and upbraideth much; he openeth his mouth like a crier; today he lendeth, and tomorrow will he ask it again; such an one is to be hated of God and man" (*Ecclesiasticus* 20: 14, 15). The same writer warns against "upbraiding speeches before friends" (*Ecclesiasticus* 41: 22). There is a kind of giver who gives only with a view to getting more than he gives; who gives only to gratify his vanity and his sense of power by putting the recipient under an obligation which he will never be allowed to forget; who gives and then continuously casts up the gift that he has given. But God gives with generosity. Philemon, the Greek poet, called God "the lover of gifts," not in the sense of loving to receive gifts, but in the sense of loving to give them. Nor does God cast up his gifts; he gives with all the splendour of his love, because it is his nature to give.

(ii) We must remember *how the asker must ask*. He must ask without doubts. He must be sure of both the power and the desire of God to give. If he asks in doubt, his mind is like the broken water of the sea, driven hither and thither by any chance wind. Mayor says that he is like a cork carried by the waves, now near the shore, now far away. Such a man is unstable in his ways. Hort suggests that the picture is of a man who is drunk, staggering from side to side on the road and getting nowhere. James says vividly that such a man is *dipsuchos,* which literally means a man with two souls, or two minds, inside him. One believes, the other disbelieves; and the man is a walking civil war in which trust and distrust of God wage a continual battle against each other.

If we are to use aright the experiences of life to beget a sterling character, we must ask wisdom from God. And when we ask, we must remember the absolute generosity of God and see to it that we ask believing that we shall receive what God knows it is good and right for us to have.

AS EACH MAN NEEDS

James 1: 9–11

> Let the lowly brother be proud of his exaltation; and let the rich brother be proud of his humiliation; for he will pass away like a flower of the field. The sun rises with the scorching wind and withers the grass, and the flower wilts, and the beauty of its form is destroyed. So the rich will wither away in all his ways.

As James saw it, Christianity brings to every man what he needs. As Mayor put it "As the despised poor learns self-respect, so the proud rich learns self-abasement."

(i) Christianity brings to the poor man a new sense of his own value. (*a*) He learns that he matters *in the Church*. In the early church there were no class distinctions. It could happen that the slave was the minister of the congregation, preaching and dispensing the sacrament, while the master was no more than a humble member. In the Church the social distinctions of the world are obliterated and none matters more than any other. (*b*) He learns that he matters *in the world*. It is the teaching of Christianity that every man in this world has a task to do. Every man is of use to God and even if he be confined to a bed of pain, the power of his prayers can still act on the world of men. (*c*) He learns that he matters *to God*. As Muretus said long ago, "Call no man worthless for whom Christ died."

(ii) Christianity brings to the rich man a new sense of self-abasement. The great peril of riches is that they tend to give a man a false sense of security. He feels that he is safe; he feels that he has the resources to cope with anything and to buy himself out of any situation he may wish to avoid.

James draws a vivid picture, very familiar to the people of Palestine. In the desert places, if there is a shower of rain, the thin green shoots of grass will sprout; but one day's burning sunshine will make them vanish as if they had never been. The *scorching heat* is the *kausōn*. The *kausōn* was the south-east wind, the Simoon. It came straight from the deserts and burst on Palestine like a blast of hot air when an oven door is opened. In an hour it could wipe out all vegetation.

This is a picture of what a life dependent on riches can be like. A man who puts his trust in riches is trusting in things which the chances and changes of life can take from him at any moment. Life itself is uncertain. At the back of James's mind there is Isaiah's picture: "All flesh is grass, and all its beauty is like the flower of the field. The grass withers, the flower fades, when the breath of the Lord blows upon it; surely the people is grass" (*Isaiah* 40: 6, 7; cp. *Psalm* 103: 15).

James's point is this. If life is so uncertain and man so vulnerable, calamity and disaster may come at any moment. Since that is so, a man is a fool to put all his trust in things— like wealth—which he may lose at any moment. He is only wise if he puts his trust in things which he cannot lose.

So, then, James urges the rich to cease to put their trust in that which their own power can amass. He urges them to admit their essential human helplessness and humbly to put their trust in God, who alone can give the things which abide for ever.

THE CROWN OF LIFE

James 1: 12

Happy is the man who meets trial with steadfast constancy because, when he has shown himself of sterling worth, he will receive the crown of life which he has promised to those who love him.

To the man who meets trials in the right way there is joy here and hereafter.

(i) In this life he becomes a man of sterling worth. He is *dokimos*; he is like metal which is cleansed of all alloy. The weaknesses of his character are eradicated; and he emerges strong and pure.

(ii) In the life to come he receives *the crown of life*. There is far more than one thought here. In the ancient world the crown (*stephanos*) had at least four great associations.

(*a*) The crown of flowers was worn at times of joy, at weddings and at feasts (cp. *Isaiah* 28: 1, 2; *Song of Solomon* 3: 11). The crown was the sign of festive joy.

(*b*) The crown was the mark of royalty. It was worn by kings and by those in authority. Sometimes this was the crown of gold; sometimes it was the linen band, or fillet, worn around the brows (cp. *Psalm* 21: 3; *Jeremiah* 13: 18).

(*c*) The crown of laurel leaves was the victor's crown in the games, the prize which the athlete coveted above all (cp. 2 *Timothy* 4: 8).

(*d*) The crown was the mark of honour and of dignity. The instructions of parents can bring a crown of grace to those who listen to them (*Proverbs* 1: 9); Wisdom provides a man with a crown of glory (*Proverbs* 4: 9); in a time of disaster and dishonour it can be said, "The crown has fallen from our head" (*Lamentations* 5: 16).

We do not need to choose between these meanings. They are all included. The Christian has a *joy* that no other man can ever have. Life for him is like being for ever at a feast. He has a *royalty* that other men have never realized for, however humble his earthly circumstances, he is the child of God. He has a *victory* which others cannot win, for he meets life and all its demands in the conquering power of the presence of Jesus Christ. He has a new *dignity,* for he is ever conscious that God thought him worth the life and death of Jesus Christ.

What is the crown? It is the *crown of life*; and that phrase means that it is *the crown which consists of life*. The crown of the Christian is a new kind of living which is life indeed; through Jesus Christ he has entered into life more abundant.

James says that if the Christian meets the testings of life in the steadfast constancy which Christ can give, life becomes infinitely more splendid than ever it was before. The struggle is the way to glory, and the very struggle itself is a glory.

PUTTING THE BLAME ON GOD

James 1: 13–15

> Let no man say when he is tempted, "My temptation comes from
> God." For God himself is untemptable by evil and tempts no man.
> But temptation comes to every man, because he is lured on and
> seduced by his own desire; then desire conceives and begets sin; and,
> when sin has reached its full development, it spawns death.

AT the back of this passage lies a Jewish way of belief to which
all of us are to some extent prone. James is here rebuking the
man who puts the blame for temptation on God.

Jewish thought was haunted by the inner division that is in
every man. It was the problem which haunted Paul: "I delight
in the law of God in my inmost self, but I see in my members
another law at war with the law of my mind, and making me
captive to the law of sin which dwells in my members" (*Romans*
7: 22, 23). Every man was pulled in two directions. Purely as
an interpretation of experience the Jews arrived at the doctrine
that in every man there were two tendencies. They called them
the *Yetser Hatob, the good tendency,* and the *Yetser Hara, the
evil tendency.* This simply stated the problem; it did not explain
it. In particular, it did not say where the evil tendency came
from. So Jewish thought set out to try to explain that.

The writer of *Ecclesiasticus* was deeply impressed with the
havoc that the evil tendency causes. "O *Yetser Hara,* why wast
thou made to fill the earth with thy deceit?" (*Ecclesiasticus*
37: 3). In his view the evil tendency came from Satan, and
man's defence against it was his own will. "God made man
from the beginning and he delivered him into the hand of him
who took him for a prey. He left him in the power of his will.
If thou willest, thou wilt observe the commandments, and
faithfulness is a matter of thy good pleasure" (*Ecclesiasticus*
15: 14, 15).

There were Jewish writers who traced this evil tendency right
back to the Garden of Eden. In the apocryphal work, *The
Life of Adam and Eve,* the story is told. Satan took the form

of an angel and, speaking through the serpent, put into Eve the desire for the forbidden fruit and made her swear that she would give the fruit to Adam as well. "When he had made me swear," says Eve, "he ascended up into the tree. But in the fruit he gave me to eat *he placed the poison of his malice,* that is, of his lust. For lust is the beginning of all sin. And he bent down the bough to the earth, and I took of the fruit and ate it." In this conception it was Satan himself who succeeded in inserting the evil tendency into man; and that evil tendency is identified with the lust of the flesh. A later development of this story was that the beginning of all sin was in fact Satan's lust for Eve.

The Book of Enoch has two theories. One is that the fallen angels are responsible for sin (85). The other is that man himself is responsible for it. "Sin has not been sent upon the earth, but man himself created it" (98: 4).

But every one of these theories simply pushes the problem one step further back. Satan may have put the evil tendency into man; the fallen angels may have put it into man; man may have put it into himself. But where did it *ultimately* come from?

To meet this problem, certain of the Rabbis took a bold and dangerous step. They argued that, since God has created everything, he must have created the evil tendency also. So we get Rabbinic sayings such as the following. "God said, It repents me that I created the evil tendency in man; for had I not done so, he would not have rebelled against me. I created the evil tendency; I created the law as a means of healing. If you occupy yourself with the law, you will not fall into the power of it. God placed the good tendency on a man's right hand, and the evil on his left." The danger is obvious. It means that in the last analysis a man can blame God for his own sin. He can say, as Paul said, "It is no longer I that do it, but sin which dwells in me" (*Romans* 7: 15–24). Of all strange doctrines surely the strangest is that God is ultimately responsible for sin.

THE EVASION OF RESPONSIBILITY

James 1: 13–15 (*continued*)

FROM the beginning of time it has been man's first instinct to blame others for his own sin. The ancient writer who wrote the story of the first sin in the Garden of Eden was a first-rate psychologist with a deep knowledge of the human heart. When God challenged Adam with his sin, Adam's reply was, "The woman whom thou gavest to be with me, she gave me of the tree, and I ate." And when God challenged Eve with her action, her answer was, "The serpent beguiled me, and I ate." Adam said, "Don't blame me; blame Eve." Eve said, "Don't blame me; blame the serpent" (*Genesis* 3: 12, 13).

Man has always been an expert in evasion.

Robert Burns wrote:

> Thou know'st that Thou hast formed me
> 　With passions wild and strong;
> And list'ning to their witching voice
> 　Has often led me wrong.

In effect, he is saying that his conduct was as it was because God made him as he was. The blame is laid on God. So men blame their fellows, they blame their circumstances, they blame the way in which they are made, for the sin of which they are guilty.

James sternly rebukes that view. To him what is responsible for sin is man's own evil desire. Sin would be helpless if there was nothing in man to which it could appeal. Desire is something which can be nourished or stifled. A man can control and even, by the grace of God, eliminate it if he deals with it at once. But he can allow his thoughts to follow certain tracks, and his steps to take him into certain places and his eyes to linger on certain things; and so foment desire. He can so hand himself over to Christ and be so engaged on good things that there is no time or place left for evil desire. It is idle hands for which Satan finds mischief to do; it is the unexercised mind and the uncommitted heart which are vulnerable.

If a man encourages desire long enough, there is an inevitable consequence. *Desire becomes action.*

Further, it was the Jewish teaching that sin produced death. *The life of Adam and Eve* says that the moment Eve ate of the fruit she caught a glimpse of death. The word which James uses in verse 15, and which the Authorized and the Revised Standard Versions translate *brings forth* death, is an animal word for birth; and it means that sin *spawns* death. Mastered by desire, man becomes less than a man and sinks to the level of the brute creation.

The great value of this passage is that it urges upon man his personal responsibility for sin. No man was ever born without desire for some wrong thing. And, if a man deliberately encourages and nourishes that desire until it becomes full-grown and monstrously strong, it will inevitably issue in the action which is sin—and that is the way to death. Such a thought—and all human experience admits it to be true—must drive us to that grace of God which alone can make and keep us clean, and which is available to all.

GOD'S CONSTANCY FOR GOOD

James 1: 16–18

My dear brothers, do not be deceived. Every good gift and every perfect boon comes down from the Father of lights, with whom there is none of that changeableness which comes from changing shadows. Of his own purpose he has begotten us by the word of truth so that we might be, as it were, the first-fruits of his created things.

ONCE again James stresses the great truth that every gift that God sends is good. Verse 17 might well be translated: "All giving is good." That is to say, there is nothing which comes from God which is not good. There is a strange phenomenon here in the Greek. The phrase which we have translated, "Every good gift and every perfect boon," is, in fact, a perfect hexameter line of poetry. Either James had a rhythmic ear for a fine cadence or he is quoting from some work which we do not know.

What he is stressing is the unchangeableness of God. To do so he uses two astronomical terms. The word he uses for changeableness is *parallagē,* and the word for the turn of the shadow is *tropē.* Both these words have to do with the variation which the heavenly bodies show, the variation in the length of the day and of the night, the apparent variation in the course of the sun, the phases of waxing and waning, the different brilliance at different times of the stars and the planets. Variability is characteristic of all created things. God is the creator of the lights of heaven—the sun, the moon, the stars. The Jewish morning prayer says, "Blessed be the Lord God who hath formed the lights." The lights change but he who created them never changes.

Further, his purpose is altogether gracious. *The word of truth* is the gospel; and by the sending of that gospel it is God's purpose that man should be reborn into a new life. The shadows are ended and the certain word of truth has come.

That rebirth is a rebirth into the family and the possession of God. In the ancient world it was the law that all first-fruits were sacred to God. They were offered in grateful sacrifice to God because they belonged to him. So, when we are reborn by the true word of the gospel, we become the property of God, even as the first-fruits of the harvest did.

James insists that, so far from ever tempting man, God's gifts are invariably good. In all the chances and changes of a changing world they never vary. And God's supreme object is to re-create life through the truth of the gospel, so that men should know that they belong by right to him.

WHEN TO BE QUICK AND WHEN TO BE SLOW

James 1: 19, 20

All this, my dear brothers, you already know. Let every man be quick to hear, slow to speak, slow to anger; for the anger of man does not produce the righteousness which God desires.

THERE are few wise men who have not been impressed by the dangers of being too quick to speak and too unwilling to listen. A most interesting list could be compiled of the things in which it is well to be quick and the things in which it is well to be slow. In the Sayings of the Jewish Fathers we read: "There are four characters in scholars. Quick to hear and quick to forget; his gain is cancelled by his loss. Slow to hear and slow to forget; his loss is cancelled by his gain. Quick to hear and slow to forget; he is wise. Slow to hear and quick to forget; this is an evil lot." Ovid bids men to be slow to punish, but swift to reward. Philo bids a man to be swift to benefit others, and slow to harm them.

In particular the wise men were impressed by the necessity of being slow to speak. Rabbi Simeon said, "All my days I have grown up among the wise, and have not found aught good for a man but silence . . . Whoso multiplies words occasions sin." Jesus, the son of Sirach, writes, "Be swift to hear the word that thou mayest understand . . . If thou hast understanding, answer thy neighbour; if not, lay thy hand upon thy mouth, lest thou be surprised in an unskilful word, and be confounded" (*Ecclesiasticus* 5: 11, 12). *Proverbs* is full of the perils of too hasty speech. "When words are many, transgression is not lacking, but he who restrains his lips is prudent" (*Proverbs* 10: 19). "He who guards his mouth preserves his life; he who opens wide his lips comes to ruin" (*Proverbs* 13: 3). "Even a fool who keeps silent is considered wise" (*Proverbs* 17: 28). "Do you see a man who is hasty in his words? There is more hope for a fool than for him" (*Proverbs* 29: 20).

Hort says that the really good man will be much more anxious to listen to God than arrogantly, garrulously and stridently to shout his own opinions. The classical writers had the same idea. Zeno said, "We have two ears but only one mouth, that we may hear more and speak less." When Demonax was asked how a man might rule best, he answered, "Without anger, speaking little, and listening much." Bias said, "If you hate quick speaking, you will not fall into error." The tribute was once paid to a great linguist that he could be

silent in seven different languages. Many of us would do well
to listen more and to speak less.

It is James's advice that we should also be *slow to anger*.
He is probably meeting the arguments of some that there is a
place for the blazing anger of rebuke. That is undoubtedly true;
the world would be a poorer place without those who blazed
against the abuses and the tyrannies of sin. But too often this is
made an excuse for petulant and self-centred irritation.

The *teacher* will be tempted to be angry with the slow and
backward and still more with the lazy scholar. But, except on
the rarest occasions, he will achieve more by encouragement
than by the lash of the tongue. The *preacher* will be tempted
to anger. But "don't scold" is always good advice to him; he
loses his power whenever he does not make it clear by every
word and gesture that he loves his people. When anger gives
the impression in the pulpit of dislike or contempt it will not
convert the souls of men. The *parent* will be tempted to anger.
But a parent's anger is much more likely to produce a still more
stubborn resistance than it is to control and direct. The accent
of love always has more power than the accent of anger; and
when anger becomes constant irritability, petulant annoyance,
carping nagging, it always does more harm than good.

To be slow to speak, slow to anger, quick to listen is always
good policy for life.

THE TEACHABLE SPIRIT

James 1: 21

> So then strip yourself of all filthiness and of the excrescence of vice,
> and in gentleness receive the inborn word which is able to save
> your souls.

JAMES uses a series of vivid words and pictures.

He tells his readers to strip themselves of all vice and
filthiness. The word he uses for *strip* is the word used for
stripping off one's clothes. He bids his hearers get rid of all
defilement as a man strips off soiled garments or as a snake
sloughs off its skin.

Both the words he uses for *defilement* are vivid. The word we have translated *filthiness* is *ruparia*; and it can be used for the filth which soils clothes or soils the body. But it has one very interesting connection. It is a derivative of *rupos* and, when *rupos* is used in a medical sense, it means *wax in the ear*. It is just possible that it still retains that meaning here; and that James is telling his readers to get rid of everything which would stop their ears to the true word of God. When wax gathers in the ear, it can make a man deaf; and a man's sins can make him deaf to God. Further, James talks of the *excrescence* (*perisseia*) of vice. He thinks of vice as tangled undergrowth or a cancerous growth which must be cut away.

He bids them receive the *inborn word* in gentleness. The word for inborn is *emphutos*, and is capable of two general meanings.

(i) It can mean *inborn* in the sense of *innate* as opposed to acquired. If James uses it in that way he is thinking of much the same thing as Paul was thinking of when he spoke of the Gentiles doing the works of the law by nature because they have a kind of law in their hearts (*Romans* 2: 14, 15); it is the same picture as the Old Testament picture of the law "very near you; it is in your mouth, and in your heart" (*Deuteronomy* 30: 14). It is practically equal to our word *conscience*. If this is its meaning here, James is saying that there is an instinctive knowledge of good and evil in a man's heart whose guidance we should at all times obey.

(ii) It can mean *inborn* in the sense of *implanted,* as a seed is planted in the ground. In 4 *Ezra* 9: 31 we read of God saying: "Behold, I sow my law in you, and you shall be glorified in it for ever." If James is using the word in this sense, the idea may well go back to the Parable of the Sower (*Matthew* 13: 1–8), which tells how the seed of the word is sown into the hearts of men. Through his prophets and his preachers, and above all through Jesus Christ, God sows his truth into the hearts of men and the man who is wise will receive it and welcome it.

It may well be that we are not required to make a choice between these two meanings. It may well be that James is implying that knowledge of the true word of God comes to us from *two* sources, from the depths of our own being, and from the Spirit of God and the teaching of Christ and the preaching of men. From inside and from outside come voices telling us the right way; and the wise man will listen and obey.

He will receive the word with *gentleness. Gentleness* is an attempt to translate the untranslatable word *prautēs.* This is a great Greek word which has no precise English equivalent. Aristotle defined it as the mean between excessive anger and excessive angerlessness; it is the quality of the man whose feelings and emotions are under perfect control. Andronicus Rhodius, commenting on Aristotle, writes, "*Prautēs* is moderation in regard to anger . . . You might define *prautēs* as serenity and the power, not to be lead away by emotion, but to control emotion as right reason dictates." The Platonic *definitions* say that *prautēs* is the regulation of the movement of the soul caused by anger. It is the temperament (*krasis*) of a soul in which everything is mixed in the right proportions.

No one can ever find one English word to translate what is a one word summary of the truly teachable spirit. The teachable spirit is *docile* and *tractable,* and therefore humble enough to learn. The teachable spirit is *without resentment* and *without anger* and is, therefore, able to face the truth, even when it hurts and condemns. The teachable spirit is not blinded by its own overmastering *prejudices* but is clear-eyed to the truth. The teachable spirit is not seduced by *laziness* but is so self-controlled that it can willingly and faithfully accept the discipline of learning. *Prautēs* describes the perfect conquest and control of everything in a man's nature which would be a hindrance to his seeing, learning and obeying the truth.

HEARING AND DOING

James 1: 22–24

Prove yourselves to be doers of the word, and not only hearers, for those who think that hearing is enough deceive themselves. For, if a man is a hearer of the word and not a doer of it, he is like a man

who looks in a mirror at the face which nature gave him. A glance
and he is gone; and he immediately forgets what kind of man he is.

AGAIN James presents us with two of the vivid pictures of
which he is such a master. First of all, he speaks of the man
who goes to the church meeting and listens to the reading and
expounding of the word, and who thinks that that listening
has made him a Christian. He has shut his eyes to the fact that
what is read and heard in Church must then be lived out. It
is still possible to identify Church attendance and Bible reading
with Christianity but this is to take ourselves less than half the
way; the really important thing is to turn that to which we have
listened into action.

Second, James says such a man is like one who looks in a
mirror—ancient mirrors were made, not of glass, but of highly
polished metal—sees the smuts which disfigure his face and the
dishevelment of his hair, and goes away and forgets what he
looks like, and so omits to do anything about it. In his listening
to the true word a man has revealed to him that which he is
and that which he ought to be. He sees what is wrong and what
must be done to put it right; but, if he is only a hearer, he remains just as he is, and all his hearing has gone for nothing.

James does well to remind us that what is heard in the holy
place must be lived in the market place—or there is no point
in hearing at all.

THE TRUE LAW

James 1: 25

He who looks into the perfect law, which is the law in the observance
of which a man finds freedom, and who abides in it and shows
himself not a forgetful hearer but an active doer of the word, will be
blessed in all his action.

THIS is the kind of passage in *James* which Luther so much
disliked. He disliked the idea of law altogether, for with Paul
he would have said, "Christ is the end of the law" (*Romans*
10: 4). "James," said Luther, "drives us to law and works."

And yet beyond all doubt there is a sense in which James is right. There is an ethical law which the Christian must seek to put into action. That law is to be found first in the Ten Commandments and then in the teaching of Jesus.

James calls that law two things.

(i) He calls it the *perfect law*. There are three reasons why the law is perfect. (*a*) It is God's law, given and revealed by him. The way of life which Jesus laid down for his followers is in accordance with the will of God. (*b*) It is perfect in that it cannot be bettered. The Christian law is the law of love; and the demand of love can never be satisfied. We know well, when we love some one, that even though we gave them all the world and served them for a lifetime, we still could not satisfy or deserve their love. (*c*) But there is still another sense in which the Christian law is perfect. The Greek word is *teleios* which nearly always describes perfection towards some given end. Now, if a man obeys the law of Christ, he will fulfil the purpose for which God sent him into the world; he will be the person he ought to be and will make the contribution to the world he ought to make. He will be perfect in the sense that he will, by obeying the law of God, realize his God-given destiny.

(ii) He calls it the *law of liberty*; that is, the law in the keeping of which a man finds his true liberty. All the great men have agreed that it is only in obeying the law of God that a man becomes truly free. "To obey God," said Seneca, "is liberty." "The wise man alone is free," said the Stoics, "and every foolish man is a slave." Philo said "All who are under the tyranny of anger or desire or any other passion are altogether slaves; all who live with the law are free." So long as a man has to obey his own passions and emotions and desires, he is nothing less than a slave. It is when he accepts the will of God that he becomes really free—for then he is free to be what he ought to be. His service is perfect freedom and in doing his will is our peace.

TRUE WORSHIP

James 1: 26, 27

> If anyone thinks that he is a worshipper of God and yet does not
> bridle his tongue, his worship is an empty thing. This is pure and
> undefiled worship, as God the Father sees it, to visit the orphans
> and the widows, and to keep oneself unspotted from the world.

WE must be careful to understand what James is saying here.
The Revised Standard Version translates the phrases at the
beginning of verse 27: "*Religion* that is pure and undefiled is
. . ." The word translated religion is *thrēskeia,* and its
meaning is not so much *religion* as *worship* in the sense of the
outward expression of religion in ritual and liturgy and
ceremony. What James is saying is, "The finest ritual and the
finest liturgy you can offer to God is service of the poor and
personal purity." To him real worship did not lie in elaborate
vestments or in magnificent music or in a carefully wrought
service; it lay in the practical service of mankind and in the
purity of one's own personal life. It is perfectly possible for a
Church to be so taken up with the beauty of its buildings and
the splendour of its liturgy that it has neither the time nor the
money for practical Christian service; and that is what James
is condemning.

In fact James is condemning only what the prophets had
condemned long ago. "God," said the Psalmist, "is a father of
the fatherless, and protector of widows" (*Psalm* 68: 5). It was
Zechariah's complaint that the people pulled away their
shoulders and made their hearts as adamant as stone at the
demand to execute true justice, to show mercy and compassion
every man to his brother, to oppress not the widow, the
fatherless, the stranger and the poor, and not to entertain evil
thoughts against another within the heart (*Zechariah* 7: 6–10).
It was Micah's complaint that all ritual sacrifices were useless
if a man did not do justice and love kindness and walk humbly
before God (*Micah* 6: 6–8).

All through history men have tried to make ritual and liturgy

a substitute for sacrifice and service. They have made religion
splendid *within* the Church at the expense of neglecting it
outside the Church. This is by no means to say that it is wrong
to seek to offer the noblest and the most splendid worship
within God's house; but it is to say that all such worship is
empty and idle unless it sends a man out to love God by loving
his fellow-men and to walk more purely in the tempting ways
of the world.

RESPECT OF PERSONS

James 2: 1

> My brothers, you cannot really believe that you have faith in our
> glorious Lord Jesus Christ, and yet continue to have respect of
> persons.

RESPECT of persons is the New Testament phrase for undue
and unfair partiality; it means pandering to someone, because
he is rich or influential or popular. It is a fault which the New
Testament consistently condemns. It is a fault of which the
orthodox Jewish leaders completely acquitted Jesus. Even they
were bound to admit that there was no respect of persons with
him (*Luke* 20: 21; *Mark* 12: 14; *Matthew* 22: 16). After his
vision of the sheet with the clean and unclean animals upon it,
the lesson that Peter learned was that with God there is no
respect of persons (*Acts* 10: 34). It was Paul's conviction that
Gentile and Jew stand under a like judgment in the sight of
God, for with God there is no favouritism (*Romans* 2: 11). This
is a truth which Paul urges on his people again and again
(*Ephesians* 6: 9; *Colossians* 3: 25).

The word itself is curious—*prosōpolēmpsia*. The noun comes
from the expression *prosōpon lambanein. Prosōpon* is the *face*;
and *lambanein* here means *to lift up*. The expression in Greek
is a literal translation of a Hebrew phrase. To lift up a person's
countenance was to regard him with favour, in contradistinction perhaps to *casting down his countenance*.

Originally it was not a bad word at all; it simply meant *to accept a person with favour*. Malachi asks if the governor will be pleased with the people and *will accept their persons,* if they bring him blemished offerings (*Malachi* 1: 8, 9). But the word rapidly acquired a bad sense. It soon began to mean, not so much to favour a person, as to show favouritism, to allow oneself to be unduly influenced by a person's social status or prestige or power or wealth. Malachi goes on to condemn that very sin when God accuses the people of not keeping his ways and of being *partial in their judgments* (*Malachi* 2: 9). The great characteristic of God is his complete impartiality. In the Law it was written, "You shall do no injustice in judgment; you shall not be partial to the poor or defer to the great, but in righteousness shall you judge your neighbour" (*Leviticus* 19: 15). There is a necessary emphasis here. A person may be unjust because of the snobbery which truckles to the rich; and may be equally unjust because of the inverted snobbery which glorifies the poor. "The Lord," said Ben Sirach, "is judge and with him is no respect of persons" (*Ecclesiasticus* 35: 12).

The Old and New Testaments unite in condemning that partiality of judgment and favouritism of treatment which comes of giving undue weight to a man's social standing, wealth or worldly influence. And it is a fault to which every one is more or less liable. "The rich and the poor meet together," says *Proverbs,* "the Lord is the maker of them all" (*Proverbs* 22: 2). "It is not meet," says Ben Sirach, "to despise the poor man that hath understanding; neither is it fitting to magnify a sinful man that is rich" (*Ecclesiasticus* 10: 23). We do well to remember that it is just as much respect of persons to truckle to the mob as it is to pander to a tyrant.

THE PERIL OF SNOBBERY WITHIN THE CHURCH

James 2: 2–4

For, if a man comes into your assembly with his fingers covered with gold rings and dressed in elegant clothes and a poor man comes in

dressed in shabby clothes, and you pay special attention to the man
who is dressed in elegant clothes and you say to him: "Will you
sit here, please?" and you say to the poor man, "You stand there!"
or, "Squat on the floor beside my footstool!" have you not drawn
distinctions within your minds, and have you not become judges
whose thoughts are evil?"

IT is James's fear that snobbery may invade the Church. He
draws a picture of two men entering the Christian assembly.
The one is well-dressed and his fingers are covered with gold
rings. The more ostentatious of the ancients wore rings on
every finger except the middle one, and wore far more than one
on each finger. They even hired rings to wear when they wished
to give an impression of special wealth. "We adorn our fingers
with rings," said Seneca, "and we distribute gems over every
joint." Clement of Alexandria recommends that a Christian
should wear only one ring, and that he should wear it on his little
finger. It ought to have on it a religious emblem, such as a
dove, a fish or an anchor; and the justification for wearing it
is that it might be used as a seal.

So, then, into the Christian assembly comes an elegantly
dressed and much beringed man. The other is a poor man,
dressed in poor clothes because he has no others to wear and
unadorned by any jewels. The rich man is ushered to a special
seat with all ceremony and respect; while the poor man is
bidden to stand, or to squat on the floor, beside the footstool
of the well-to-do.

That the picture is not overdrawn is seen from certain
instructions in some early service order books. Ropes quotes
a typical passage from the Ethiopic *Statutes of the Apostles*:
"If any other man or woman enters in fine clothes, either a
man of the district or from other districts, being brethren, thou,
presbyter, while thou speakest the word which is concerning
God, or while thou hearest or readest, thou shalt not respect
persons, nor leave thy ministering to command places for
them, but remain quiet, for the brethren shall receive them,
and if they have no place for them, the lover of brothers and
sisters, will rise, and leave a place for them . . . And if a poor

man or woman of the district or of other districts should come in and there is no place for them, thou, presbyter, make place for such with all thy heart, even if thou wilt sit on the ground, that there should not be the respecting of the person of man but of God." Here is the same picture. It is even suggested that the leader of the service might be liable, when a rich man entered, to stop the service and to conduct him to a special seat.

There is no doubt that there must have been social problems in the early church. The Church was the only place in the ancient world where social distinctions did not exist. There must have been a certain initial awkwardness when a master found himself sitting next to his slave or when a master arrived at a service in which his slave was actually the leader and the dispenser of the Sacrament. The gap between the slave, who in law was nothing more than a living tool, and the master was so wide as to cause problems of approach on either side. Further, in its early days the Church was predominantly poor and humble; and therefore if a rich man was converted and came to the Christian fellowship, there must have been a very real temptation to make a fuss of him and treat him as a special trophy for Christ.

The Church must be the one place where all distinctions are wiped out. There can be no distinctions of rank and prestige when men meet in the presence of the King of glory. There can be no distinctions of merit when men meet in the presence of the supreme holiness of God. In his presence all earthly distinctions are less than the dust and all earthly righteousness is as filthy rags. In the presence of God all men are one.

In verse 4 there is a problem of translation. The word *diekrithēte* can have two meanings. (i) It can mean, "You are wavering in your judgments, if you act like that." That is to say, "If you pay special honour to the rich, you are torn between the standards of the world and the standards of God and you can't make up your mind which you are going to apply." (ii) It may mean, "You are guilty of making class distinctions which in the Christian fellowship should not exist." We prefer the second meaning, because James goes on to say, "If you

do that, you are judges whose thoughts are evil." That is to
say, "You are breaking the commandment of him who said,
'Judge not that you be not judged' " (*Matthew* 7: 1).

THE RICHES OF POVERTY
AND THE POVERTY OF RICHES

James 2: 5–7

Listen, my dear brothers. Did God not choose those who are poor
by the world's valuation to be rich because of their faith and to be
heirs of the Kingdom which he has promised to those who love him?
But you dishonour the poor man. Do not the rich oppress you, and
is it not they who drag you to the law-courts? And is it not they who
abuse the fair name by which you have been called?

"GOD," said Abraham Lincoln, "must love the common
people because he made so many of them." Christianity has
always had a special message for the poor. In Jesus's first
sermon in the synagogue at Nazareth his claim was: "He has
anointed me to preach good news to the poor" (*Luke* 4: 18).
His answer to John's puzzled inquiries as to whether or not he
was God's Chosen One culminated in the claim: "The poor
have good news preached to them" (*Matthew* 11: 5). The first
of the Beatitudes was "Blessed are the poor in spirit, for theirs
is the Kingdom of Heaven" (*Matthew* 5: 3). And Luke is even
more definite: "Blessed are you poor; for yours is the Kingdom
of God (*Luke* 6: 20). During the ministry of Jesus, when he
was banished from the synagogues and took to the open road
and the hillside and the seaside, it was the crowds of common
men and women to whom his message came. In the days of the
early church it was to the crowds that the street preachers
preached. In fact the message of Christianity was that those
who mattered to no one else mattered intensely to God. "For
consider your call, brethren," wrote Paul to the Corinthians,
"not many of you were wise according to worldly standards,
not many were powerful, not many were of noble birth"
(1 *Corinthians* 1: 26).

It is not that Christ and the Church do not want the great and the rich and the wise and the mighty; we must beware of an inverted snobbery, as we have already seen. But it was the simple fact that the gospel offered so much to the poor and demanded so much from the rich, that it was the poor who were swept into the Church. It was, in fact, the common people who heard Jesus gladly and the rich young ruler who went sorrowfully away because he had great possessions. James is not shutting the door on the rich—far from that. He is saying that the gospel of Christ is specially dear to the poor and that in it there is a welcome for the man who has none to welcome him, and that through it there is a value set on the man whom the world regards as valueless.

In the society which James inhabited the rich oppressed the poor. They dragged them to the law-courts. No doubt this was for debt. At the bottom end of the social scale men were so poor that they could hardly live and moneylenders were plentiful and extortionate. In the ancient world there was a custom of summary arrest. If a creditor met a debtor on the street, he could seize him by the neck of his robe, nearly throttling him, and literally drag him to the law-courts. That is what the rich did to the poor. They had no sympathy; all they wanted was the uttermost farthing. It is not riches that James is condemning; it is the conduct of riches without sympathy.

It is the rich who abuse the name by which the Christians are called. It may be the name *Christian* by which the heathen first called the followers of Christ at Antioch and which was given at first as a jest. It may be the name of Christ, which was pronounced over a Christian on the day of his baptism. The word James uses for *called* (*epikaleisthai*) is the word used for a wife taking her husband's name in marriage or for a child being called after his father. The Christian takes the name of Christ; he is called after Christ. It is as if he was married to Christ, or born and christened into the family of Christ.

The rich and the masters would have many a reason for insulting the name Christian. A slave who became a Christian

would have a new *independence*; he would no longer cringe at
his master's power, punishment would cease to terrorize him
and he would meet his master clad in a new manhood. He
would have a new *honesty*. That would make him a better slave,
but it would also mean he could no longer be his master's
instrument in sharp practice and petty dishonesty as once he
might have been. He would have a new *sense of worship*; and
on the Lord's Day he would insist on leaving work aside in
order that he might worship with the people of God. There
would be ample opportunity for a master to find reasons for
insulting the name of Christian and cursing the name of Christ.

THE ROYAL LAW

James 2: 8–11

> If you perfectly keep the royal law, as the Scripture has it: "You
> must love your neighbour as yourself," you do well. But if you
> treat people with respect of persons, such conduct is sin and you
> stand convicted by the law as transgressors. For, if a man keeps the
> whole law and yet fails to keep it in one point, he becomes guilty
> of transgressing the law as a whole. For he who said, "Do not
> commit adultery," also said, "Do not kill." If you do not commit
> adultery but kill, you become a transgressor of the law.

THE connection of thought with the previous passage is this.
James has been condemning those who pay special attention
to the rich man who enters the Church. "But," they might
answer, "the law tells me to love my neighbour as myself.
Therefore we are under duty to welcome the man when he
comes to Church." "Very well," answers James, "If you are
really welcoming the man because you love him as you do
yourself, and you wish to give him the welcome you yourself
would wish to receive, that is fine. But, if you are giving him
this special welcome because he is a rich man, that is respect
of persons and that is wrong—and so far from keeping the law,
you **are** in fact breaking it. You don't love your neighbour, or

you would not neglect the poor man. What you love is wealth—and that is not what the law commands."

James calls the great injunction to love our neighbour as ourselves the *royal law*. There can be various meanings of the phrase. It may mean the law which is of *supreme excellence*; it may mean *the law which is given by the King of the kings*; it may mean *the king of all laws*; it may mean *the law that makes men kings and is fit for kings*. To keep that greatest law is to become king of oneself and a king among men. It is a law fit for those who are royal, and able to make men royal.

James goes on to lay down a great principle about the law of God. To break any part of it is to become a transgressor. The Jew was very apt to regard the law as a series of detached injunctions. To keep one was to gain credit; to break one was to incur debt. A man could add up the ones he kept and subtract the ones he broke and so emerge with a credit or a debit balance. There was a Rabbinic saying, "Whoever fulfils only one law, good is appointed to him; his days are prolonged and he will inherit the land." Again many of the Rabbis held that "the Sabbath weighs against all precepts," and to keep it was to keep the law.

As James saw it, the *whole* law was the will of God; to break any part of it was to infringe that will and therefore to be guilty of sin. That is perfectly true. To break any part of the law is to become a transgressor in principle. Even under human justice a man becomes a criminal when he has broken one law. So James argues: "No matter how good you may be in other directions, if you treat people with respect of persons, you have acted against the will of God and you are a transgressor."

There is a great truth here which is both relevant and practical. We may put it much more simply. A man may be in nearly all respects a good man; and yet he may spoil himself by one fault. He may be moral in his action, pure in his speech, meticulous in his devotion. But he may be hard and self-righteous; rigid and unsympathetic; and, if so, his goodness is spoiled.

We do well to remember that, though we may claim to

have done many a good thing and to have resisted many an
evil thing, there may be something in us by which everything
is spoiled.

THE LAW OF LIBERTY AND THE LAW OF MERCY

James 2: 12, 13

> So speak and so act as those who are going to be judged under the
> law of liberty. For he who acts without mercy will have judgment
> without mercy. Mercy triumphs over judgment.

As he comes to the end of a section, James reminds his readers
of two great facts of the Christian life.

(i) The Christian lives under the law of liberty, and it is by
the law of liberty he will be judged. What he means is this.
Unlike the Pharisee and the orthodox Jew, the Christian is not
a man whose life is governed by the external pressure of a whole
series of rules and regulations imposed on him from without.
He is governed by the inner compulsion of love. He follows
the right way, the way of love to God and love to men, not
because any external law compels him to do so nor because
any threat of punishment frightens him into doing so, but
because the love of Christ within his heart makes him desire to
do so.

(ii) The Christian must ever remember that only he who
shows mercy will find mercy. This is a principle which runs
through all Scripture. Ben Sirach wrote, "Forgive thy
neighbour the hurt that he hath done thee, so shall thy sins
also be forgiven. One man beareth hatred against another, and
doth he seek pardon from the Lord? He showeth no mercy to
a man who is like himself; and doth he ask forgiveness for
his own sins?" (*Ecclesiasticus* 28: 2–5). Jesus said, "Blessed are
the merciful for they shall obtain mercy" (*Matthew* 5: 7). "If
you forgive men their trespasses, your heavenly Father also
will forgive you; but if you do not forgive men their trespasses,

neither will your Father forgive your trespasses" (*Matthew* 6: 14, 15). "Judge not that you be not judged, for with the judgment you pronounce you will be judged" (*Matthew* 7: 1, 2). He tells of the condemnation which fell upon the unforgiving servant and ends the parable by saying, "So, also, my heavenly Father will do to every one of you, if you do not forgive your brother from your heart" (*Matthew* 18: 22–35).

Scripture teaching is agreed that he who would find mercy must himself be merciful. And James goes even further, for in the end he says that mercy triumphs over judgment; by which he means that in the day of judgment the man who has shown mercy will find that his mercy has even blotted out his own sin.

FAITH AND WORKS

James 2: 14–26

My brothers, what use is it if a man claims to have faith and has no deeds to show? Are you going to claim that his faith is able to save him? If a brother or sister has nothing to wear, and if they have not enough for their daily food, and if one of you says to them, "Go in peace! Be warmed and fed!" and yet does not give them the essentials of bodily existence, what use is that? So, if faith too has no deeds to show, by itself it is dead.

But someone may well say, "Have you faith?" My answer is, "I have deeds. Show me your faith apart from your deeds, and I will show you my faith by means of my deeds." You say that you believe that there is one God. Excellent! The demons also believe the same thing—and shudder in terror.

Do you wish for proof, you empty creature, that faith without deeds is ineffective? Was not our father Abraham proved righteous in virtue of deeds when he was ready to offer Isaac his own son upon the altar? You see how his faith co-operated with his deeds and how his faith was completed by his deeds, and so there was fulfilled the passage of Scripture which says, "Abraham believed in God, and it was reckoned to him for righteousness, for he was the friend of God." You see that it is by deeds that a man is proved righteous, and not only by faith.

In the same way was Rahab the harlot not also proved righteous
by deeds, when she received the messengers and sent them away by
another way? For just as the body without breath is dead, so faith
without works is dead.

THIS is a passage which we must take as a whole before we
look at it in parts, for it is so often used in an attempt to
show that James and Paul were completely at variance. It is
apparently Paul's emphasis that a man is saved by faith alone
and that deeds do not come into the process at all. "For we
hold that a man is justified by faith apart from works of law"
(*Romans* 3: 28). "A man is not justified by works of the law,
but through faith in Jesus Christ . . . because by works of the
law shall no one be justified" (*Galatians* 2: 16). It is often
argued that James is not simply differing from Paul but is
flatly contradicting him. This is a matter we must investigate.

(i) We begin by noting that James's emphasis is in fact a
universal New Testament emphasis. It was the preaching of
John the Baptist that men should prove the reality of their
repentance by the excellence of their deeds (*Matthew* 3: 8;
Luke 3: 8). It was Jesus's preaching that men should so live
that the world might see their good works and give the glory
to God (*Matthew* 5: 16). He insisted that it was by their fruits
that men must be known and that a faith which expressed
itself in words only could never take the place of one which
expressed itself in the doing of the will of God (*Matthew* 7:
15–21).

Nor is this emphasis missing from Paul himself. Apart from
anything else, there can be few teachers who have ever stressed
the ethical effect of Christianity as Paul does. However
doctrinal and theological his letters may be, they never fail to
end with a section in which the expression of Christianity in
deeds is insisted upon. Apart from that general custom Paul
repeatedly makes clear the importance he attaches to deeds as
part of the Christian life. He speaks of God who will render
to every man according to his works (*Romans* 2: 6). He insists
that every one of us shall give account of himself to God
(*Romans* 14: 12). He urges men to put off the works of

darkness and put on the armour of light (*Romans* 13: 12). Every man shall receive his own reward according to his labour (1 *Corinthians* 3: 8). We must all appear before the judgment seat of Christ so that every one may receive good or evil, according to what he has done in the body (2 *Corinthians* 5: 10). The Christian has to put off the old nature and all its deeds (*Colossians* 3: 9).

The fact that Christianity must be ethically demonstrated is an essential part of the Christian faith throughout the New Testament.

(ii) The fact remains that James reads as if he were at variance with Paul; for in spite of all that we have said Paul's main emphasis is upon grace and faith and James's upon action and works. But this must be said—what James is condemning is not Paulinism but a perversion of it. The essential Pauline position in one sentence was: "Believe in the Lord Jesus and you will be saved" (*Acts* 16: 31). But clearly the significance we attach to this demand will entirely depend on the meaning we attach to *believe*. There are two kinds of belief.

There is belief which is purely intellectual. For instance, I believe that the square on the hypotenuse of a right-angled triangle equals the sum of the squares on the other two sides; and if I had to, I could prove it—but it makes no difference to my life and living. I accept it, but it has no effect upon me.

There is another kind of belief. I believe that five and five make ten, and, therefore, I will resolutely refuse to pay more than ten pence for two fivepenny bars of chocolate. I take that fact, not only into my mind, but into my life and action.

What James is arguing against is the first kind of belief, the acceptance of a fact without allowing it to have any influence upon life. The devils are intellectually convinced of the existence of God; they, in fact, tremble before him; but their belief does not alter them in the slightest. What Paul held was the second kind of belief. For him to believe in Jesus meant to take that belief into every section of life and to live by it.

It is easy to pervert Paulinism and to emasculate *believe* of all effective meaning; and it is not really Paulinism but a misunderstood form of it that James condemns. He is condemning profession without practice and with that condemnation Paul would have entirely agreed.

(iii) Even allowing for that, there is still a difference between James and Paul—*they begin at different times in the Christian life*. Paul begins *at the very beginning*. He insists that no man can ever earn the forgiveness of God. The initial step must come from the free grace of God; a man can only accept the forgiveness which God offers him in Jesus Christ.

James begins much later *with the professing Christian,* the man who claims to be already forgiven and in a new relationship with God. Such a man, James rightly says, must live a new life for he is a new creature. He has been *justified*; he must now show that he is *sanctified*. With that Paul would have entirely agreed.

The fact is that no man can be saved by works; but equally no man can be saved without producing works. By far the best analogy is that of a great human love. He who is loved is certain that he does not deserve to be loved; but he is also certain that he must spend his life trying to be worthy of that love.

The difference between James and Paul is a difference of starting-point. Paul starts with the great basic fact of the forgiveness of God which no man can earn or deserve; James starts with the professing Christian and insists that a man must prove his Christianity by his deeds. We are not saved *by* deeds; we are saved *for* deeds; these are the twin truths of the Christian life. Paul's emphasis is on the first and James's is on the second. In fact they do not contradict but complement each other; and the message of both is essential to the Christian faith in its fullest form. As the paraphrase has it:

> Let all who hold this faith and hope
> 　In holy deeds abound;
> Thus faith approves itself sincere,
> 　By active virtue crown'd.

PROFESSION AND PRACTICE

James 2: 14–17

My brothers, what use is it, if a man claims to have faith and has no deeds to show? Are you going to claim that his faith is able to save him? If a brother or sister has nothing to wear and if they have not enough for their daily food, and if one of you says to them, "Go in peace! Be warmed and fed!" and yet does not give them the essentials of bodily existence, what use is that? So, if faith too has no deeds to show, by itself it is dead.

THE one thing that James cannot stand is profession without practice, words without deeds. He chooses a vivid illustration of what he means. Suppose a man to have neither clothes to protect him nor food to feed him; and suppose his so-called friend to express the sincerest sympathy for his sad plight; and suppose that sympathy stops with words and no effort is made to alleviate the plight of the unfortunate man, what use is that? What use is sympathy without some attempt to turn that sympathy into practical effect? Faith without deeds is dead. This is a passage which would appeal specially to a Jew.

(i) To a Jew almsgiving was of paramount importance. So much so that righteousness and almsgiving mean one and the same thing. Almsgiving was considered to be a man's one defence when he was judged by God. "Water will quench a flaming fire," writes Ben Sirach, "and alms maketh an atonement for sin" (*Ecclesiasticus* 3: 30). In *Tobit* it is written, "Everyone who occupieth himself in alms shall behold the face of God, as it is written, I will behold thy face by almsgiving" (*Tobit* 4: 8–10). When the leaders of the Jerusalem Church agreed that Paul should go to the Gentiles the one injunction laid upon him was not to forget the poor (*Galatians* 2: 10). This stress on practical help was one of the great and lovely marks of Jewish piety.

(ii) There was a strain of Greek religion to which this stress on sympathy and almsgiving was quite alien. The Stoics aimed at *apatheia,* the complete absence of feeling. The aim of life was serenity. Emotion disturbs serenity. The way to perfect calm was to annihilate all emotion. Pity was a mere disturbance of the detached philosophic calm in which a man should aim to live. So Epictetus lays it down that only he who disobeys the divine command will ever feel grief or pity (*Discourses* 3: 24, 43). When Virgil in the *Georgics* (2: 498) draws the picture of the perfectly happy man, he has no pity for the poor and no grief for the sorrowing, for such emotions would only upset his own serenity. This is the very opposite of the Jewish point of view. For the Stoic blessedness meant being wrapped up in his own philosophic detachment and calm; for the Jew it meant actively sharing in the misfortunes of others.

(iii) In his approach to this subject James is profoundly right. There is nothing more dangerous than the repeated ex-periencing of a fine emotion with no attempt to put it into action. It is a fact that every time a man feels a noble impulse without taking action, he becomes less likely ever to take action. In a sense it is true to say that a man has no right to feel sympathy unless he at least tries to put that sympathy into action. An emotion is not something in which to luxuriate; it is something which at the cost of effort and of toil and of discipline and of sacrifice must be turned into the stuff of life.

NOT "EITHER OR", BUT "BOTH AND"

James 2: 18, 19

> But some one may well say, "Have you faith?" My answer is, "I have deeds. Show me your faith apart from your deeds and I will show you my faith by means of my deeds." You say that you believe there is one God. Excellent! The demons also believe the same thing—and shudder in terror.

JAMES is thinking of a possible objector who says, "Faith is a fine thing; and works are fine things. They are both perfectly genuine manifestations of real religion. But the one man does not necessarily possess both. One man will have faith and another will have works. Well, then, you carry on with your works and I will carry on with my faith; and we are both being truly religious in our own way." The objector's view is that faith and works are alternative expressions of the Christian religion. James will have none of it. It is not a case of *either* faith *or* works; it is necessarily a case of *both* faith *and* works.

In many ways Christianity is falsely represented as an "either or" when it must properly be a "both and".

(i) In the well-proportioned life there must be *thought* and *action*. It is tempting and it is common to think that one may be either a *man of thought* or a *man of action*. The man of thought will sit in his study thinking great thoughts; the man of action will be out in the world doing great deeds. But that is wrong. The thinker is only half a man unless he turns his thoughts into deeds. He will scarcely even inspire men to action unless he comes down into the battle and shares the arena with them. As Kipling had it:

> O England is a garden and such gardens are not made
> By saying, "O how beautiful," and sitting in the shade;
> While better men than we began their working lives
> By digging weeds from garden paths with broken dinner knives.

Nor can anyone be a real man of action unless he has thought out the great principles on which his deeds are founded.

(ii) In the well-proportioned life there must be *prayer* and *effort*. Again it is tempting to divide men into two classes— the saints who spend life secluded on their knees in constant devotion and the toilers who labour in the dust and the heat of the day. But it will not do. It is said that Martin Luther was close friends with another monk. The other was as fully persuaded of the necessity of the Reformation as Luther was. So they made an arrangement. Luther would go down into the world and fight the battle there; the other would remain in his cell praying for the success of Luther's labours. But one night the monk had a dream. In it he saw a single reaper engaged on the impossible task of reaping an immense field by himself. The lonely reaper turned his head and the monk saw his face was the face of Martin Luther; and he knew that he must leave his cell and his prayers and go to help. It is, of course, true that there are some who, because of age or bodily weakness, can do nothing other than pray; and their prayers are indeed a strength and a support. But if any normal person thinks that prayer can be a substitute for effort, his prayers are merely a way of escape. Prayer and effort must go hand in hand.

(iii) In any well-proportioned life there must be *faith* and *deeds*. It is only through deeds that faith can prove and demonstrate itself; and it is only through faith that deeds will be attempted and done. Faith is bound to overflow into action; and action begins only when a man has faith in some great cause or principle which God has presented to him.

THE PROOF OF FAITH

James 2: 20–26

Do you wish for proof, you empty creature, that faith without deeds is ineffective? Our father Abraham was proved righteous in consequence of deeds, when he was ready to offer Isaac his son upon the altar. You see how his faith co-operated with his deeds and how his faith was completed by his deeds, and so there was fulfilled the passage of Scripture which says, "Abraham believed in God, and it was reckoned to him for righteousness and he was called the friend of God." You see that it is by deeds that a man is proved righteous and not only by faith. In the same way was Rahab the harlot not also proved righteous by deeds, when she received the messengers and sent them away by another way? For just as the body without the breath is dead, so faith without deeds is dead.

JAMES offers two illustrations of the point of view on which he is insisting. Abraham is the great example of faith; but Abraham's faith was proved by his willingness to sacrifice Isaac at the apparent demand of God. Rahab was a famous figure in Jewish legend. She had sheltered the spies sent to spy out the Promised Land (*Joshua* 2: 1–21). Later legend said that she became a proselyte to the Jewish faith, that she married Joshua and that she was a direct ancestress of many priests and prophets, including Ezekiel and Jeremiah. It was her treatment of the spies which proved that she had faith.

Paul and James are both right here. Unless Abraham had had faith he would never have answered the summons of God. Unless Rahab had had faith, she would never have taken the risk of identifying her future with the fortunes of Israel. And yet, unless Abraham had been prepared to obey God to the uttermost, his faith would have been unreal; and unless Rahab had been prepared to risk all to help the spies, her faith would have been useless.

These two examples show that faith and deeds are not opposites; they are, in fact, inseparables. No man will ever be moved to action without faith; and no man's faith is genuine unless it moves him to action. Faith and deeds are opposite sides of a man's experience of God.

THE TEACHER'S PERIL

James 3: 1

My brothers, it is a mistake for many of you to become teachers, for you must be well aware that those of us who teach will receive a greater condemnation.

IN the early church the teachers were of first rate importance. Wherever they are mentioned, they are mentioned with honour. In the Church at Antioch they are ranked with the prophets who sent out Paul and Barnabas on the first missionary journey (*Acts* 13: 1). In Paul's list of those who hold great gifts within the Church they come second only to the apostles and to the prophets (1 *Corinthians* 12: 28; cp. *Ephesians* 4: 11). The apostles and the prophets were for ever on the move. Their field was the whole Church; and they did not stay long in any one congregation. But the teachers worked within a congregation, and their supreme importance was that it must have been to them that the converts were handed over for instruction in the facts of the Christian gospel and for edification in the Christian faith. It was the teacher's awe-inspiring responsibility that he could put the stamp of his own faith and knowledge on those who were entering the Church for the first time.

In the New Testament itself we get glimpses of teachers who failed in their responsibility and became false teachers. There were teachers who tried to turn Christianity into another kind of Judaism and tried to introduce circumcision and the keeping of the law (*Acts* 15: 24). There were teachers who lived out nothing of the truth which they taught, whose life was a contradiction of their instruction and who did nothing but bring dishonour on the faith they represented (*Romans* 2: 17–29). There were some who tried to teach before they themselves knew anything (1 *Timothy* 1: 6, 7); and others who pandered to the false desires of the crowd (2 *Timothy* 4: 3).

But, apart altogether from the false teachers, it is James's conviction that teaching is a dangerous occupation for any man. His instrument is speech and his agent the tongue. As Ropes puts it, James is concerned to point out "the responsibility of teachers and the dangerous character of the instrument they have to use."

The Christian teacher entered into a perilous heritage. In the Church he took the place of the Rabbi in Judaism. There were many great and saintly Rabbis, but the Rabbi was treated in a way that was liable to ruin the character of any man. His very name means, "My great one." Everywhere he went he was treated with the utmost respect. It was actually held that a man's duty to his Rabbi exceeded his duty to his parents, because his parents only brought him into the life of this world but his teacher brought him into the life of the world to come. It was actually said that if a man's parents and a man's teacher were captured by an enemy, the Rabbi must be ransomed first. It was true that a Rabbi was not allowed to take money for teaching and that he was supposed to support his bodily needs by working at a trade; but it was also held that it was a specially

pious and meritorious work to take a Rabbi into the household
and to support him with every care. It was desperately easy
for a Rabbi to become the kind of person whom Jesus depicted,
a spiritual tyrant, an ostentatious ornament of piety, a lover of
the highest place at any function, a person who gloried in the
almost subservient respect shown to him in public (*Matthew*
23 : 4–7). Every teacher runs the risk of becoming "Sir Oracle."
No profession is more liable to beget spiritual and intellectual
pride.

There are two dangers which every teacher must avoid. In
virtue of his office he will either be teaching those who are
young in years or those who are children in the faith. He
must, therefore, all his life struggle to avoid two things. He
must have every care that he is teaching the truth, and not his
own opinions or even his own prejudices. It is fatally easy for
a teacher to distort the truth and to teach, not God's version,
but his own. He must have every care that he does not
contradict his teaching by his life, continually, as it were, not,
"Do as I do," but, "Do as I say." He must never get into
the position when his scholars and students cannot hear what
he says for listening to what he is. As the Jewish Rabbis
themselves said, "Not learning but doing is the foundation,
and he who multiplies words multiplies sin" (*Sayings of the
Fathers* 1 : 18).

It is James's warning that the teacher has of his own choice
entered into a special office; and is, therefore, under the greater
condemnation, if he fails in it. The people to whom James was
writing coveted the prestige of the teacher; James demanded
that they should never forget the responsibility.

THE UNIVERSAL DANGER

James 3 : 2

> There are many things in which we all slip up; but if a man never
> slips up in his speech, he is a perfect man, able to keep the whole
> body also on the rein.

JAMES sets down two ideas which were woven into Jewish thought and literature.

(i) There is no man in this world who does not sin in something. The word James uses means *to slip up*. "Life," said Lord Fisher, the great sailor, "is strewn with orange peel." Sin is so often not deliberate but the result of a slip up when we are off our guard. This universality of sin runs all through the Bible. "None is righteous, no not one," quotes Paul. "For all have sinned and fall short of the glory of God" (*Romans* 3: 10, 23). "If we say we have no sin," says John, "we deceive ourselves, and the truth is not in us" (1 *John* 1: 8). "There is not a righteous man on earth who does good and never sins," said the preacher (*Ecclesiastes* 7: 20). "There is no man," says the Jewish sage, "among them that be born, but he hath dealt wickedly; and among the faithful there is none who hath not done amiss" (2 *Esdras* 8: 35). There is no room for pride in human life, for there is not a man upon earth who has not some blot of which to be ashamed. Even the pagan writers have the same conviction of sin. "It is the nature of man to sin both in private and in public life," said Thucydides (3: 45). "We all sin," said Seneca, "some more grievously, some more lightly" (*On Clemency* 1: 6).

(ii) There is no sin into which it is easier to fall and none which has graver consequences than the sin of the tongue. Again this idea is woven into Jewish thought. Jesus warned men that they would give account for every word they spoke. "By your words you will be justified; and by your words you will be condemned" (*Matthew* 12: 36, 37). "A soft answer turns away wrath; but a harsh word stirs up anger. . . . A gentle tongue is a tree of life; but perverseness in it breaks the spirit" (*Proverbs* 15: 1–4).

Of all Jewish writers, Jesus ben Sirach, the writer of *Ecclesiasticus,* was most impressed with the terrifying potentialities of the tongue. "Honour and shame is in talk; and the tongue of man is his fall. Be not called a whisperer, and lie not in wait with the tongue; for a foul shame is upon the thief, and an evil condemnation upon the double tongue. . . .

Instead of a friend become not an enemy; for thereby thou shalt inherit an ill name, shame and reproach; even so shall a sinner that hath a double tongue" (*Ecclesiasticus* 5: 13–6: 1). "Blessed is the man who has not slipped with his mouth" (14: 1). "Who is he that hath not offended with his tongue?" (19: 15). "Who shall set a watch before my mouth and a seal of wisdom upon my lips, that I shall not suddenly fall by them and my tongue destroy me not?" (22: 27).

He has a lengthy passage which is so nobly and passionately put that it is worth quoting in full:

> Curst the whisperer and the double-tongued; for such have destroyed many that were at peace. A backbiting tongue hath disquieted many and driven them from nation to nation; strong cities hath it pulled down and overthrown the houses of great men. It hath cut in pieces the forces of people and undone strong nations. A backbiting tongue hath cast out virtuous women and deprived them of their labours. Whoso hearkeneth unto it shall never find rest and never dwell quietly, neither shall he have a friend in whom he may repose. The stroke of the whip maketh marks in the flesh: but the stroke of the tongue breaketh the bones. Many have fallen by the edge of the sword; but not so many as have fallen by the tongue. Well is he that is defended from it and has not passed through the venom thereof; who hath not drawn the yoke thereof, nor hath been bound in her bands. For the yoke thereof is a yoke of iron and the bands thereof are bands of brass. The death thereof is an evil death, the grave were better than it. . . . Look that thou hedge thy possession about with thorns and bind up thy silver and gold and weigh thy words in a balance and make a bridle for thy lips and make a door and bar for thy mouth. Beware thou slide not by it, lest thou fall before him that lieth in wait and thy fall be incurable unto death (28: 13–26).

LITTLE BUT POWERFUL

James 3: 3–5a

If we put bits into horses' mouths to make them obedient to us, we can control the direction of their whole body as well. Look at ships, too. See how large they are and how they are driven by rough winds, and see how their course is altered by a very small rudder, wherever the pressure of the steersman desires. So, too, the tongue is a little member of the body, but it makes arrogant claims for itself.

It might be argued against James's terror of the tongue that it is a very small part of the body to make such a fuss about and to which to attach so much importance. To combat that argument James uses two pictures.

(i) We put a bit into the mouth of a horse, knowing that if we can control its mouth, we can control its whole body. So James says that if we can control the tongue, we can control the whole body; but if the tongue is uncontrolled, the whole life is set on the wrong way.

(ii) A rudder is very small in comparison with the size of a ship; and yet, by exerting pressure on that little rudder, the steersman can alter the course of the ship and direct it to safety. Long before, Aristotle had used this same picture when he was talking about the science of mechanics: "A rudder is small and it is attached to the very end of the ship, but it has such power that by this little rudder, and by the power of one man—and that a power gently exerted—the great bulk of ships can be moved." The tongue also is small, yet it can direct the whole course of a man's life.

Philo called the mind the charioteer and steersman of man's life; it is when the mind controls every word and is itself controlled by Christ that life is safe.

James is not for a moment saying that silence is better than speech. He is not pleading for a Trappist life where speech is forbidden. He is pleading for the control of the tongue. Aristippus the Greek had a wise saying, "The conqueror of pleasure is not the man who never uses it. He is the man who uses pleasure as a rider guides a horse or a steersman directs a ship, and so directs them wherever he wishes." Abstention from anything is never a complete substitute for control in its use. James is not pleading for a cowardly silence but for a wise use of speech.

A DESTRUCTIVE FIRE

James 3: 5b, 6

> See how great a forest how little a fire can set alight. And the tongue
> is a fire; in the midst of our members the tongue stands for the whole
> wicked world, for it defiles the whole body and sets on fire the
> ever-recurring cycle of creation, and is itself set on fire by hell.

THE damage the tongue can cause is like that caused by a
forest fire. The picture of the forest fire is common in the Bible.
It is the prayer of the Psalmist that God may make the wicked
like chaff before the wind; and that his tempest may destroy
them as fire consumes the forest and the flame sets the
mountains ablaze (*Psalm* 83: 13, 14). Isaiah says "wickedness
burns like a fire, it consumes briers and thorns; it kindles the
thickets of the forest" (*Isaiah* 9: 18). Zechariah speaks of "a
blazing pot in the midst of wood, like a flaming torch among
sheaves" (*Zechariah* 12: 6). The picture was one the Jews of
Palestine knew well. In the dry season the scanty grass and
low-growing thorn bushes and scrub were as dry as tinder. If
they were set on fire, the flames spread like a wave which there
was no stopping.

The picture of the tongue as a fire is also a common Jewish
picture. "A worthless man plots evil, and his speech is like a
scorching fire," says the writer of the *Proverbs* (*Proverbs*
16: 27). "As pitch and tow, so a hasty contention kindleth
fire" (*Ecclesiasticus* 28: 11). There are two reasons why the
damage which the tongue can do is like a fire.

(i) It is wide-ranging. The tongue can damage at a distance.
A chance word dropped at one end of the country or the town
can finish up by bringing grief and hurt at the other. The
Jewish Rabbis had this picture: "Life and death are in the
hand of the tongue. Has the tongue a hand? No, but as the
hand kills, so the tongue. The hand kills only at close quarters;
the tongue is called an arrow because it kills at a distance. An
arrow kills at forty or fifty paces, but of the tongue it is said
(*Psalm* 73: 9), 'They set their mouths against the heavens, and

their tongue struts through the earth.' It ranges over the whole earth and reaches to heaven." That, indeed, is the peril of the tongue. A man can ward off a blow with the hand, for the striker must be in his presence. But a man can drop a malicious word, or repeat a scandalous and untrue story, about someone whom he does not even know or about someone who stays hundreds of miles away, and cause infinite harm.

(ii) It is uncontrollable. In the tinder-dry conditions of Palestine a forest fire was almost immediately out of control; and no man can control the damage of the tongue. "Three things come not back—the spent arrow, the spoken word and the lost opportunity." There is nothing so impossible to kill as a rumour; there is nothing so impossible to obliterate as an idle and malignant story. Let a man, before he speaks, remember that once a word is spoken it is gone from his control; and let him think before he speaks because, although he cannot get it back, he will most certainly answer for it.

THE CORRUPTION WITHIN

James 3: 5b, 6 (*continued*)

WE must spend a little longer on this passage, because in it there are two specially difficult phrases.

(i) The tongue, says the Revised Standard Version is *an unrighteous world*. That ought to be *the* unrighteous world. In our bodies, that is to say, the tongue stands for the whole wicked world. In Greek the phrase is *ho kosmos tēs adikias,* and we shall best get at its meaning by remembering that *kosmos* can have two meanings.

(*a*) It can mean *adornment,* although this is less usual. The phrase, therefore, could mean that the tongue is *the adornment of evil*. That would mean that it is the organ which can make evil attractive. By the tongue men can make the worse appear the better reason; by the tongue men can excuse and justify their wicked ways; by the tongue men can persuade others into sin. There is no doubt that this gives excellent sense; but it is doubtful if the phrase really can mean that.

(*b*) *Kosmos* can mean *world*. In almost every part of the New Testament *kosmos* means the world with more than a suggestion of *the evil world*. The world cannot receive the Spirit (*John* 14: 17). Jesus manifests himself to the disciples but not to the world (*John* 14: 22). The world hates him and therefore hates his disciples (*John* 15: 18, 19). Jesus's kingdom is not of this world (*John* 18: 36). Paul condemns the wisdom of this world (1 *Corinthians* 1: 20). The Christian must not be conformed to this world (*Romans* 12: 2). When *kosmos* is used in this sense it means *the world without God,* the world in its ignorance of, and often its hostility to, God. Therefore, if we call the tongue the evil *kosmos*, it means that it is that part of the body which is without God. An uncontrolled tongue is like a world hostile to God. It is the part of us which disobeys him.

(ii) The second difficult phrase is what the Revised Standard Version translates *the cycle of nature* (*trochos geneseōs*). It literally means *the wheel of being*.

The ancients used the picture of the wheel to describe life in four different ways.

(i) The wheel is a circle, a rounded and complete whole, and, therefore, the wheel of life can mean *the totality of life*.

(ii) Any particular point in the wheel is always moving up or down. Therefore, the wheel of life can stand for *the ups and downs of life*. In this sense the phrase very nearly means the wheel of fortune, always changing and always variable.

(iii) The wheel is circular; it is always turning back upon itself in exactly the same circle; therefore, the wheel came to stand for *the cyclical repetition of life,* the weary round of an existence which is ever repeating itself without advancing.

(iv) The phrase had one particular technical use. The Orphic religion believed that the human soul was continually undergoing a process of birth and death and rebirth; and the aim of life was to escape from this treadmill into infinite being. So the Orphic devotee who had achieved could say, "I have flown out of the sorrowful, weary wheel." In this sense the wheel of life can stand for *the weary treadmill of constant reincarnation*.

It is unlikely that James knew anything about Orphic reincarnation. It is not at all likely that any Christian would think in terms of a cyclical life which was not going anywhere. It is not likely that a Christian would be afraid of the chances and changes of life. Therefore, the phrase most probably means *the whole of life and living*. What James is saying is that the tongue can kindle a destructive fire which can destroy all life; and the tongue itself is kindled with the very fire of hell. Here indeed is its terror.

BEYOND ALL TAMING

James 3: 7, 8

> Every kind of beast and bird, and reptile and fish, is and has been tamed for the service of mankind; but no man can tame the tongue. It is a restless evil, full of deadly poison.

THE idea of the taming of the animal creation in the service of mankind is one which often occurs in Jewish literature. We get it in the creation story. God said of man, "Let them have dominion over the fish of the sea, and over the birds of the air, and over every living thing that moves upon the earth" (*Genesis* 1: 28). It is, in fact, to that verse that James is very likely looking back. The same promise is repeated to Noah: "And the fear of you and the dread of you shall be upon every beast of the earth, and upon every bird of the air, upon everything that creeps on the ground and all the fish of the sea; into your hand they are delivered (*Genesis* 9: 2). The writer of *Ecclesiasticus* repeats the same idea: "God put the fear of man upon all flesh, and gave him dominion over beasts and fowls" (*Ecclesiasticus* 17: 4). The Psalmist thought on the same lines: "Thou hast given him dominion over the works of thy hands; thou hast put all things under his feet; all sheep and oxen, and also the beasts of the field; the birds of the air, and the fish of the sea, whatever passes along the paths of the sea" (*Psalm* 8: 6–8). The Roman world knew of tame fish in the fish-ponds which were in the open central hall or *atrium* of a Roman house. The serpent was the emblem of Aesculapius, and in his temples tame serpents glided about and were supposed to be incarnations of the god. People who were ill slept in the temples of Aesculapius at night, and if one of these tame serpents glided over them, that was supposed to be the healing touch of the god.

Man's ingenuity has tamed every wild creature in the sense of controlling and making useful; that, says James, is what no man by his own unaided efforts has ever been able to do with the tongue.

BLESSING AND CURSING

James 3: 9–12

> With it we bless the Lord and Father and with it we curse the men who have been made in the likeness of God. From the same mouth there emerge blessing and cursing. These things should not be so, my brothers. Surely the one stream from the same cleft in the rock does not gush forth fresh and salt water? Surely, brothers, a fig-tree cannot produce olives, nor a vine figs, nor can salt water produce fresh water?

WE know only too well from experience that there is a cleavage in human nature. In man there is something of the ape and something of the angel, something of the hero and something of the villain, something of the saint and much of the sinner. It is James's conviction that nowhere is this contradiction more evident than in the tongue.

With it, he says, we bless God. This was specially relevant to a Jew. Whenever the name of God was mentioned, a Jew must respond: "Blessed be he!" Three times a day the devout Jew had to repeat the *Shemoneh Esreh,* the famous eighteen prayers called *Eulogies,* every one of which begins, "Blessed be thou, O God." God was indeed *eulogētos, The Blessed One,* the One who was continually blessed. And yet the very mouths and tongues which had frequently and piously blessed God, were the very same mouths and tongues which cursed fellowmen. To James there was something unnatural about this; it was as unnatural as for a stream to gush out both fresh and salt water or a bush to bear opposite kinds of fruit. Unnatural and wrong such things might be, but they were tragically common.

Peter could say, "Even if I must die with you, I will not deny you" (*Matthew* 26: 35), and that very same tongue of his denied Jesus with oaths and curses (*Matthew* 26: 69–75). The John who said, "Little children, love one another," was the same who had once wished to call down fire from heaven in order to blast a Samaritan village out of existence (*Luke* 9: 51–56). Even the tongues of the apostles could say very different things.

John Bunyan tells us of Talkative: "He was a saint abroad and a devil at home." Many a man speaks with perfect courtesy to strangers and even preaches love and gentleness, and yet snaps with impatient irritability at his own family. It has not been unknown for a man to speak with piety on Sunday and to curse a squad of workmen on Monday. It has not been unknown for a man to utter the most pious sentiments one day and to repeat the most questionable stories the next. It has not been unknown for a woman to speak with sweet graciousness at a religious meeting and then to go outside to murder someone's reputation with a malicious tongue.

These things, said James, should not be. Some drugs are at once poisons and cures; they are benefits to a man when wisely controlled by his doctor but harmful when used unwisely. The tongue can bless or curse; it can wound or soothe; it can speak the fairest or the foulest things. It is one of life's hardest and plainest duties to see that the tongue does not contradict itself but speaks only such words as we would wish God to hear.

THE MAN WHO OUGHT NEVER
TO BE A TEACHER

James 3: 13, 14

Who among you is a man of wisdom and of understanding? Let him show by the loveliness of his behaviour that all he does is done with gentleness. If in your hearts you have a zeal that is bitter, and selfish ambition, do not be arrogantly boastful about your attainments, for you are false to the truth.

JAMES goes back, as it were, to the beginning of the chapter. His argument runs like this: "Is there any of you who wishes to be a real sage and a real teacher? Then let him live a life of such beautiful graciousness that he will prove to all that gentleness is enthroned as the controlling power within his heart. For, if he has a fanatical bitterness and is obviously controlled by selfish and personal ambition, then, whatever claims he makes in his arrogance, all he does is to be false to the truth which he professes to teach."

James uses two interesting words. His word for zeal is *zēlos*. *Zēlos* need not be a bad word. It could mean the noble emulation which a man felt when confronted with some picture of greatness and goodness. But there is a very narrow dividing line between noble emulation and ignoble envy. The word he uses for *selfish ambition* is *eritheia* which was also a word with no necessarily bad meaning. It originally meant *spinning for hire* and was used of serving women. Then it came to mean any work done for pay. Then it came to mean the kind of work done solely for what could be got out of it. Then it entered politics and came to mean that selfish ambition which was out for self and for nothing else and was ready to use any means to gain its ends.

A scholar and a teacher is always under a double temptation.

(i) He is under the temptation to *arrogance*. Arrogance was the besetting sin of the Rabbis. The greatest of the Jewish teachers were well aware of that. In *The Sayings of the Fathers* we read, "He that is arrogant in decision is foolish, wicked,

puffed up in spirit." It was the advice of one of the wise men:
"It rests with thy colleagues to choose whether they will adopt
thy opinion: it is not for thee to force it upon them." Few
are in such constant spiritual peril as teachers and preachers.
They are used to being listened to and to having their words
accepted. All unconsciously they tend, as Shakespeare had it,
to say,

> "I am Sir Oracle,
> And when I ope my lips let no dog bark!"

It is very difficult to be a teacher or a preacher and to remain
humble; but it is absolutely necessary.

(ii) He is under the temptation to *bitterness*. We know how
easily "learned discussion can produce passion." The *odium
theologicum* is notorious. Sir Thomas Browne has a passage on
the savagery of scholars to each other: "Scholars are men of
peace, they bear no arms, but their tongues are sharper than
Actius's razor; their pens carry farther, and give a louder
report than thunder: I had rather stand the shock of a basilisco,
than the fury of a merciless pen." Philip Lilley reminds us
that Dr. H. F. Stewart said that the arguments of Pascal with
the Jesuits reminded him of Alan Breck's fight with the crew
of the *Covenant* in Stevenson's *Kidnapped*: "The sword in his
hand flashed like quicksilver into the middle of our flying
enemies, and at every flash came the scream of a man hurt."
One of the most difficult things in the world is to argue without
passion and to meet arguments without wounding. To be
utterly convinced of one's own beliefs without at the same time
being bitter to those of others is no easy thing; and yet it is a
first necessity for the Christian teacher and scholar.

We may find in this passage four characteristics of the wrong
kind of teaching.

(i) It is *fanatical*. The truth it holds is held with unbalanced
violence rather than with reasoned conviction.

(ii) It is *bitter*. It regards its opponents as enemies to be
annihilated rather than as friends to be persuaded.

(iii) It is *selfishly ambitious*. It is, in the end, more eager to display itself than to display the truth, and it is interested more in the victory of its own opinions than in the victory of the truth.

(iv) It is *arrogant*. Its attitude is pride in its knowledge rather than humility in its ignorance. The real scholar will be far more aware of what he does not know than of what he knows.

THE WRONG KIND OF WISDOM

James 3: 15, 16

Such wisdom is not the wisdom which comes down from above, but is earthly, characteristic of the natural man, inspired by the devil. For where there is envy and selfish ambition, there is disorder and every evil thing.

THIS bitter and arrogant wisdom, so-called, is very different from real wisdom. James first of all describes it in itself, and then in its effects. In itself it is three things.

(i) It is earthly. Its standards and sources are earthly. It measures success in worldly terms; and its aims are worldly aims.

(ii) It is characteristic of the natural man. The word James uses is difficult to translate. It is *psuchikos,* which comes from *psuchē*. The ancients divided man into three parts—body, soul and spirit. The body (*sōma*) is our physical flesh and blood; the soul (*psuchē*) is the physical life which we share with the beasts; the spirit (*pneuma*) is that which man alone possesses, which differentiates him from the beasts, which makes him a rational creature and kin to God. This is a little confusing for us, because we are in the habit of using *soul* in the same sense as the ancient people used *spirit*. James is saying that this wrong kind of wisdom is no more than an animal kind of thing; it is the kind of wisdom which makes an animal snap and snarl with no other thought than that of prey or personal survival.

(iii) It is devilish. Its source is not God, but the devil. It produces the kind of situation which the devil delights in, not God.

James then describes this arrogant and bitter wisdom in its effects. The most notable thing about it is that it issues in disorder. That is to say, instead of bringing people together, it drives them apart. Instead of producing peace, it produces strife. There is a kind of person who is undoubtedly clever, with acute brain and skilful tongue; but his effect, nevertheless, in any committee, in any church, in any group, is to cause trouble and to disturb personal relationships. It is a sobering thing to remember that the wisdom he possesses is devilish rather than divine.

THE TRUE WISDOM (1)

James 3: 17, 18

The wisdom which comes from above is first pure, then peaceable, considerate, willing to yield, full of mercy and of good fruits, undivided in mind, without hypocrisy. For the seed which one day produces the reward which righteousness brings can only be sown when personal relationships are right and by those whose conduct produces such relationships.

THE Jewish sages were always agreed that the true wisdom came from above. It was not the attainment of man but the gift of God. *Wisdom* describes this wisdom as "the breath of the power of God, and a pure influence flowing from the glory of the Almighty" (*Wisdom of Solomon* 7: 25). The same book prays, "Give me the wisdom that sitteth by thy throne" (*Wisdom* 9: 4); and again, "O send her from Thy holy heavens, and from the throne of thy glory" (*Wisdom* 9: 8). Ben Sirach began his book with the sentence, "All wisdom cometh from the Lord, and is with him for ever" (*Ecclesiasticus* 1: 1); and he makes Wisdom say, "I came out of the mouth of the Most High" (*Ecclesiasticus* 24: 3). With one voice the Jewish sages agreed that wisdom came to men from God.

James uses eight words to describe this wisdom, and every one has a great picture in it.

(i) The true wisdom is *pure*. The Greek is *hagnos* and its root meaning is *pure enough to approach the gods*. At first it had only a ceremonial meaning and meant nothing more than that a man had gone through the right ritual cleansings. So, for instance, Euripides can make one of his characters say, "My hands are pure, but my heart is not." At this stage *hagnos* describes ritual, but not necessarily moral, purity. But as time went on the word came to describe the moral purity which alone can approach the gods. On the Temple of Aesculapius at Epidaurus there was the inscription at the entrance: "He who would enter the divine temple must be pure (*hagnos*); and purity is to have a mind which thinks holy thoughts." The true wisdom is so cleansed of all ulterior motives and of self that it has become pure enough to see God. Worldly wisdom might well wish to escape God's sight; the true wisdom is able to bear his very scrutiny.

(ii) The true wisdom is *eirēnikos*. We have translated this *peaceable* but it has a very special meaning. *Eirēnē* means peace, and when it is used of men its basic meaning is *right relationships between man and man, and between man and God*. The true wisdom produces right relationships. There is a kind of clever and arrogant wisdom which separates man from man, and which makes a man look with superior contempt on his fellows. There is a kind of cruel wisdom which takes a delight in hurting others with clever, but cutting, words. There is a kind of depraved wisdom which seduces men away from their loyalty to God. But the true wisdom at all times brings men closer to one another and to God.

(iii) The true wisdom is *epieikēs*. Of all Greek words in the New Testament this is the most untranslatable. Aristotle defined it as that "which is just beyond the written law" and as "justice and better than justice" and as that "which steps in to correct things when the law itself becomes unjust." The man who is *epieikēs* is the man who knows when it is actually wrong to apply the strict letter of the law. He knows how to forgive when strict justice gives him a perfect right to condemn. He knows how to make allowances, when not to stand upon his rights, how to temper justice with mercy, always remembers that there are greater things in the world than rules and regulations. It is impossible to find an English word to translate this quality. Matthew Arnold called it "sweet reasonableness" and it is the ability to extend to others the kindly consideration we would wish to receive ourselves.

THE TRUE WISDOM (2)

James 3: 17, 18 (*continued*)

(iv) The true wisdom is *eupeithēs*. Here we must make a choice between two meanings. (*a*) *Eupeithēs* can mean *ever ready to obey*. The first of William Law's rules for life was, "To fix it deep in my mind that I have but one business upon my hands, to seek for eternal happiness by doing the will of God." If we take the word in this sense, it means that the truly wise man is for ever ready to obey whenever God's voice comes to him. (*b*) *Eupeithēs* can mean *easy to persuade,* not in the sense of being pliable and weak, but in the sense of not being stubborn and of being willing to listen to reason and to appeal. Coming as it does after *epieikēs,* it probably bears this second meaning here. The true wisdom is not rigid but is willing to listen and skilled in knowing when wisely to yield.

(v) We take the next two terms together. The true wisdom is *full of mercy* (*eleos*) *and good fruits. Eleos* is a word which acquired a new meaning in Christian thought. The Greeks defined it as *pity for the man who is suffering unjustly*; but Christianity means far more than that by *eleos.* (*a*) In Christian thought *eleos* means mercy for the man who is in trouble, even if the trouble is his own fault. Christian pity is the reflection of God's pity; and that went out to men, not only when they were suffering unjustly, but when they were suffering through their own fault. We are so apt to say of someone in trouble, "It is his own fault; he brought it on himself," and, therefore, to feel no responsibility for him. Christian mercy is mercy for any man who is in trouble, even if he has brought that trouble on himself. (*b*) In Christian thought *eleos* means mercy which issues in good fruits, that is, which issues in practical help. Christian pity is not merely an emotion; it is action. We can never say that we have truly pitied anyone until we have helped him.

(vi) The true wisdom is *adiakritos, undivided*. This means that it is not wavering and vacillating; it knows its own mind, chooses its course and abides by it. There are those who think that it is clever never to make one's mind up about anything. They speak about having an open mind and about suspending judgment. But the Christian wisdom is based on the Christian certainties which come to us from God through Jesus Christ.

(vii) The true wisdom is *anupokritos, without hypocrisy*. That is to say, it is not a pose and does not deal in deception. It is honest; it never pretends to be what it is not; and it never acts a part to gain its own ends.

Finally, James says something which every Christian Church and every Christian group should have written on its heart. The Revised Standard Version correctly translates the Greek literally: "The harvest of righteousness is sown in peace by those who make peace." This is a highly compressed sentence. Let us remember that peace, *eirēnē*, means *right relationships between man and man*. So, then, what James is saying is this, "We are all trying to reap the harvest which a good life brings. But the seeds which bring the rich harvest can never flourish in any atmosphere other than one of right relationships between man and man. And the only people who can sow these seeds and reap the reward are those whose life work it has been to produce such right relationships."

That is to say, nothing good can ever grow in an atmosphere where men are at variance with one another. A group where there is bitterness and strife is a barren soil in which the seeds of righteousness can never grow and out of which no reward can ever come. The man who disturbs personal relationships

and is responsible for strife and bitterness has cut himself off
from the reward which God gives to those who live his life.

MAN'S PLEASURE OR GOD'S WILL?

James 4: 1–3

> Whence come feuds and whence come fights among you? Is this
> not their source—do they not arise because of these desires for
> pleasures which carry on their constant warring campaign within
> your members? You desire but you do not possess; you murder;
> you covet but you cannot obtain. You fight and war but you do
> not possess, because you do not ask. You ask but you do not receive,
> because you ask wrongly, for your only desire is to spend what you
> receive on your own pleasures.

JAMES is setting before his people a basic question—whether
their aim in life is to submit to the will of God or to gratify
their own desires for the pleasures of this world? He warns
that, if pleasure is the policy of life, nothing but strife and
hatred and division can possibly follow. He says that the result
of the over-mastering search for pleasure is *polemoi* (wars) and
machai (battles). He means that the feverish search for pleasure
issues in long-drawn-out resentments which are like wars, and
sudden explosions of enmity which are like battles. The ancient
moralists would have thoroughly agreed with him.

When we look at human society we so often see a seething
mass of hatred and strife. Philo writes, "Consider the continual
war which prevails among men even in times of peace, and
which exists not only between nations and countries and cities,
but also between private houses, or, I might rather say, is
present with every individual man; observe the unspeakable
raging storm in men's souls that is excited by the violent rush
of the affairs of life; and you may well wonder whether anyone
can enjoy tranquility in such a storm, and maintain calm
amidst the surge of this billowing sea."

The root cause of this unceasing and bitter conflict is nothing
other than desire. Philo points out that the Ten Command-

ments culminate in the forbidding of covetousness or desire, for desire is the worst of all the passions of the soul. "Is it not because of this passion that relations are broken, and this natural goodwill changed into desperate enmity? that great and populous countries are desolated by domestic dissensions? and land and sea filled with ever new disasters by naval battles and land campaigns? For the wars famous in tragedy . . . have all flowed from one source—desire either for money or glory or pleasure. Over these things the human race goes mad." Lucian writes, "All the evils which come upon man— revolutions and wars, stratagems and slaughters—spring from desire. All these things have as their fountain-head the desire for more." Plato writes, "The sole cause of wars and revolutions and battles is nothing other than the body and its desires." Cicero writes, "It is insatiable desires which over- turn not only individual men, but whole families, and which even bring down the state. From desires there spring hatred, schisms, discords, seditions and wars." Desire is at the root of all the evils which ruin life and divide men.

The New Testament is clear that this overmastering desire for the pleasures of this world is always a threatening danger to the spiritual life. It is the cares and riches and pleasures of this life which combine to choke the good seed (*Luke* 8: 14). A man can become a slave to passions and pleasures and when he does malice and envy and hatred enter into life (*Titus* 3: 3).

The ultimate choice in life lies between pleasing oneself and pleasing God; and a world in which men's first aim is to please themselves is a battleground of savagery and division.

THE CONSEQUENCES OF THE PLEASURE-DOMINATED LIFE

James 4: 1–3 (*continued*)

THIS pleasure-dominated life has certain inevitable con- sequences.

(i) It sets men at each other's throats. Desires, as James sees it, are inherently warring powers. He does not mean that they war within a man—although that is also true—but that they set men warring against each other. The basic desires are for the same things—for money, for power, for prestige, for worldly possessions, for the gratification of bodily lusts. When all men are striving to possess the same things, life inevitably becomes a competitive arena. They trample each other down in the rush to grasp them. They will do anything to eliminate a rival. Obedience to the will of God draws men together, for it is that will that they should love and serve one another; obedience to the craving for pleasure drives men apart, for it drives them to internecine rivalry for the same things.

(ii) The craving for pleasure drives men to shameful deeds. It drives them to envy and to enmity; and even to murder. Before a man can arrive at a deed there must be a certain driving emotion in his heart. He may restrain himself from the things that the desire for pleasure incites him to do; but so long as that desire is in his heart he is not safe. It may at any time explode into ruinous action.

The steps of the process are simple and terrible. A man allows himself to desire something. That thing begins to dominate his thoughts; he finds himself involuntarily thinking about it in his waking hours and dreaming of it when he sleeps. It begins to be what is aptly called a *ruling passion*. He begins to form imaginary schemes to obtain it; and these schemes may well involve ways of eliminating those who stand in his way. For long enough all this may go on in his mind. Then one day the imaginings may blaze into action; and he may find himself taking the terrible steps necessary to obtain his desire. Every crime in this world has come from desire which was first only a feeling in the heart but which, being nourished long enough, came in the end to action.

(iii) The craving for pleasure in the end shuts the door of prayer. If a man's prayers are simply for the things which will gratify his desires, they are essentially selfish and, therefore, it is not possible for God to answer them. The true end of prayer is to say to God, "Thy will be done." The prayer of the man who is pleasure-dominated is: "My desires be satisfied." It is one of the grim facts of life that a selfish man can hardly ever pray aright; no one can ever pray aright until he removes self from the centre of his life and puts God there.

In this life we have to choose whether to make our main object our own desires or the will of God. And, if we choose our own desires, we have thereby separated ourselves from our fellow-men and from God.

INFIDELITY TO GOD

James 4 : 4–7

> Renegades to your vows, do you not know that love for this world is enmity to God? Whoever makes it his aim to be the friend of this world thereby becomes the enemy of God. Do you think that the saying of Scripture is only an idle saying: "God jealously yearns for the spirit which he has made to dwell within us"? But God gives the more grace. That is why Scripture says, "God sets himself against the haughty, but gives grace to the humble." So, then, submit yourselves to God. Resist the devil and he will flee from you; draw near to God and he will draw near to you.

THE Authorized Version makes this passage even more difficult than it is. In it the warning is addressed to *adulterers* and *adulteresses*. In the correct text the word occurs only in the feminine. Further, the word is not intended to be taken literally; the reference is not to physical but to spiritual adultery. The whole conception is based on the common Old Testament idea of Jahweh as the husband of Israel and Israel as the bride of God. "Your Maker is your husband; the Lord of hosts is his name" (*Isaiah* 54 : 5). "Surely as a faithless wife leaves her husband, so have you been faithless to me, O house of Israel, says the Lord" (*Jeremiah* 3 : 20). This idea of Jahweh as the husband and the nation of Israel as the wife, explains the way in which the Old Testament constantly expresses spiritual infidelity in terms of physical adultery. To make a covenant with the gods of a strange land and to sacrifice to them and to intermarry with their people is "to play the harlot after their gods" (*Exodus* 34: 15, 16). It is God's forewarning to Moses that the day will come when the people "will rise and play the harlot after the strange gods of the land, where they go to be among them," and that they will forsake him (*Deuteronomy* 31: 16). It is Hosea's complaint that the people have played the harlot and forsaken God (*Hosea* 9: 1). It is in this spiritual sense that the New Testament speaks of "an *adulterous* generation" (*Matthew* 16: 4; *Mark* 8: 38). And the picture came into Christian thought in the conception of the Church as the Bride of Christ (2 *Corinthians* 11: 1, 2; *Ephesians* 5: 24–28; *Revelation* 19: 7; 21: 9).

This form of expression may offend some delicate modern ears; but the picture of Israel as the bride of God and of God as the husband of Israel has something very precious in it. It means that to disobey God is like breaking the marriage vow. It means that all sin is sin against love. It means that our relationship to God is not like the distant relationship of king and subject or master and slave, but like the intimate relationship of husband and wife. It means that when we sin we break God's heart, as the heart of one partner in a marriage may be broken by the desertion of the other.

FRIENDSHIP WITH THE WORLD AND ENMITY WITH GOD

James 4: 4–7 (*continued*)

IN this passage James says that love of the world is enmity with God and that he who is the friend of the world thereby becomes the enemy of God. It is important to understand what he means.

(i) This is not spoken out of contempt for the world. It is not spoken from the point of view which regards earth as a desert drear and which denigrates everything in the natural world. There is a story of a Puritan who was out for a walk in the country with a friend. The friend noticed a very lovely flower at the roadside and said, "That is a lovely flower." The Puritan replied, "I have learned to call nothing lovely in this lost and sinful world." That is not James's point of view; he would have agreed that this world is the creation of God; and like Jesus he would have rejoiced in its beauty.

(ii) We have already seen that the New Testament often uses the word *kosmos* in the sense *of the world apart from God.* There are two New Testament passages which well illustrate what James means. Paul writes, "The mind that is set on the flesh is hostile to God; . . . those who are in the flesh cannot please God" (*Romans* 8: 7, 8). What he means is that those who insist on assessing everything by purely human standards are necessarily at variance with God. The second passage is one of the most poignant epitaphs on the Christian life in all literature: "Demas, in love with this present world, has deserted me" (2 *Timothy* 4: 10). The idea is that of *worldliness.* If material things are the things to which he dedicates his life, clearly he cannot dedicate his life to God. In that sense the man who has dedicated his life to the world is at enmity with God.

(iii) The best commentary on this saying is that of Jesus: "No one can serve two masters" (*Matthew* 6: 24). There are two attitudes to the things of this world and the things of time. We may be so dominated by them that the world becomes our master. Or we may so use them as to serve our fellow-men and prepare ourselves for eternity, in which case the world is not our master but our servant. A man may either use the world or be used by it. To use the world as the servant of God and men is to be the friend of God, for that is what God meant the world to be. To use the world as the controller and dictator of life is to be at enmity with God, for that is what God never meant the world to be.

GOD THE JEALOUS LOVER

James 4: 4–7 (*continued*)

VERSE 5 is exceedingly difficult. To begin with, it is cited as a quotation from Scripture, but there is no part of Scripture of which it is, in fact, anything like a recognizable quotation. We may either assume that James is quoting from some book now lost which he regarded as Scripture; or, that he is summing up in one sentence what is the eternal sense of the Old Testament and not meaning to quote any particular passage.

Further, the translation is difficult: There are two alternative renderings which in the end give much the same sense. "He (that is, God) jealously yearns for the devotion of the spirit which he has made to dwell within us," or, "The Spirit which God has made to dwell within us jealously yearns for the full devotion of our hearts."

In either case the meaning is that God is the jealous lover who will brook no rival. The Old Testament was never afraid to apply the word *jealous* to God. Moses says of God to the people: "They stirred him to jealousy with strange gods" (*Deuteronomy* 32: 16). He hears God say, "They have stirred me to jealousy with what is no God" (*Deuteronomy* 32: 21). In insisting on his sole right to worship, God in the Ten Commandments says, "I the Lord your God am a jealous God" (*Exodus* 20: 5). "You shall worship no other god, for the Lord whose name is Jealous is a jealous God" (*Exodus* 34: 14). Zechariah hears God say, "Thus says the Lord of hosts: I am jealous for Zion with great jealousy" (*Zechariah* 8: 2). *Jealous* comes from the Greek *zēlos* which has in it the idea of burning heat. The idea is that God loves men with such a passion that he cannot bear any other love within the hearts of men.

It may be that *jealous* is a word which nowadays we find it difficult to connect with God, for it has acquired a lower significance; but behind it is the amazing truth that God is the lover of the souls of men. There is a sense in which love must be diffused among all men and over all God's children; but there is also a sense in which love gives and demands an exclusive devotion to one person. It is profoundly true that a man can be in love only with one person at one time; if he thinks otherwise, he does not know the meaning of love.

THE GLORY OF HUMILITY
AND THE TRAGEDY OF PRIDE

James 4: 4–7 (*continued*)

JAMES goes on to meet an almost inevitable reaction to this picture of God as the jealous lover. If God is like that, how can any man give to him the devotion he demands? James's answer is that, if God makes a great demand, he gives great grace to fulfil it; and the greater the demand, the greater the grace God gives.

But grace has a constant characteristic—a man cannot receive it until he has realized his need of it, and has come to God humbly pleading for help. Therefore, it must always remain true that God sets himself against the proud and gives lavishly of his grace to the humble. "God opposes the proud, but gives grace to the humble." This is a quotation from *Proverbs* 3: 34; and it is made again in 1 *Peter* 5: 5.

What is this destructive *pride*? The word for *proud* is *huperēphanos* which literally means *one who shows himself above other people*. Even the Greeks hated pride. Theophrastus described it as "a certain contempt for all other people." Theophylact, the Christian writer, called it, "the citadel and summit of all evils." Its real terror is that it is a thing of the heart. It means *haughtiness*; but the man who suffers from it might well appear to be walking in downcast humility, while all the time there is in his heart a vast contempt for all his fellow-men. It shuts itself off from God for three reasons.

(i) *It does not know its own need.* It so admires itself that it recognizes no need to be supplied. (ii) *It cherishes its own independence.* It will be beholden to no man and not even to God. (iii) *It does not recognize its own sin.* It is occupied with thinking of its own goodness and never realizes that it has any sin from which it needs to be saved. A pride like that cannot receive help, because it does not know that it needs help, and, therefore, it cannot ask.

The humility for which James pleads is no cringing thing. It has two great characteristics.

(i) It knows that if a man takes a resolute stand against the devil, he will prove him a coward. "The devil," as Hermas puts it, "can wrestle against the Christian, but he cannot throw him." This is a truth of which the Christians were fond, for Peter says the same thing (1 *Peter* 5: 8, 9). The great example and inspiration is Jesus in his own temptations. In them Jesus showed that the devil is not invincible; when he is confronted with the word of God, he can be put to flight. The Christian has the humility which knows that he must fight his battles with the tempter, not in his own power, but in the power of God.

(ii) It knows that it has the greatest privilege of all, access to God. This is a tremendous thing, for the right of approach to God under the old order of things belonged only to the priests (*Exodus* 19: 22). The office of the priest was to come near to God for sin-stained people (*Ezekiel* 44: 13). But through the work of Jesus Christ any man can come boldly before the throne of God, certain that he will find mercy and grace to help in time of need (*Hebrews* 4: 16). There was a time when only the High Priest might enter the Holy of Holies, but we have a new and a living way, a better hope by which we draw near to God (*Hebrews* 7: 19).

The Christian must have humility, but it is a humility which gives him dauntless courage and knows that the way to God is open to the most fearful saint.

GODLY PURITY

James 4: 8–10

Cleanse your hands, you sinners, and purify your hearts, you double-minded. Be afflicted and mourn and weep. Let your laughter be turned to sorrow, and your joy to gloom. Humble yourself before God and then he will exalt you.

IN James's thought the ethical demand of Christianity is never far away. He has talked about the grace which God gives to the humble and which enables a man to meet his great demands. But James is sure that there is something needed beyond asking and passive receiving. He is sure that moral effort is a prime necessity.

His appeal is addressed to *sinners*. The word used for sinner is *hamartōlos,* which means the hardened sinner, the man whose sin is obvious and notorious. Suidas defines *hamartōloi* as "those who choose to live in company with disobedience to the law, and who love a corrupt life." From such people James demands a moral reform which will embrace both their outward conduct and their inner desires. He demands both clean hands and a pure heart (*Psalm* 24: 4).

The phrase *cleanse your hands* originally denoted nothing more than ceremonial cleansing, the ritual washing with water which made a man ceremonially fit to approach the worship of God. The priests must wash and bathe themselves before they entered on their service (*Exodus* 30: 19–21; *Leviticus* 16: 4). The orthodox Jew must ceremonially wash his hands before he ate (*Mark* 7: 3). But men came to see that God required much more than an outward washing; and so the phrase came to stand for moral purity. "I wash my hands in innocence," says the Psalmist (*Psalm* 26: 6). It is Isaiah's demand that men should "wash yourselves; make yourselves clean," and that is equated with ceasing to do evil (*Isaiah* 1: 16). In the letter to Timothy men are urged to lift holy hands to God in prayer (1 *Timothy* 2: 8). The history of the phrase shows a deepening consciousness of what God demanded. Men began by thinking in terms of an outward washing, a ritual thing; and ended by seeing that the demand of God was moral, not ritual.

Biblical thought demands a fourfold cleansing. It demands a cleansing of the *lips* (*Isaiah* 6: 5, 6). It demands a cleansing

of the *hands* (*Psalm* 24: 4). It demands a cleansing of the *heart*
(*Psalm* 73: 13). It demands a cleansing of the *mind* (*James*
4: 8). That is to say, the ethical demand of the Bible is that a
man's words and deeds and emotions and thoughts should all
be purified. Inwardly and outwardly a man must be clean, for
only the pure in heart shall see God (*Matthew* 5: 8).

THE GODLY SORROW

James 4: 8–10 (*continued*)

IN his demand for a godly sorrow James is going back to the
fact that Jesus had said, "Blessed are those who mourn for they
shall be comforted" (*Matthew* 5: 4; *Luke* 6: 20–26). We must
not read into this passage something James does not mean.
He is not denying the joy of the Christian life. He is not
demanding that men should live a gloom-encompassed life in a
shadowed world. He is doing two things. He is pleading for
sobriety in place of frivolousness, and is doing so with all the
intensity of one whose natural instincts are puritan; and he is
describing, not the *end,* but the *beginning* of the Christian life.
He demands three things.

(i) He demands what he calls *affliction.* The verb is *talaipōrein*
and it can describe—Thucydides so uses it—the experiences of
an army whose food has gone done and who have no shelter
from the stormy weather. What James is demanding is a
voluntary abstinence from lavish luxury and effeminate
comfort. He is talking to people who are in love with the world;
and he is pleading with them not to make luxury and
comfort the standards by which they judge all life. It is
discipline which produces the scholar; it is rigorous training
which creates the athlete; and it is a wise abstinence which
produces the Christian who knows how to use the world and
its gifts aright.

(ii) He demands that they should *mourn,* that their laughter
should be turned to sorrow and their joy to gloom. Here, James

is describing the *first* step of the Christian life which is taken when a man is confronted with God and with his own sin. That is a daunting experience. When Wesley preached to the miners of Kingswood, they were moved to such grief that the tears made runnels as they ran down the grime of their faces. But that is by no means the end of the Christian life. The terrible sorrow of the realization of sin moves on to the thrilling joy of sins forgiven. But to get to the second stage a man must go through the first. James is demanding that these self-satisfied, luxury-loving, unworried hearers of his should be confronted with their sins and should be ashamed, grief-stricken and afraid; for only then can they reach out for grace and go on to a joy far greater than their earthbound pleasures.

(iii) He demands that they should *weep*. It is perhaps not reading too much into this to say that James may well be thinking of *tears of sympathy*. Up to this time these luxury-loving people have lived in utter selfishness, quite insensitive to what the poet called "the world's rain of tears." James is insisting that the griefs and the needs of others should pierce the armour of their own pleasure and comfort. A man is not a Christian until he becomes aware of the poignant cry of that humanity for which Christ died.

So, then, in words deliberately chosen to waken the sleeping soul, James demands that his hearers should substitute the way of abstinence for the way of luxury; that they should become aware of their own sins and mourn for them; and that they should become conscious of the world's need and weep for it.

THE GODLY HUMILITY

James 4: 8–10 (*continued*)

JAMES concludes with the demand for a godly humility. All through the Bible there runs the conviction that it is only the humble who can know the blessings of God. God will save the humble person (*Job* 22: 29). A man's pride will bring him low; but honour shall uphold the humble in spirit (*Proverbs* 29: 23). God dwells on high, but he is also with him that is of a humble and a contrite spirit (*Isaiah* 57: 15). They that fear the Lord will humble their souls in his sight, and the greater a man is the more he ought to humble himself, if he is to find favour in the sight of God (*Ecclesiasticus* 2: 17; 3: 17). Jesus himself repeatedly declared that it was the man who humbled himself who alone would be exalted (*Matthew* 23: 12; *Luke* 14: 11).

Only when a man realizes his own ignorance will he ask God's guidance. Only when a man realizes his own poverty in the things that matter will he pray for the riches of God's grace. Only when a man realizes his weakness in necessary things will he come to draw upon God's strength. Only when a man realizes his own sin will he realize his need of a Saviour and of God's forgiveness.

In life there is one sin which can be said to be the basis of all others; and that is forgetting that we are creatures and that God is creator. When a man realizes his essential creatureliness, he realizes his essential helplessness and goes to the source from which that helplessness can alone be supplied.

Such a dependence begets the only real independence; for then a man faces life not in his own strength but in God's and is given victory. So long as a man regards himself as independent of God he is on the way to ultimate collapse and to defeat.

THE SIN OF JUDGING OTHERS

James 4: 11, 12

Stop talking harshly about each other. He who speaks harshly of his brother, or who judges his brother, speaks harshly of the law and judges the law; and, if you judge the law, you are not a doer of the law but a judge of it. One is law-giver and judge, he who is able to save and to destroy. Who are you to judge your neighbour?

THE word James uses for *to speak harshly of,* or, *to slander* is *katalalein.* Usually this verb means to slander someone when he is not there to defend himself. This sin slander (the noun is *katalalia*) is condemned all through the Bible. It is the Psalmist's accusation against the wicked man: "You sit and speak against your brother; you slander your own mother's son" (*Psalm* 50: 20). The Psalmist hears God saying, "Him who slanders his neighbour secretly I will destroy" (*Psalm* 101: 5). Paul lists it among the sins which are characteristic of the unredeemed evil of the pagan world (*Romans* 1: 30); and it is one of the sins which he fears to find in the warring Church of Corinth (2 *Corinthians* 12: 20). It is significant to note that in both these passages *slander* comes in immediate connection with *gossip. Katalalia* is the sin of those who meet in corners and gather in little groups and pass on confidential titbits of information which destroy the good name of those who are not there to defend themselves. The same sin is condemned by Peter (1 *Peter* 2: 1).

There is great necessity for this warning. People are slow to realize that there are few sins which the Bible so unsparingly condemns as the sin of irresponsible and malicious gossip. There are few activities in which the average person finds more delight than this; to tell and to listen to the slanderous story—especially about some distinguished person—is for most people a fascinating activity. We do well to remember what God thinks of it. James condemns it for two fundamental reasons.

(i) It is a breach of the royal law that we should love our neighbour as ourselves (*James* 2: 8; *Leviticus* 19: 18). Obviously a man cannot love his neighbour as himself and speak slanderous evil about him. Now, if a man breaks a law knowingly, he sets himself above the law. That is to say, he has made himself a judge of the law. But a man's duty is not to judge the law, but to obey it. So the man who speaks evil of his neighbour has appointed himself a judge of the law and taken to himself the right to break it, and therefore stands condemned.

(ii) It is an infringement of the prerogative of God. To slander our neighbour is, in fact, to pass judgment upon him. And no human being has any right to judge any other human; the right of judgment belongs to God alone.

It is God alone who is able to save and to destroy. This great prerogative runs all through Scripture. "I kill and I make alive," says God (*Deuteronomy* 32: 39). "The Lord kills and brings to life," says Hannah in her prayer (1 *Samuel* 2: 6). "Am I God to kill and to make alive?" is the shocked question of the Israelite king to whom Naaman came with a demand for a cure for his leprosy (2 *Kings* 5: 7). Jesus warns that we should not fear men, who at the worst can only kill the body, but should fear him who can destroy both body and soul (*Matthew* 10: 28). As the Psalmist had it, it is to God alone that the issues of life and of death belong (*Psalm* 68: 20). To judge another is to take to ourselves a right to do what God alone has the right to do; and he is a reckless man who deliberately infringes the prerogatives of God.

We might think that to speak evil of our neighbour is not a very serious sin. But Scripture would say that it is one of the worst of all because it is a breach of the royal law and an infringement of the rights of God.

THE MISTAKEN CONFIDENCE

James 4: 13–17

> Come now, you who say, "Today, or tomorrow, we will go into this city, and we will spend a year there, and we will trade and make a profit." People like you do not know what will happen tomorrow. What is your life like? You are like a mist which appears for a little time and then disappears. And yet you talk like that instead of saying, "If the Lord wills, we shall live, and we shall do this or that." As it is, you make your arrogant claims in your braggart ways. All such arrogant claims are evil. So then, if a man knows what is good and does not do it, that to him is sin.

HERE again is a contemporary picture which James's readers would recognize, and in which they might well see their own portrait. The Jews were the great traders of the ancient world; and in many ways that world gave them every opportunity to practise their commercial abilities. This was an age of the founding of cities; and often when cities were founded and their founders were looking for citizens to occupy them, citizenship was offered freely to the Jews, for where the Jews came money and trade followed. So the picture is of a man looking at a map. He points at a certain spot on it, and says, "Here is a new city where there are great trade chances. I'll go there; I'll get in on the ground floor; I'll trade for a year or so; I'll make my fortune and come back rich." James's answer is that no man has a right to make confident plans for the future, for he does not know what even a day may bring forth. Man may propose but God disposes.

The essential uncertainty of the future was deeply impressed on the minds of men of all nations. The Hebrew sage wrote, "Do not boast about tomorrow, for you do not know what a day may bring forth" (*Proverbs* 27: 1). Jesus told his story of the rich but foolish man who made his fortune and built up his plans for the future, and forgot that his soul might be required of him that very night (*Luke* 12: 16–21). Ben Sirach wrote, "There is that waxeth rich by his wariness and pinching, and this is the portion of his reward: whereas, he saith, 'I have found rest and now will eat continually of my goods'; and yet he knoweth not what time shall come upon him and that death approacheth; and that he must leave these things to others and die" (*Ecclesiasticus* 11: 18, 19). Seneca said: "How foolish it is for a man to make plans for his life, when not even tomorrow is in his control." And again: "No man has such rich friends that he can promise himself tomorrow." The Rabbis had a proverb: "Care not for the morrow, for ye know not what a day may bring forth. Perhaps you may not find tomorrow." Dennis Mackail was the friend of Sir James Barrie. He tells that, as Barrie grew older, he would never make an arrangement for even a social engagement at any distant date. "Short notice now!" he would always say.

James goes on. This uncertainty of life is not a cause either for fear or for inaction. It is a reason for realizing our complete dependence on God. It has always been the mark of a serious-minded man that he makes his plans in such dependence. Paul writes to the Corinthians: "I will come to you soon, if the Lord wills" (1 *Corinthians* 4: 19). "I hope to spend some time with you, if the Lord permits" (1 *Corinthians* 16: 7). Xenophon writes, "May all these things be, if the gods so will. If anyone wonders that we often find the phrase written, 'if the gods will,' I would have him to know that, once he has experienced the risks of life, he will not wonder nearly so much." Plato relates a conversation between Socrates and Alcibiades. Alcibiades says: "I will do so if you wish, Socrates." Socrates answers, "Alcibiades, that is not the way to talk. And how ought you to speak? You ought to say, 'If *God* so wishes.' " Minucius Felix writes, " ' God grant it'— it comes instinctively to the ordinary man to speak like that." Constantly among the Arabs there is heard the expressions: "Imsh' Allah—if Allah wills." The curious thing is that there seems to have been no corresponding phrase which the Jews used. In this they had to learn.

The true Christian way is not to be terrorized into fear and paralysed into inaction by the uncertainty of the future; but to commit the future and all our plans into the hands of God, always remembering that these plans may not be within God's purpose.

The man who does not remember that, is guilty of arrogant boasting. The word is *alazoneia*. *Alazoneia* was originally the characteristic of the wandering quack. He offered cures which were no cures and boasted of things that he was not able to do. The future is not within the hands of men and no man can arrogantly claim that he has power to decide it.

James ends with a threat. If a man knows that a thing is wrong and still continues to do it, that to him is sin. James is in effect saying, "You have been warned; the truth has been placed before your eyes." To continue now in the self-confident habit of seeking to dispose of one's own life is sin for the man who has been reminded that the future is not in his hands but in God's.

THE WORTHLESSNESS OF RICHES

James 5: 1–3

> Come now, you rich, weep and wail at the miseries which are coming
> upon you. Your wealth is rotten and your garments are food for
> moths. Your gold and silver are corroded clean through with rust;
> and their rust is proof to you of how worthless they are. It is a rust
> which will eat into your very flesh like fire. It is a treasure indeed
> that you have amassed for yourselves in the last days!

IN the first six verses of this chapter James has two aims. First,
to show the ultimate worthlessness of all earthly riches; and
second, to show the detestable character of those who possess
them. By doing this he hopes to prevent his readers from
placing all their hopes and desires on earthly things.

If you knew what you were doing, he says to the rich, you
would weep and wail for the terror of the judgment that is
coming upon you at the Day of the Lord. The vividness of the
picture is increased by the word which James uses for *to wail.*
It is the verb *ololuzein,* which is onomatopoetic and carries its
meaning in its very sound. It means even more than to wail, it
means *to shriek,* and in the Authorized Version is often
translated *to howl;* and it depicts the frantic terror of those on
whom the judgment of God has come (*Isaiah* 13: 6; 14: 31;
15: 2, 3; 16: 7; 23: 1, 14; 65: 14; *Amos* 8: 3). We might well
say that it is the word which describes those undergoing the
tortures of the damned.

All through this passage the words are vivid and pictorial
and carefully chosen. In the east there were three main sources
of wealth and James has a word for the decay of each of them.

There were corn and grain. That is the wealth which grows
rotten (*sēpein*).

There were garments. In the east garments were wealth.
Joseph gave changes of garments to his brothers (*Genesis* 45:
22). It was for a beautiful mantle from Shinar. that Achan
brought disaster on the nation and death on himself and his
family (*Joshua* 7: 21). It was changes of garments that Samson

promised to anyone who would solve his riddle (*Judges* 14: 12).
It was garments that Naaman brought as a gift to the prophet
of Israel and to obtain which Gehazi sinned his soul (2 *Kings*
5: 5, 22). It was Paul's claim that he had coveted no man's
money or apparel (*Acts* 20: 33). These garments, which are so
splendid, will be food for moths (*sētobrōtos*, cp. *Matthew* 6: 19).

The climax of the world's inevitable decay comes at the end.
Even their gold and silver will be rusted clean through
(*katiasthai*). The point is that gold and silver do not actually
rust; so James in the most vivid way is warning men that even
the most precious and apparently most indestructible things
are doomed to decay.

This rust is proof of the impermanence and ultimate
valuelessness of all earthly things. More, it is a dread warning.
The desire for these things is like a dread rust eating into men's
bodies and souls. Then comes a grim sarcasm. It is a fine
treasure indeed that any man who concentrates on these things
is heaping up for himself at the last. The only treasure he will
possess is a consuming fire which will wipe him out.

It is James's conviction that to concentrate on material
things is not only to concentrate on a decaying delusion; it is
to concentrate on self-produced destruction.

THE SOCIAL PASSION OF THE BIBLE

James 5: 1–3 (*continued*)

NOT even the most cursory reader of the Bible can fail to be
impressed with the social passion which blazes through its
pages. No book condemns dishonest and selfish wealth with
such searing passion as it does. The book of the prophet Amos
was called by J. E. McFadyen "The Cry for Social Justice."
Amos condemns those who store up violence and robbery in
their palaces (*Amos* 3: 10). He condemns those who tread on
the poor and themselves have houses of hewn stone and
pleasant vineyards—which in the wrath of God they will never

enjoy (*Amos* 5: 11). He lets loose his wrath on those who give short weight and short measure, who buy the poor for silver and the needy for a pair of shoes, and who palm off on the poor the refuse of their wheat. "I will never forget any of their deeds," says God (*Amos* 8: 4–7). Isaiah warns those who build up great estates by adding house to house and field to field (*Isaiah* 5: 8). The sage insists that he who trusts in riches shall fall (*Proverbs* 11: 28). Luke quotes Jesus as saying, "Woe to you that are rich!" (*Luke* 6: 24). It is only with difficulty that those who have riches enter into the Kingdom of God (*Luke* 18: 24). Riches are a temptation and a snare; the rich are liable to foolish and hurtful lusts which end in ruin, for the love of money is the root of all evils (1 *Timothy* 6: 9, 10).

In the inter-testamental literature there is the same note. "Woe to you who acquire silver and gold in unrighteousness. . . . They shall perish with their possessions, and in shame will their spirits be cast into the furnace of fire" (*Enoch* 97: 8). In the *Wisdom of Solomon* there is a savage passage in which the sage makes the selfish rich speak of their own way of life as compared with that of the righteous. "Come on, therefore, let us enjoy the good things that are present; and let us speedily use created things like as in youth. Let us fill ourselves with costly wine and ointments: and let no flower of the spring pass by us. Let us crown ourselves with rosebuds before they be withered; let there be no meadow but our luxury shall pass through it. Let none of us go without his part of our voluptuousness; let us leave tokens of our joyfulness in every place; for this is our portion, and our lot is this. Let us oppress the poor righteous man, let us not spare the widow, nor reverence the ancient grey hairs of the aged. . . . Therefore, let us lie in wait for the righteous; because he is not for our turn and is clean contrary to our doings; he upbraideth us with our offending of the law, and objecteth to our infamy, the sins of our way of life" (*Wisdom of Solomon* 2: 6–12).

One of the mysteries of social thought is how the Christian religion ever came to be regarded as "the opiate of the people" or to seem an other-worldly affair. There is no book in any

literature which speaks so explosively of social injustice as the
Bible, nor any book which has proved so powerful a social
dynamic. It does not condemn wealth as such but there is no
book which more strenuously insists on wealth's responsibility
and on the perils which surround a man who is abundantly
blessed with this world's goods.

THE WAY OF SELFISHNESS AND ITS END

James 5: 4–6

> Look you, the pay of the reapers who reaped your estates, the pay
> kept back from them by you, cries against you, and the cries of those
> who reaped have come to the ears of the Lord of Hosts. On the
> earth you have lived in soft luxury and played the wanton; you have
> fattened your hearts for the day of slaughter. You condemned, you
> killed the righteous man, and he does not resist you.

HERE is condemnation of selfish riches and warning of where
they must end.

(i) The selfish rich have gained their wealth by injustice.
The Bible is always sure that the labourer is worthy of his hire
(*Luke* 10: 7; 1 *Timothy* 5: 18). The day labourer in Palestine
lived on the very verge of starvation. His wage was small; it
was impossible for him to save anything; and if the wage was
withheld from him, even for a day, he and his family simply
could not eat. That is why the merciful laws of Scripture again
and again insist on the prompt payment of his wages to the
hired labourer. "You shall not oppress a hired servant who
is poor and needy. . . . You shall give him his hire on the day
he earns it, before the sun goes down (for he is poor, and sets
his heart upon it); lest he cry against you to the Lord, and it be
sin in you" (*Deuteronomy* 24: 14, 15). "The wages of a hired
servant shall not remain with you all night until the morning"
(*Leviticus* 19: 13). "Do not say to your neighbour, 'Go, and
come again, tomorrow I will give it'—when you have it with
you" (*Proverbs* 3: 27, 28). "Woe to him that builds his house

by unrighteousness and his upper rooms by injustice; who makes his neighbour serve him for nothing, and does not give him his wages" *(Jeremiah* 22: 13). "Those that oppress the hireling in his wages" are under the judgment of God *(Malachi* 3: 5). "He that taketh away his neighbour's living, the bread gotten by sweat, slayeth him; and he that defraudeth the labourer of his hire, defraudeth his Maker, and shall receive a bitter reward, for he is brother to him that is a blood-shedder" *(Ecclesiasticus* 34: 22). "Let not the wages of any man which hath wrought for thee tarry with thee, but give it him out of hand" *(Tobit* 4: 14).

The law of the Bible is nothing less than the charter of the labouring man. The social concern of the Bible speaks in the words of the Law and of the Prophets and of the Sages alike. Here it is said that the cries of the harvesters have reached the ears of the Lord of hosts! The hosts are the hosts of heaven, the stars and the heavenly powers. It is the teaching of the Bible in its every part that the Lord of the universe is concerned for the rights of the labouring man.

(ii) The selfish rich have used their wealth selfishly. They have lived in soft luxury and have played the wanton. The word translated *to live in soft luxury* is *truphein*. It comes from a root which means *to break down*; and it describes the soft living which in the end saps and destroys a man's moral fibre. The word translated *to play the wanton* is *spatalan*. It is a much worse word; it means to live in lewdness and lasciviousness. It is the condemnation of the selfish rich that they have used their possessions to gratify their own love of comfort and to satisfy their own lusts, and that they have forgotten all duty to their fellow-men.

(iii) But anyone who chooses this pathway has also chosen its end. The end of specially fattened cattle is that they will be slaughtered for some feast; and those who have sought this easy luxury and selfish wantonness are like men who have fattened themselves for the day of judgment. The end of their pleasure is grief and the goal of their luxury is death. Selfishness always leads to the destruction of the soul.

(iv) The selfish rich have slain the unresisting righteous man. It is doubtful to whom this refers. It could be a reference to Jesus. "You denied the Holy and Righteous One and asked for a murderer to be granted to you" (*Acts* 3: 14). It is Stephen's charge that the Jews always slew God's messengers even before the coming of the Just One (*Acts* 7: 52). It is Paul's declaration that God chose the Jews to see the Just One although they rejected him (*Acts* 22: 14). Peter says that Christ suffered for our sins, the just for the unjust (1 *Peter* 3: 18). The suffering servant of the Lord offered no resistance. He opened not his mouth and like a sheep before his shearers he was dumb (*Isaiah* 53: 7), a passage which Peter quotes in his picture of Jesus (1 *Peter* 2: 23). It may well be that James is saying that in their oppression of the poor and the righteous man, the selfish rich have crucified Christ again. Every wound that selfishness inflicts on Christ's people is another wound inflicted on Christ.

It may be that James is not specially thinking of Jesus when he speaks about the righteous man but of the evil man's instinctive hatred of the good man. We have already quoted the passage in *The Wisdom of Solomon* which describes the conduct of the rich. That passage goes on: "He (the righteous man) professeth to have the knowledge of God, and he calleth himself the child of the Lord. He was made to reprove our thoughts. He is grievous unto us even to behold: for his life is not like other men's, his ways are of another fashion. We are esteemed of him as counterfeits: he abstaineth from our ways as from filthiness: he pronounceth the end of the just to be blessed, and maketh his boast that God is his Father. Let us see if his words be true: and let us prove what shall happen in the end of him. For if the just man be the son of God, he will help him and deliver him from the hand of his enemies. Let us examine him with despitefulness and torture, that we may know his meekness and prove his patience. Let us condemn him with a shameful death: for by his own saying he shall be respected" (*Wisdom of Solomon* 2: 13–30). These, says the Sage, are the words of men whose wickedness has blinded them.

Alcibiades, the friend of Socrates, for all his great talents often lived a riotous and debauched life. And there were times when he said to Socrates: "Socrates, I hate you; for every time I see you, you show me what I am." The evil man would gladly eliminate the good man, for he reminds him of what he is and of what he ought to be.

WAITING FOR THE COMING OF THE LORD

James 5: 7–9

> Brothers, have patience until the coming of the Lord. Look you, the farmer waits for the precious fruit of the earth, patiently waiting for it until it receives the early and the late rains. So do you too be patient. Make firm your hearts for the coming of the Lord is near. Brothers, do not complain against each other, that you may not be condemned. Look you, the judge stands at the door.

THE early church lived in expectation of the immediate Second Coming of Jesus Christ; and James exhorts his people to wait with patience for the few years which remain. The farmer has to wait for his crops until the early and the late rains have come. The early and the late rains are often spoken of in Scripture, for they were all-important to the farmer of Palestine (*Deuteronomy* 11: 14; *Jeremiah* 5: 24; *Joel* 2: 23). The early rain was the rain of late October and early November without which the seed would not germinate. The late rain was the rain of April and May without which the grain would not mature. The farmer needs patience to wait until nature does her work; and the Christian needs patience to wait until Christ comes.

During that waiting they must confirm their faith. They must not blame one another for the troubles of the situation in which they find themselves for, if they do, they will be breaking the commandment which forbids Christians to judge one another (*Matthew* 7: 1); and if they break that commandment, they will be condemned. James has no doubt of the nearness of the coming of Christ. The judge is at the door, he says, using a phrase which Jesus himself had used (*Mark* 13: 29; *Matthew* 24: 33).

It so happened that the early church was mistaken. Jesus Christ did not return within a generation. But it will be of interest to gather up the New Testament's teaching about the Second Coming so that we may see the essential truth at its heart.

We may first note that the New Testament uses three different words to describe the Second Coming of Jesus Christ.

(i) The commonest is *parousia,* a word which has come into English as it stands. It is used in *Matthew* 24: 3, 27, 37, 39; 1 *Thessalonians* 2: 19; 3: 13; 4: 15; 5: 23; 2 *Thessalonians* 2: 1; 1 *Corinthians* 15: 23; 1 *John* 2: 28; 2 *Peter* 1: 16; 3: 4). In secular Greek this is the ordinary word for someone's presence or arrival. But it has two other usages, one of which became quite technical. It is used of the invasion of a country by an army; and specially it is used of the visit of a king or a governor to a province of his empire. So, then, when this word is used of Jesus, it means that his Second Coming is the final invasion of earth by heaven and the coming of the King to receive the final submission and adoration of his subjects.

(ii) The New Testament also uses the word *epiphaneia* (*Titus* 2: 13; 2 *Timothy* 4: 1; 2 *Thessalonians* 2: 9). In ordinary Greek this word has two special usages. It is used of the appearance of a god to his worshipper; and it is used of the accession of an emperor to the imperial power of Rome. So, then, when this word is used of Jesus, it means that his Second Coming is God appearing to his people, both to those who are waiting for him and to those who are disregarding him.

(iii) Finally the New Testament uses the word *apokalupsis* (1 *Peter* 1: 7, 13). *Apokalupsis* in ordinary Greek means an *unveiling* or a *laying bare*; and when it is used of Jesus, it means that his Second Coming is the laying bare of the power and glory of God come upon men.

Here, then, we have a series of great pictures. The Second Coming of Jesus is the arrival of the King; it is God appearing to his people and mounting his eternal throne; it is God directing on the world the full blaze of his heavenly glory.

THE COMING OF THE KING

James 5: 7–9 (*continued*)

WE may now gather up briefly the teaching of the New Testament about the Second Coming and the various uses it makes of the idea.

(i) The New Testament is clear that no man knows the day or the hour when Christ comes again. So secret, in fact, is that time that Jesus himself does not know it; it is known to God alone (*Matthew* 24: 36; *Mark* 13: 32). From this basic fact one thing is clear. Human speculation about the time of the Second Coming is not only useless, it is blasphemous; for surely no man should seek to gain a knowledge which is hidden from Jesus Christ himself and resides only in the mind of God.

(ii) The one thing that the New Testament does say about the Second Coming is that it will be as sudden as the lightning and as unexpected as a thief in the night (*Matthew* 24: 27, 37, 39; 1 *Thessalonians* 5: 2; 2 *Peter* 3: 10). We cannot wait to get ready when it comes; we must be ready for its coming.

So, the New Testament urges certain duties upon men.

(i) They must be for ever on the watch (1 *Peter* 4: 7). They are like servants whose master has gone away and who, not knowing when he will return, must have everything ready for his return, whether it be at morning, at midday, or at evening (*Matthew* 24: 36–51).

(ii) Long delay must not produce despair or forgetfulness (2 *Peter* 3: 4). God does not see time as men do. To him a thousand years are as a watch in the night and even if the years pass on, it does not mean that he has either changed or abandoned his design.

(iii) Men must use the time given them to prepare for the coming of the King. They must be sober (1 *Peter* 4: 7). They must get to themselves holiness (1 *Thessalonians* 3: 13). By the grace of God they must become blameless in body and in spirit (1 *Thessalonians* 5: 23). They must put off the works of darkness and put on the armour of light now that the day is far spent (*Romans* 13: 11–14). Men must use the time given them to make themselves such that they can greet the coming of the King with joy and without shame.

(iv) When that time comes, they must be found in fellowship. Peter uses the thought of the Second Coming to urge men to love and mutual hospitality (1 *Peter* 4: 8, 9). Paul commands that all things be done in love—*Maran atha*—the Lord is at hand (1 *Corinthians* 16: 14, 22). He says that our *forbearance* must be known to all men because the Lord is at hand (*Philippians* 4: 5). The word translated *forbearance* is *epieikes* which means the spirit that is more ready to offer forgiveness than to demand justice. The writer to the Hebrews demands mutual help, mutual Christian fellowship, mutual encouragement because the day is coming near (*Hebrews* 10: 24, 25). The New Testament is sure that in view of the Coming of Christ we must have our personal relationships right with our fellow-men. The New Testament would urge that no man ought to end a day with an unhealed breach between himself and a fellowman, lest in the night Christ should come.

(v) John uses the Second Coming as a reason for urging men to abide in Christ (1 *John* 2: 28). Surely the best preparation for meeting Christ is to live close to him every day.

Much of the imagery attached to the Second Coming is Jewish, part of the traditional apparatus of the last things in the ancient Jewish mind. There are many things which we are not meant to take literally. But the great truth behind all the temporary pictures of the Second Coming is that this world is not purposeless but going somewhere, that there is one divine far-off event to which the whole creation moves.

THE TRIUMPHANT PATIENCE

James 5: 10, 11

Brothers, take as an example of patience in hardship the prophets who spoke in the name of the Lord. Look you, we count those who endure blessed. You have heard of Job's steadfast endurance and you have seen the conclusion of his troubles which the Lord gave to him, and you have proof that the Lord is very kind and merciful.

IT is always a comfort to feel that others have gone through
what we have to go through. James reminds his readers that
the prophets and the men of God could never have done their
work and borne their witness had they not patiently endured.
He reminds them that Jesus himself had said that the man who
endured to the end was blessed for he would be saved
(*Matthew* 24: 13).

Then he quotes the example of Job, of whom in the
synagogue discourses they had often heard. We generally speak
of the *patience* of Job which is the word the Authorized Version
uses. But patience is far too passive a word. There is a sense in
which Job was anything but patient. As we read the tremendous
drama of his life we see him passionately resenting what has
come upon him, passionately questioning the conventional
arguments of his so-called friends, passionately agonizing over
the terrible thought that God might have forsaken him. Few
men have spoken such passionate words as he did; but the great
fact about him is that in spite of all the agonizing questionings
which tore at his heart, he never lost his faith in God. "Behold,
he will slay me; I have no hope;" (*Job* 13: 15). "My witness is
in heaven, and he that vouches for me is on high" (*Job* 16: 19).
"I know that my redeemer lives" (*Job* 19: 25). His is no
unquestioning submission; he struggled and questioned, and
sometimes even defied, but the flame of his faith was never
extinguished.

The word used of him is that great New Testament word
hupomonē, which describes, not a passive patience, but that
gallant spirit which can breast the tides of doubt and sorrow
and disaster and come out with faith still stronger on the other
side. There may be a faith which never complained or
questioned; but still greater is the faith which was tortured by
questions and still believed. It was the faith which held grimly
on that came out on the other side, for "the Lord blessed the
latter days of Job more than his beginning" (*Job* 42: 12).

There will be moments in life when we think that God has
forgotten, but if we cling to the remnants of faith, at the end
we, too, shall see that God is very kind and very merciful.

THE NEEDLESSNESS AND THE FOLLY OF OATHS

James 5: 12

> Above all things, my brothers, do not swear, neither by heaven nor
> by earth nor by any other oath. Let your yes be a simple yes and
> your no a simple no, lest you fall under judgment.

JAMES is repeating the teaching of Jesus in the Sermon on the
Mount (*Matthew* 5: 33–37), teaching which was very necessary
in the days of the early church. James is not thinking of what
we call bad language but of confirming a statement or a
promise or an undertaking by an oath. In the ancient world,
there were two evil practices.

(i) There was a distinction—especially in the Jewish world—
between oaths which were binding and oaths which were not
binding. Any oath in which the name of God was directly used
was considered to be definitely binding; but any oath in which
direct mention of the name of God was not made was held not
to be binding. The idea was that, once God's name was
definitely used, he became an active partner in the transaction,
but he did not become a partner unless his name was so
introduced. The result of this was that it became a matter of
skill and sharp practice to find an oath which was not binding.
This made a mockery of the whole practice of confirming
anything by an oath.

(ii) There was in this age an extraordinary amount of oath-
taking. This in itself was quite wrong. For one thing, the value
of an oath depends to a large extent on the fact of it being
very seldom necessary to take one. When oaths became a
commonplace, they ceased to be respected as they ought to be.
For another thing, the practice of taking frequent oaths was
nothing other than a proof of the prevalence of lying and
cheating. In an honest society no oath is needed; it is only when
men cannot be trusted to tell the truth that they have to be
put upon oath.

In this the ancient writers on morals thoroughly agreed with
Jesus. Philo says, "Frequent swearing is bound to beget perjury

and impiety." The Jewish Rabbis said, "Accustom not thyself to vows, for sooner or later thou wilt swear false oaths." The Essenes forbade all oaths. They held that if a man required an oath to make him tell the truth, he was already branded as untrustworthy. The great Greeks held that the best guarantee of any statement was not an oath but the character of the man who made it; and that the ideal was to make ourselves such that no one would ever think of demanding an oath from us because he would be certain that we would always speak the truth.

The New Testament view is that every word is spoken in the presence of God and ought, therefore, to be true; and it would agree that the Christian must be known to be a man of such honour that it will be quite unnecessary ever to put him on oath. The New Testament would not entirely condemn oaths but it would deplore the human tendency to falsehood which on occasion makes oaths necessary.

A SINGING CHURCH

James 5: 13–15

> Is any among you in trouble? Let him pray. Is any in good spirits? Let him sing a hymn. Is any among you sick? Let him call in the elders of the Church; and let them anoint him with oil in the name of the Lord, and pray over him; and the believing prayer will restore to health the ailing person, and the Lord will enable him to rise from his bed; and even if he has committed sin, he will receive forgiveness.

HERE we have set out before us certain dominant characteristics of the early church.

It was a *singing church*; the early Christians were always ready to burst into song. In Paul's description of the meetings of the Church at Corinth, we find singing an integral part (1 *Corinthians* 14: 15, 26). When he thinks of the grace of God going out to the Gentiles, it reminds him of the joyous saying of the Psalmist: "I will praise thee among the Gentiles, and sing to thy name" (*Romans* 15: 9; cp. *Psalm* 18: 49). The

Christians they speak to each other in psalms and hymns and spiritual songs, singing and making melody in their hearts to the Lord (*Ephesians* 5 : 19). The word of Christ dwells in them, and they teach and admonish each other in psalms and hymns and spiritual songs, singing with thankfulness in their hearts to the Lord (*Colossians* 3 : 16). There was a joy in the heart of the Christians which issued from their lips in songs of praise for the mercy and the grace of God.

The fact is that the heathen world has always been sad and weary and frightened. Matthew Arnold wrote a poem describing its bored weariness.

> "On that hard Pagan world disgust
>   And secret loathing fell;
> Deep weariness and sated lust
>   Made human life a hell.
> In his cool hall, with haggard eyes,
>   The Roman noble lay;
> He drove abroad in furious guise
>   Along the Appian Way;
> He made a feast, drank fierce and fast,
>   And crowned his hair with flowers—
> No easier nor no quicker past
>   The impracticable hours."

In contrast with that weary mood the accent of the Christian is singing joy. That was what impressed John Bunyan when he heard four poor old women talking, as they sat at a door in the sun: "Methought they spake, as if joy did make them speak." When Bilney, the martyr, grasped the wonder of redeeming grace, he said, "It was as if dawn suddenly broke on a dark night." Archibald Lang Fleming, the first Bishop of the Arctic, tells of the saying of an Eskimo hunter: "Before you came the road was dark and we were afraid. Now we are not afraid, for the darkness has gone away and all is light as we walk the Jesus way."

Always the church has been a singing Church. When Pliny, governor of Bithynia, wrote to Trajan, the Roman Emperor, in A.D. 111 to tell him of this new sect of Christians, he said that his information was that "they are in the habit of meeting on a certain fixed day before it is light, when they sing in alternate verses a hymn to Christ as God." In the orthodox Jewish synagogue, since the Fall of Jerusalem in A.D. 70, there has been no music, for, when they worship, they remember a tragedy; but in the Christian Church, from the beginning until now, there has been the music of praise, for the Christian remembers an infinite love and enjoys a present glory.

A HEALING CHURCH

James 5: 13–15 (*continued*)

ANOTHER great characteristic of the early church was that it was a *healing* Church. Here it inherited its tradition from Judaism. When a Jew was ill, it was to the Rabbi he went rather than to the doctor; and the Rabbi anointed him with oil—which Galen the Greek doctor called "the best of all medicines"—and prayed over him. Few communities can have been so devotedly attentive to their sick as the early church was. Justin Martyr writes that numberless demoniacs were healed by the Christians when all other exorcists had been helpless to cure them and all drugs had been unavailing. Irenaeus, writing far down the second century, tells us that the sick were still healed by having hands laid on them. Tertullian, writing midway through the third century, says that no less a person than the Roman Emperor, Alexander Severus, was healed by anointing at the hands of a Christian called Torpacion and that in his gratitude he kept Torpacion as a guest in his palace until the day of his death.

One of the earliest books concerning Church administration is the *Canons of Hippolytus*, which goes back to the end of the second century or the beginning of the third. It is there laid down that men who have the gift of healing are to be ordained as presbyters after investigation has been made to ensure that they really do possess the gift and that it comes from God.

That same book gives the noble prayer used at the consecration of the local bishops, part of which runs: "Grant unto him, O Lord, ... the power to break all the chains of the evil power of the demons, to cure all the sick, and speedily to subdue Satan beneath his feet." In the *Clementine Letters* the duties of the deacons are laid down; and they include the rule: "Let the deacons of the Church move about intelligently and act as eyes for the bishop. ... Let them find out those who are sick in the flesh, and bring such to the notice of the main body who know nothing of them, that they may visit them, and supply their wants." In the *First Epistle of Clement* the prayer of the Church is: "Heal the sick; raise up the weak; cheer the faint-hearted." A very early Church code lays it down that each congregation must appoint at least one widow to take care of women who are sick. For many centuries the Church consistently used anointing as a means of healing the sick. In fact it is important to note that the sacrament of unction, or anointing, was in the early centuries always designed as a means of cure, and not as a preparation for death as it now is in the Roman Catholic Church. It was not until A.D. 852 that this sacrament did, in fact, become the Sacrament of Extreme Unction, administered to prepare for death.

The Church has always cared for her sick; and in her there has always resided the gift of healing. The social gospel is not an appendix to Christianity; it is the very essence of the Christian faith and life.

A PRAYING CHURCH

James 5: 16–18

Confess your sins to each other, and pray for each other, that you may be healed. The prayer of a good man, when it is set to work, is very powerful. Elijah was a man with the same emotions as ourselves, and he prayed earnestly that it should not rain, and for three years and six months no rain fell upon the earth. And he prayed again and the heaven gave rain; and the earth put forth her fruit.

THERE are in this passage three basic ideas of Jewish religion.

(i) There is the idea that all sickness is due to sin. It was a deeply-rooted Jewish belief that where there were sickness and suffering, there must have been sin. "There is no death without guilt," said the Rabbis, "and no suffering without sin." The Rabbis, therefore, believed that before a man could be healed of his sickness his sins must be forgiven by God. Rabbi Alexandrai said, "No man gets up from his sickness until God has forgiven him all his sins." That is why Jesus began his healing of the man with the palsy by saying, "My son, your sins are forgiven" (*Mark* 2: 5). The Jew always identified suffering and sin. Nowadays we cannot make this mechanical identification; but this remains true—that no man can know any health of soul or mind or body until he is right with God.

(ii) There is the idea that, to be effective, confession of sin has to be made to men, and especially to the person wronged, as well as to God. In a very real sense it is easier to confess sins to God than to confess them to men; and yet in sin there are two barriers to be removed—the barrier it sets up between us and God, and the barrier it sets up between us and our fellow-men. If both these barriers are to be removed, both kinds of confession must be made. This was, in fact, the custom of the Moravian Church and Wesley took it over for his earliest Methodist classes. They used to meet two or three times a week "to confess their faults to one another and to pray for one another that they might be healed." This is clearly a principle which must be used with wisdom. It is quite true that there may be cases where confession of sin to each other may do infinitely more harm than good; but where a barrier has been erected because of some wrong which has been done, a man must put himself right both with God and his fellow-man.

(iii) Above all, there is the idea that no limits can be set to the power of prayer. The Jews had a saying that he who prays surrounds his house with a wall stronger than iron. They said, "Penitence can do something; but prayer can do everything." To them prayer was nothing less than contacting the power of God; it was the channel through which the strength and grace of God were brought to bear on the troubles and problems of life. How much more must this be so for a Christian?

Tennyson wrote:

> "More things are wrought by prayer
> Than this world dreams of. Wherefore, let thy voice
> Rise like a fountain for me night and day.
> For what are men better than sheep or goats
> That nourish a blind life within the brain,
> If, knowing God, they lift not hands of prayer
> Both for themselves and those who call them friend?
> For so the whole round earth is every way
> Bound by gold chains about the feet of God."

As the Jew saw it, and as indeed it is, to cure the ills of life we need to be right with God and right with men, and we need to bring to bear upon men through prayer the mercy and the might of God.

Before we leave this passage there is one interesting technical fact that we must note. It quotes Elijah as an example of the power of prayer. This is an excellent illustration of how Jewish rabbinic exegesis developed the meaning of Scripture. The full story is in 1 *Kings* 17 and 18. The *three years and six months*—a period also quoted in *Luke* 4:25—is a deduction from 1 *Kings* 18:1. Further, the Old Testament narrative does not say that either the coming or the cessation of the drought was due to the prayers of Elijah; he was merely the prophet who announced its coming and its going. But the Rabbis always studied Scripture under the microscope. In 1 *Kings* 17:1 we read: "As the Lord the God of Israel lives, *before whom I stand,* there shall be neither dew nor rain these years, except by my word." Now the Jewish attitude of prayer was *standing before God*; and so in this phrase the Rabbis found what was to them an indication that the drought was the result of the prayers of Elijah. In 1 *Kings* 18:42 we read that Elijah went up to Carmel, *bowed himself down upon the earth* and put his face between his knees. Once again the Rabbis saw the attitude of agonizing prayer; and so found what was to them an indication that it was the prayer of Elijah which brought the drought to an end.

THE TRUTH WHICH MUST BE DONE

James 5: 19, 20

My brothers, if any among you wanders from the truth and if anyone turns him again to the right way, let him know that he who has turned a sinner from his wandering way will save his brother's soul from death and will hide a multitude of his own sins.

IN this passage there is set down the great differentiating characteristic of Christian truth. It is something from which a man can *wander*. It is not only intellectual, philosophical and abstract; it is always moral truth.

This comes out very clearly when we go to the New Testament and look at the expressions which are used in connection with truth. Truth is something which a man must *love* (2 *Thessalonians* 2: 10); it is something which a man must *obey* (*Galatians* 5: 7); it is something which a man must *display in life* (2 *Corinthians* 4: 2); it is something which must be *spoken in love* (*Ephesians* 4: 15); it is something which must be *witnessed to* (*John* 18: 37); it is something which must be *manifested in a life of love* (1 *John* 3: 19); it is something which *liberates* (*John* 8: 32); and it is something which is *the gift of the Holy Spirit,* sent by Jesus Christ (*John* 16: 13, 14).

Clearest of all is the phrase in *John* 3: 21, *he who does what is true.* That is to say, *Christian truth is something which must be done.* It is not only the object of the search of the mind; it is always moral truth issuing in action. It is not only something to be studied but something to be done; not only something to which a man must submit only his mind but something to which he must submit his whole life.

THE SUPREME HUMAN ACHIEVEMENT

James 5: 19, 20 (*continued*)

JAMES finishes his letter with one of the greatest and most uplifting thoughts in the New Testament; and yet one which occurs more than once in the Bible. Suppose a man goes wrong and strays away; and suppose a fellow-Christian rescues him from the error of his ways and brings him back to the right path. That man has not only saved his brother's soul, he has covered a multitude of his own sins. In other words, to save another's soul is the surest way to save one's own.

Mayor points out that Origen has a wonderful passage in one of his Homilies in which he indicates these six ways in which a man may gain forgiveness of his sins—by baptism, by martyrdom, by almsgiving (*Luke* 11: 41), by the forgiveness of others (*Matthew* 6: 14), by love (*Luke* 7: 47), and by converting a sinner from the evil of his ways. God will forgive much to the man who has been the means of leading another brother back to him.

This is a thought which shines forth every now and then from the pages of Scripture. Jeremiah says, "If you utter what is precious, and not what is worthless, you shall be as my mouth" (*Jeremiah* 15: 19). Daniel writes: "And those who are wise shall shine like the brightness of the firmament; and those who turn many to righteousness, like the stars for ever and ever" (*Daniel* 12: 3). The advice to the young Timothy is: "Take heed to yourself, and to your teaching; for by so doing you will save both yourself and your hearers" (1 *Timothy* 4: 16).

There is a saying of the Jewish Fathers: "Whosoever makes a man righteous, sin prevails not over him." Clement of Alexandria says that the true Christian reckons that which benefits his neighbour his own salvation. It is told that an ultra-evangelical lady once asked Wilberforce, the liberator of the slaves, if his soul was saved. "Madame," he answered, "I have been so busy trying to save the souls of others that I have had no time to think of my own." It has been said that those who bring sunshine into the lives of others cannot keep it from themselves; and certainly those who bring the lives of others to God cannot keep God out of their own. The highest honour God can give is bestowed upon him who leads another to God; for the man who does that does nothing less than share in the work of Jesus Christ, the Saviour of men.

THE LETTERS OF PETER

INTRODUCTION TO THE
FIRST LETTER OF PETER

First Peter belongs to that group of New Testament letters which are known as the *Catholic* or *General* Epistles. Two explanations of that title have been offered.

(i) It is suggested that these letters were so called because they were addressed to the Church at large, in contradistinction to the Pauline letters which were addressed to individual churches. But that is not so. *James* is addressed to a definite, though widely scattered, community. It is written to the twelve tribes who are scattered abroad (*James* 1: 1). It needs no argument that *Second* and *Third John* are addressed to definite communities; and, although *First John* has no specific address, it is clearly written with the needs and perils of a particular community in mind. *First Peter* itself is written to the strangers scattered abroad through Pontus, Galatia, Cappadocia, Asia and Bithynia (1 *Peter* 1: 1). It is true that these General Epistles have a wider range than the letters of Paul; at the same time, they all have a definite community in mind.

(ii) So we must turn to the second explanation—that these letters were called *Catholic* or *General* because they were accepted as Scripture by the whole Church in contradistinction to that large number of letters which enjoyed a local and temporary authority but never universally ranked as Scripture. At the time when these letters were being written there was an outbreak of letter-writing in the Church. We still possess many of the letters which were then written—the letter of Clement of Rome to Corinth, the letter of Barnabas, the letters of Ignatius and the letters of Polycarp. All were regarded as very precious in the Churches to which they were written but were never regarded as having authority throughout the Church; on the other hand the *Catholic* or *General* Epistles gradually won a place in Scripture and were accepted by the whole Church. Here is the true explanation of their title.

THE LOVELY LETTER

Of all the General Epistles it is probably true that *First Peter* is the best known and loved, and the most read. No one has ever been in any doubt about its charm. Moffatt writes of it: "The beautiful spirit of the pastoral shines through any translation of the Greek text. 'Affectionate, loving, lowly, humble,' are Izaak Walton's quaternion of adjectives for the Epistles of James, John and Peter, but it is *First Peter* which deserves them pre-eminently." It is written out of the love of a pastor's heart to help people who were going through it and on whom worse things were still to come. "The key-note," says Moffatt, "is steady encouragement to endurance in conduct and innocence in character." It has been said that its distinctive characteristic is *warmth*. E. J. Goodspeed wrote: "*First Peter* is one of the most moving pieces of persecution literature." To this day it is one of the easiest letters in the New Testament to read, for it has never lost its winsome appeal to the human heart.

THE MODERN DOUBT

Until a comparatively short time ago few would have raised any doubts about the authenticity of *First Peter*. Renan, who was by no means a conservative critic, wrote of it: "The First Epistle is one of the writings of the New Testament which are most anciently and most unanimously cited as genuine." But in recent times the Petrine authorship of the letter has been widely questioned. The commentary by F. W. Beare, published in 1947, goes the length of saying, "There can be no possible doubt that 'Peter' is a pseudonym." That is to say, Beare has no doubt that someone else wrote this letter under the name of Peter. We shall go on in fairness to investigate that view; but first we shall set out the traditional view—which we ourselves unhesitatingly accept—of the date and authorship of this letter. This is that *First Peter* was written from Rome by Peter himself, about the year A.D. 67, in the days immediately following the first persecution of the Christians by Nero, to the Christians in those parts of Asia Minor named in the address. What is the evidence for this early date and, therefore, for the Petrine authorship?

THE SECOND COMING

When we go to the letter we find that expectation of the second coming of Christ is in the very forefront of its thought. Christians are being kept for the salvation which is to be revealed at the last time (1: 5). Those who keep the faith will be saved from the coming judgment (1: 7). Christians are to hope for the grace which will come at the revelation of Jesus Christ (1: 13). The day of visitation is expected (2: 12). The end of all things is at hand (4: 7). Those who suffer with Christ will also rejoice with Christ when his glory is revealed (4: 13). Judgment is to begin at the house of God (4: 17). The writer himself is sure that he will be a sharer in the glory to come (5: 1). When the Chief Shepherd shall appear the faithful Christian will receive a crown of glory (5: 4).

From beginning to end of the letter the second coming is in the forefront of the writer's mind. It is the motive for steadfastness in the faith, for the loyal living of the Christian life and for gallant endurance amidst the sufferings which have come and will come upon them.

It would be untrue to say that the second coming ever dropped out of Christian belief, but it did recede from the forefront of Christian belief as the years passed and Christ did not return. It is, for instance, significant that in *Ephesians*, one of Paul's latest letters, there is no mention of it. On this ground it is reasonable to suppose that *First Peter* is early and comes from the days when the Christians vividly expected the return of their Lord at any moment.

SIMPLICITY OF ORGANIZATION

It is clear that *First Peter* comes from a time when the organization of the Church is very simple. There is no mention of deacons; nor of the *episkopos*, the bishop, who begins to emerge in the Pastoral Epistles and becomes prominent in Ignatius's letters in the first half of the second century. The only Church officials mentioned are the elders. "I exhort the elders among you, as a fellow-elder" (5: 1). On this ground, also, it is reasonable to suppose that *First Peter* comes from an early date.

THE THEOLOGY OF THE EARLY CHURCH

What is most significant of all is that the theology of *First Peter* is the theology of the very early church. E. G. Selwyn has made a detailed study of this; and he has proved beyond all question that the theological ideas of *First Peter* are exactly the same as those we meet in the recorded sermons of Peter in the early chapters of *Acts*.

The preaching of the early church was based on five main ideas. One of the greatest contributions of C. H. Dodd to New Testament scholarship was his formulation of these. They form the framework of all the sermons of the early church, as recorded in *Acts*; and they are the foundation of the thought of all the New Testament writers. The summary of these basic ideas has been given the name *Kērugma,* which means the announcement or the proclamation of a herald.

These are the fundamental ideas which the Church in its first days heralded forth. We shall take them one by one and shall set down after each, first, the references in the early chapters of *Acts* and, second, the references in *First Peter*; and we will make the significant discovery that the basic ideas of the sermons of the early church and the theology of *First Peter* are precisely the same. We are not claiming, of course, that the sermons in *Acts* are verbatim reports of what was actually preached, but we believe that they give correctly the *substance* of the message of the first preachers.

(i) The age of fulfilment has dawned; the Messianic age has begun. This is God's last word. A new order is being inaugurated and the elect are summoned to join the new community. *Acts* 2: 14–16; 3: 12–26; 4: 8–12; 10: 34–43; 1 *Peter* 1: 3, 10–12; 4: 7.

(ii) This new age has come through the life, death and resurrection of Jesus Christ, all of which are in direct fulfilment of the prophecies of the Old Testament and are, therefore, the result of the definite plan and foreknowledge of God. *Acts* 2: 20–31; 3: 13, 14; 10: 43; 1 *Peter* 1: 20, 21.

(iii) By virtue of the resurrection Jesus has been exalted to the right hand of God and is the Messianic head of the new Israel. *Acts* 2: 22–26; 3: 13; 4: 11; 5: 30, 31; 10: 39–42; 1 *Peter* 1: 21; 2: 7; 2: 24; 3: 22.

(iv) These Messianic events will shortly reach their consummation in the return of Christ in glory and the judgment of the living and the dead. *Acts* 3: 19–23; 10: 42; 1 *Peter* 1: 5, 7, 13; 4: 5, 13, 17, 18; 5: 1, 4.

(v) These facts are made the grounds for an appeal for repentance, and the offer of forgiveness and of the Holy Spirit, and the promise of eternal life. *Acts* 2: 38, 39; 3: 19; 5: 31; 10: 43; 1 *Peter* 1: 13–25; 2: 1–3; 4: 1–5.

These declarations are the five main planks in the edifice of early Christian preaching, as recorded for us in the sermons of Peter in the early chapters of *Acts*. They are also the dominant ideas in *First Peter*. The correspondence is so close and so consistent that we almost certainly with entire probability see the same hand and mind in both.

QUOTATIONS FROM THE FATHERS

We may add another point to our evidence that *First Peter* is early; very early on the fathers and preachers of the Church begin to quote it. The first person to quote *First Peter* by name is Irenaeus, who lived from A.D. 130 until well into the next century. He twice quotes 1 *Peter* 1: 8: "Without having seen him you love him; though you do not now see him you believe in him and rejoice with unutterable and exalted joy." And he once quotes 1 *Peter* 2: 16, with its command not to use liberty as a cloak for maliciousness. But even before this the fathers of the Church are quoting Peter without mentioning his name. Clement of Rome, writing about A.D. 95, speaks of "the precious blood of Christ," an unusual phrase which may well come from Peter's statement that we are redeemed by the precious blood of Christ (1: 19). Polycarp, who was martyred in A.D. 155, continuously quotes Peter without using his name. We may select three passages to show how closely he gives Peter's words.

> Wherefore, girding up your loins, serve God in fear . . . believing on him who raised up our Lord Jesus Christ from the dead, and gave him glory (Polycarp; *To the Philippians* 2: 1).

> Therefore, gird up your minds . . . through him you have confidence in God, who raised him from the dead and gave him glory (1 *Peter* 1: 13, 21).

> Christ Jesus who bare our sins in his own body on the tree, who did no sin, neither was guile found in his mouth (Polycarp 8: 1).

> He committed no sin; no guile was found on his life . . . He himself bore our sins in his body on the tree (1 *Peter* 2: 22, 24).

> Having your conversation blameless among the Gentiles (Polycarp 10: 2).

> Maintain good conduct among the Gentiles (1 *Peter* 2: 12).

There can be no doubt that Polycarp is quoting Peter, although he does not name him. It takes some time for a book to acquire such an authority and familiarity that it can be quoted almost unconsciously, its language woven into the language of the Church. Once again we see that *First Peter* must be a very early book.

THE EXCELLENCE OF THE GREEK

If, however, we are defending the Petrine authorship of this letter, there is one problem we must face—and that is the excellence of the Greek. It seems impossible that it should be the work of a Galilean fisherman. New Testament scholars are at one in praising the Greek of this letter. F. W. Beare writes: "The epistle is quite obviously the work of a man of letters, skilled in all the devices of rhetoric, and able to draw on an extensive, and even learned, vocabulary. He is a stylist of no ordinary capacity, and he writes some of the best Greek in the whole New Testament, far smoother and more literary than that of the highly-trained Paul." Moffatt speaks of this letter's "plastic language and love of metaphor." Mayor says that *First Peter* has no equal in the New Testament for "sustained stateliness of rhythm." Bigg has likened certain of *First Peter's* phrases to the writing of Thucydides. Selwyn has spoken of *First Peter's* "Euripidean tenderness" and of its ability to coin compound words as Aeschylus might have done. The Greek of *First Peter* is not entirely unworthy to be set beside that of the masters of the language. It is difficult, if not impossible, to imagine Peter using the Greek language like that.

The letter itself supplies the solution to this problem. In the concluding short section Peter himself says, "By Silvanus ... I have written briefly" (1 *Peter* 5: 12). *By Silvanus—dia Silouanou*—is an unusual phrase. The Greek means that Silvanus was Peter's agent in the writing of the letter; it means that he was more than merely Peter's stenographer.

Let us approach this from two angles. First, let us enquire what we know about Silvanus. (The evidence is set out more fully in our study section on 1 *Peter* 5: 12). In all probability he is the same person as the Silvanus of Paul's letters and the Silas of *Acts*, Silas being a shortened and more familiar form of Silvanus. When we examine these passages, we find that Silas or Silvanus was no ordinary person but a leading figure in the life and counsels of the early church.

He was a prophet (*Acts* 15: 32); he was one of the "chief among the brethren" at the council of Jerusalem and one of the two chosen to deliver the decisions of the council to the Church at Antioch (*Acts* 15: 22, 27). He was Paul's chosen companion in the second missionary journey, and was with Paul both in Philippi and in Corinth (*Acts* 15: 37–40; 16: 19, 25, 29 ; 18: 5; 2 *Corinthians* 1: 19). He was associated with Paul in the initial greetings of 1 and 2 *Thessalonians* (1 *Thessalonians* 1: 1; 2 *Thessalonians* 1: 1). He was a Roman citizen (*Acts* 16: 37).

Silvanus, then, was a notable man in the early church; he was not so much the assistant as the colleague of Paul; and, since he was a Roman citizen, there is at least a possibility that he was a man of an education and culture such as Peter could never have enjoyed.

Now let us add our second line of thought. In a missionary situation, when a missionary can speak a language well enough but cannot write it very well, it is quite common for him to do one of two things in order to send a message to his people. He either writes it out in as good a style as he can, and then gets a native speaker of the language to correct his mistakes and to polish his style; or, if he has a native colleague whom he can fully trust, he tells him what he wishes said, leaves him to put the message into written form and then vets the result.

We can well imagine that this was the part Silvanus played in the writing of *First Peter*. Either he corrected and polished Peter's necessarily inadequate Greek; or he wrote in his own words what Peter wanted said, with Peter vetting the final product and adding the last personal paragraph to it.

The thought is that of Peter; but the style is that of Silvanus. And so, although the Greek is so excellent, there is no necessity to deny that the letter comes from Peter himself.

THE RECIPIENTS OF THE LETTER

The recipients of the letter are the exiles (a Christian is always a sojourner on the earth) scattered throughout Pontus, Galatia, Cappadocia, Asia and Bithynia.

Almost all of these words had a double significance. They stood for ancient kingdoms and they stood for Roman provinces to which the ancient names had been given; and the ancient kingdoms and the new provinces did not always cover the same territory. Pontus was never a province. It had originally been the kingdom of Mithradates and part of it was incorporated in Bithynia and part of it in Galatia. Galatia had originally been the kingdom of the Gauls in the area of the three cities Ancyra, Pessinus, and Tavium, but the Romans had expanded it into a much larger unit of administration, including sections of Phrygia, Pisidia, Lycaonia, and Isauria. The kingdom of Cappadocia had become a Roman province in A.D. 17 in practically its original form. Asia was not the continent of Asia as we use the term. It had been an independent kingdom, whose last king, Attalus the Third, had bequeathed it as a gift to Rome in 133 B.C. It embraced the centre of Asia Minor and was bounded on the north by Bithynia, on the south by Lycia, and on the east by Phrygia and Galatia. In popular language it was that part of Asia Minor which lay along the shores of the Aegean Sea.

We do not know why these particular districts were picked out; but this much is certain—they embraced a large area with a very large population; and the fact that they are all mentioned is one of the greatest proofs of the immense missionary activity of the early church, apart altogether from the missionary activities of Paul.

All these districts lie in the north-east corner of Asia Minor. Why they are named as a group and why they are named in this particular order, we do not know. But a glance at the map will show that, if the bearer of this letter—who may well have been Silvanus—sailed from Italy and landed at Sinope in north-east Asia Minor, a journey through these provinces would be a circular tour which would take him back to Sinope. From Sinope in Bithynia he would go south to Galatia, further south to Cappadocia, west to Asia, north again to Bithynia, and then east to arrive back in Sinope.

It is clear from the letter itself that its recipients were mainly Gentiles. There is no mention of any question of the law, a question which always arose when there was a Jewish background. Their previous condition had been one of fleshly passion (1: 14; 4: 3, 4) which fits Gentiles far better than Jews. Previously they had been no people—Gentiles outside the covenant—but now they are the people of God (2: 9, 10).

The form of his name which Peter uses also shows that this letter was intended for Gentiles for *Peter* is a Greek name. Paul calls him Cephas (1 *Corinthians* 1: 12; 3: 22; 9: 5; 15: 5; *Galatians* 1: 18; 2: 9, 11, 14); among his fellow Jews, he was known as Simeon (*Acts* 15: 14), which is the name by which he is called in *Second Peter* (1: 1). Since he uses his Greek name here, it is likely that he was writing to Greek people.

THE CIRCUMSTANCES BEHIND THE LETTER

That this letter was written in a time when persecution threatened, is abundantly clear. They are in the midst of various trials (1:6). They are likely to be falsely accused as evil-doers (3:16). A fiery ordeal is going to try them (4:12). When they suffer, they are to commit themselves to God (4:19). They may well have to suffer for righteousness' sake (3:14). They are sharing in the afflictions which the Christian brotherhood throughout the world is called upon to endure (5:9). At the back of this letter there are fiery trial, a campaign of slander and suffering for the sake of Christ. Can we identify this situation?

There was a time when the Christians had little to fear from the Roman government. In *Acts* it is repeatedly the Roman magistrates and the Roman soldiers and officials who save Paul from the fury of Jews and pagans alike. As Gibbon had it, the tribunal of the pagan magistrate proved the most assured refuge against the fury of the synagogue. The reason was that in the early days the Roman government was not able to distinguish between Jews and Christians. Within the empire Judaism was what was called a *religio licita,* a permitted religion, and Jews had full liberty to worship in their own way. It was not that the Jews did not try to enlighten the Romans as to the true facts of the situation; they did so in Corinth, for example (*Acts* 18: 12–17). But for some time the Romans simply regarded the Christians as a Jewish sect and, therefore, did not molest them.

The change came in the days of Nero and we can trace almost every detail of the story. On 19th July, A.D. 64, the great fire of Rome broke out. Rome, a city of narrow streets and high wooden tenements, was in real danger of being wiped out. The fire burned for three days and three nights, was checked, and then broke out again with redoubled violence. The Roman populace had no doubt who was responsible and put the blame on the Emperor. Nero had a passion for building; and they believed that he had deliberately taken steps to obliterate Rome so that he might build it again. Nero's responsibility must remain for ever in doubt; but it is certain that he watched the raging inferno from the tower of Maecenas and expressed himself as charmed with the flower and loveliness of the flames. It was freely said that those who tried to extinguish the fire were deliberately hindered and that men were seen to rekindle it again, when it was likely to subside. The people were overwhelmed. The ancient landmarks and the ancestral shrines had vanished; the Temple of Luna, the Ara Maxima, the great altar, the Temple of Jupiter Stator, the shrine of Vesta, their very household gods were gone. They were homeless and, in Farrar's phrase, there was "a hopeless brotherhood of wretchedness."

The resentment of the people was bitter. Nero had to divert suspicion from himself; a scapegoat had to be found. The Christians were made the scapegoat. Tacitus, the Roman historian, tells the story (*Annals* 15.44):

> Neither human assistance in the shape of imperial gifts, nor attempts to appease the gods, could remove the sinister report that the fire was due to Nero's own orders. And, so, in the hope of dissipating the rumour, he falsely diverted the charge on to a set of people to whom the vulgar gave the name of Christians, and who were detested for the abominations they perpetrated. The founder of the sect, one Christus by name, had been executed by Pontius Pilate in the reign of Tiberius; and the dangerous superstition, though put down for the moment, broke out again, not only in Judaea, the original home of the pest, but even in Rome, where everything shameful and horrible collects and is practised.

Clearly Tacitus had no doubt that the Christians were not to blame for the fire and that Nero was simply choosing them to be the scapegoats for his own crime.

Why did Nero pick on the Christians and how was it possible even to suggest that they were responsible for the fire of Rome? There are two possible answers.

(i) The Christians were already the victims of certain slanders.

(*a*) They were in the popular mind connected with the Jews. Antisemitism is no new thing and it was easy for the Roman mob to attach any crime to the Jews and, therefore, to the Christians.

(*b*) The Lord's Supper was secret, at least in a sense. It was open only to the members of the Church. And certain phrases connected with it were fruitful sources of pagan slanders, phrases about eating someone's body and drinking someone's blood. That was enough to produce a rumour that the Christians were cannibals. In time the rumour grew until it became a story that the Christians killed and ate a Gentile, or a newly born child. At the Lord's Table the Christians gave each other the kiss of peace (1 *Peter* 5: 14). Their meeting was called the *Agapē,* the Love Feast. That was enough for stories to spread that the Christian meetings were orgies of vice.

(*c*) It was always a charge against the Christians that they "tampered with family relationships." There was this much truth in such a charge that Christianity did indeed become a sword to split families, when some members of a family became Christian and some did not. A religion which split homes was bound to be unpopular.

(*d*) It was the case that the Christians spoke of a coming day when the world would dissolve in flames. Many a Christian preacher must have been heard preaching of the second coming and the fiery dissolution of all things (*Acts* 2: 19, 20). It would not be difficult to put the blame for the fire on to people who spoke like that.

There was abundant material which could be perverted into false charges against the Christians by anyone maliciously disposed to victimise them.

(ii) The Jewish faith had always appealed especially to women because of its moral standards in a world where chastity did not exist. There were, therefore, many well-born women who had embraced the Jewish faith. The Jews did not hesitate to work upon these women to influence their husbands against the Christians. We get a definite example of that in what happened to Paul and his company in Antioch of Pisidia. There it was through such women that the Jews stirred up action against Paul (*Acts* 13: 50). Two of Nero's court favourites were Jewish proselytes. There was Aliturus, his favourite actor; and there was Poppaea, his mistress. It is very likely that the Jews through them influenced Nero to take action against the Christians.

In any event, the blame for the fire was attached to the Christians and a savage outbreak of persecution occurred. Nor was it simply persecution by legal means. What Tacitus called an *ingens multitudo,* a huge multitude, of Christians perished in the most sadistic ways. Nero rolled the Christians in pitch, set light to them and used them as living torches to light his gardens. He sewed them up in the skins of wild animals and set his hunting-dogs upon them, to tear them limb from limb while they still lived.

Tacitus writes:

> Mockery of every sort was added to their deaths. Covered with the skins of beasts, they were torn by dogs and perished, or were nailed to crosses, or were doomed to the flames and burned, to serve as a nightly illumination, when daylight had expired. Nero offered his gardens for the spectacle and was exhibiting a show in the circus, while he mingled with the people in the dress of a charioteer or stood aloft on a car. Hence, even for criminals who deserve extreme and exemplary punishment, there arose a feeling of compassion; for, it was not, as it seemed, for the public good, but to glut one man's cruelty that they were being destroyed (Tacitus, *Annals* 15: 44).

The same terrible story is told by the later Christian historian, Sulipicius Severus, in his *Chronicle*:

> In the meantime, the number of Christians being now very large, it happened that Rome was destroyed by fire, while Nero was stationed at Antium. But the opinion of all cast the odium of causing the fire upon the emperor, and he was believed in this way to have sought for the glory of building a new city. And, in fact, Nero could not, by any means he tried, escape from the charge that the fire had been caused by his orders. He, therefore, turned the accusation

against the Christians and the most cruel tortures were accordingly inflicted upon the innocent. Nay, even new kinds of death were invented so that, being covered in the skins of wild beasts, they perished by being devoured by dogs, while many were crucified, or slain by fire, and not a few were set apart for this purpose, that, when the day came to a close, they should be consumed to serve for light during the night. In this way, cruelty first began to be manifested against the Christians. Afterwards, too, their religion was prohibited by laws which were enacted; and by edicts openly set forth it was proclaimed unlawful to be a Christian.

It is true that this persecution was confined originally to Rome; but the gateway to persecution had been opened and in every place they were ready victims for the mob.

Moffatt writes:

After the Neronic wave had passed over the capital, the wash of it was felt on the far shores of the provinces; the dramatic publicity of the punishment must have spread the name of Christian *urbi et orbi,* far and wide, over the entire empire; the provincials would soon hear of it, and when they desired a similar outburst at the expense of the loyal Christians, all that they needed was a proconsul to gratify their wishes and some outstanding disciple to serve as a victim.

For ever after the Christians were to live under threat. The mobs of the Roman cities knew what had happened in Rome and there were always these slanderous stories against the Christians. There were times when the mob loved blood and there were many governors ready to pander to their blood-lust. It was not Roman law but lynch law which threatened the Christians.

From now on the Christian was in peril of his life. For years nothing might happen; then some spark might set off the explosion; and the terror would break out. That is the situation at the back of *First Peter*; and it is in face of it that Peter calls his people to hope and to courage and to that lovely Christian living which alone can give the lie to the slanders with which they are attacked and which are the grounds for taking measures against them. *First Peter* was written to meet no theological heresy; it was written to strengthen men and women in jeopardy of their lives.

THE DOUBTS

We have set out in full the arguments which go to prove that Peter is really the author of the first letter which bears his name. But, as we have said, not a few first-class scholars have felt that it cannot have been his work. We ourselves accept the view that Peter is the author of the letter; but in fairness we set out the other side, largely as it is presented in the chapter on *First Peter* in *The Primitive Church* by B. H. Streeter.

STRANGE SILENCES

Bigg writes in his introduction: "There is no book in the New Testament which has earlier, better, or stronger attestation (than *First Peter*)." It is true that Eusebius, the great fourth century scholar and historian of the Church, classes *First Peter* among the books universally accepted in the early church as part of scripture (Eusebius: *Ecclesiastical History* 3.25.2). But certain things are to be noted.

(*a*) Eusebius adduces certain quotations from earlier writers to prove his contention that *First Peter* was universally accepted. This he never does in connection with the gospels or the letters of Paul; and the very fact that he feels called upon to produce his evidence in the case of *First Peter* might be held to indicate that in it he felt some necessity to prove his point, a necessity which did not exist in connection with the other books. Was there a doubt in Eusebius's own mind? Or, were there people who had to be convinced? Was the universal acceptance of *First Peter* not so unanimous after all?

(*b*) In his book, *The Canon of the New Testament*, Westcott noted that, although no one in the early church questions the right of *First Peter* to be part of the New Testament, surprisingly few of the early fathers quote it and, still more surprising, very few of the early fathers in the west and in Rome quote it. Tertullian is an immense quoter of scripture. In his writings there are 7,258 quotations from the New Testament, but only 2 of them are from *First Peter*. If Peter wrote this letter and wrote it in Rome, we would expect it to be well known and largely used in the Church of the west.

(c) The earliest known official list of New Testament books is the Muratorian Canon, so called after Cardinal Muratori who discovered it. It is the official list of New Testament books as accepted in the Church at Rome about the year A.D. 170. It is an extraordinary fact that *First Peter* does not appear at all. It can be fairly argued that the Muratorian Canon, as we possess it, is defective and that it may originally have contained a reference to *First Peter*. But that argument is seriously weakened by the next consideration.

(d) It is a fact that *First Peter* was still not in the New Testament of the Syrian Church as late as A.D. 373. It did not get in until the Syriac version of the New Testament known as the Peshitto was made about A.D. 400. We know that it was Tatian who brought the New Testament books to the Syriac-speaking Church; and he brought them to Syria from Rome when he went to Edessa and founded the Church there in A.D. 172. It could, therefore, be argued that the Muratorian Canon is correct as we possess it and that *First Peter* was not part of the Roman Church's New Testament as late as A.D. 170. This would be a very surprising fact if Peter wrote it—and actually wrote it at Rome.

When all these facts are put together, it does seem that there are some strange silences in regard to *First Peter* and that its attestation may not be as strong as is usually assumed.

FIRST PETER AND EPHESIANS

Further, there is definitely some connection between *First Peter* and *Ephesians*. There are many close parallels of thought and expression between the two and we select the following specimens of this similarity.

Blessed be the God and Father of our Lord Jesus Christ. By his great mercy we have been born anew to a living hope through the resurrection of Jesus Christ from the dead (1 *Peter* 1: 3).

Blessed be the God and Father of our Lord Jesus Christ, who

has blessed us in Christ with every spiritual blessing in the heavenly places (*Ephesians* 1: 3).

Therefore, gird up your minds, be sober, set your hope fully upon the grace that is coming to you at the revelation of Jesus Christ (1 *Peter* 1: 13).

Stand, therefore, having girded your loins with truth (*Ephesians* 6: 14).

Jesus Christ, was destined before the foundation of the world, but was made manifest at the end of the times for your sake (1 *Peter* 1: 20).

Even as he chose us in him, before the foundation of the world (*Ephesians* 1: 4).

Jesus Christ, who has gone into heaven, and is at the right hand of God, with angels and authorities and powers subject to him (1 *Peter* 3: 22).

God made him sit at his right hand in the heavenly places, far above all rule and authority, and power and dominion (*Ephesians* 1: 20, 21).

In addition, the injunctions to slaves, husbands and wives in *First Peter* and *Ephesians* are very similar.

The argument is put forward that *First Peter* is quoting *Ephesians*. Although *Ephesians* must have been written somewhere about A.D. 64, Paul's letters were not collected and edited until about A.D. 90. If, then, Peter was also writing in A.D. 64, how could he know *Ephesians*?

This is an argument to which there is more than one reply. (*a*) The injunctions to slaves, husbands and wives are part of the standardized ethical teaching given to all converts in all churches. Peter was not borrowing from Paul; both were using common stock. (*b*) All the similarities quoted can well be explained from the fact that certain phrases and lines of thought were universal in the early church. For instance, "Blessed be the God and Father of our Lord Jesus Christ," was part of the universal devotional language of the early church, which both Peter and Paul would know and use without any borrowing from each other. (*c*) Even if there was mutual borrowing, it is by no means certain that *First Peter* borrowed from *Ephesians*; the borrowing might well have been the other way round and probably was, for *First Peter* is much simpler than *Ephesians*. (*d*) Lastly, even if *First Peter* borrowed from *Ephesians,* if Peter and Paul were in Rome at the same time, it is perfectly possible that Peter could have seen a copy of *Ephesians* before it was sent to Asia Minor, and he might well have discussed its ideas with Paul.

The argument that *First Peter* must be late because it quotes from *Ephesians* seems to us very uncertain and insecure, and probably mistaken.

YOUR FELLOW-ELDER

It is objected that Peter could not well have written the sentence: "The elders among you I exhort, as a fellow-elder" (1 *Peter* 5:1). It is maintained that Peter could not have called himself an elder. He was an apostle whose function was quite different from that of an elder. The apostle was character- istically a man whose work and authority were not confined to any one congregation, but whose writ ran throughout the Church at large; whereas the elder was the governing official of the local congregation.

That is perfectly true. But it must be remembered that amongst the Jews there was no office more universally honoured than that of elder. The elder had the respect of the whole community and to him the community looked for guidance in its problems and justice in its disputes. Peter, as a Jew, would feel nothing out of place in calling himself an elder; and in so doing he would avoid the conscious claim of authority that the title of apostle might have implied, and graciously and courteously identify himself with the people to whom he spoke.

A WITNESS OF THE SUFFERINGS OF CHRIST

It is objected that Peter could not honestly have called himself a witness of Christ's sufferings, for after the arrest in the garden all the disciples forsook Jesus and fled (*Matthew* 26:56) and, apart from the beloved disciple, none was a witness of the Cross (*John* 19:26, 27). A witness of the *resurrection*

Peter could call himself, and indeed to be such was the function of an apostle (*Acts* 1: 22), but a witness of the Cross he was not. In a sense that is undeniable. And yet Peter is not here claiming to be a witness of the crucifixion, but to be a witness of the sufferings of Christ. He did see Christ suffer, in his continual rejection by men, in the poignant moments of the Last Supper, in the agony in the garden and in that moment when, after he had denied him, Jesus turned and looked on him (*Luke* 22: 61). It is an insensitive and pedestrian criticism which denies to Peter the right to say that he had been a witness of the sufferings of Christ.

PERSECUTION FOR THE NAME

The main argument for a late date for *First Peter* is drawn from its references to persecution. It is argued that *First Peter* implies that it was already a crime to be a Christian and that Christians were brought before the courts, not for any crime but for the bare fact of their faith. *First Peter* speaks about being reproached for the name of Christ (4: 14); it speaks of suffering as a Christian (4: 16). It is argued that this stage of persecution was not reached until after A.D. 100, and that prior to that date their persecution was on the score of alleged evil-doing, as in the time of Nero.

There is no doubt that this was the law by A.D. 112. At that time Pliny was governor of Bithynia. He was a personal friend of the Emperor Trajan and he had a way of referring all his difficulties to Trajan for solution. He wrote to the Emperor to tell how he dealt with the Christians. Pliny was well aware that they were law-abiding citizens to whose practices no crimes were attached. They told him that "they had been accustomed to assemble on a fixed day before daylight, and sing by turns a hymn to Christ as God; that they had bound themselves with an oath, not for any crime, but to commit neither theft, nor robbery, nor adultery, nor to break their word, and not to deny a deposit when demanded." Pliny accepted all this; but, when they were brought before him, he asked only one question. "I have asked them whether they were Christians. Those who confessed I asked a second and a third time, threatening punishment. Those who persisted I ordered to be led away to execution." Their sole crime was that of being a Christian.

Trajan replied that this was the correct proceeding and that anyone who denied being a Christian and proved it by sacrificing to the gods was immediately to be set free. From the letters it is clear that there was a good deal of information being laid against the Christians; and Trajan laid it down that no anonymous letters of information were to be accepted or acted upon (Pliny: *Letters* 96 and 97).

It is argued that this stage of persecution did not emerge until the time of Trajan; and that *First Peter,* therefore, implies a situation which must be as late as Trajan's time.

The only way in which we can settle this is to sketch the progress of persecution and the reason for it in the Roman Empire. We may do so by setting out one basic fact and three developments from it.

(i) Under the Roman system, religions were divided into two kinds. There were those which were *religiones licitae,* permitted religions; these were recognized by the state and it was open to any man to practise them. There were *religiones illicitae*; these were forbidden by the state and it was illegal for any man to practise them on pain of automatic prosecution as a criminal. It is to be noted that Roman toleration was very wide; and that any religion which did not affect public morality and civil order was certain to be permitted.

(ii) Judaism was a *religio licita*; and in the very early days the Romans, not unnaturally, did not know the difference between Judaism and Christianity. Christianity, as far as they were concerned, was merely a sect of Judaism and any tension and hostility between the two was a private quarrel which was no concern of the Roman government. Because of that in the very early days Christianity was under no danger of persecution. It enjoyed the same freedom of worship as Judaism enjoyed because it was assumed to be a *religio licita*.

(iii) The action of Nero changed the situation. However it

came about, and most likely it was by the deliberate action of the Jews, the Roman government discovered that Judaism and Christianity were different. It is true that Nero first persecuted the Christians, not for being Christians, but for burning Rome. But the fact remains that Christianity had been discovered by the government to be a separate religion.

(iv) The consequence was immediate and inevitable. Christianity was at once a prohibited religion and immediately, *ipso facto*, every Christian became an outlaw. In the Roman historian, Suetonius, we have direct evidence that this was precisely what happened. He gives a kind of list of the legislative reforms initiated by Nero:

> During his reign many abuses were severely punished and put down, and not a few new laws were made; a limit was set to expenditures; the public banquets were confined to a distribution of food; the sale of any kind of cooked viands in the taverns was forbidden, with the exception of pulse and vegetables, whereas, before, every kind of dainty was exposed for sale. Punishment was inflicted on the Christians, a class of men given to a new and mischievous superstition. He put an end to the diversions of the chariot-drivers, who from immunity of long standing claimed the right of ranging at large and amusing themselves by cheating and robbing the people. The pantomimic actors and their partisans were banished from the city.

We have quoted that passage in full because it is proof that by the time of Nero the punishment of Christians had become an ordinary police affair. It is abundantly clear that we do not need to wait until the time of Trajan for the mere fact of being a Christian to be a crime. Any time after Nero a Christian was liable to punishment and death simply for the name he bore.

This does not mean that persecution was constant and consistent; but it does mean that any Christian was liable to execution at any time, purely as a police matter. In one area a Christian might live a whole lifetime at peace; in another there might be outbreaks of persecution every few months. It depended very largely on two things. It depended on the governor himself who might either leave the Christians unmolested or equally set the processes of the law in action against them. It depended on informers. The governor might not wish to act against the Christians, but if information was laid against a Christian he had to; and there were times when the mob were out for blood, information was laid and Christians were butchered to make a Roman holiday.

To compare small things with great, the legal position of the Christians and the attitude of the Roman law can be parallelled in Britain today. There are certain actions which are illegal—to take a very small example, parking a car partly on the pavement—but which for long enough may be permitted. But if the police authorities decide to institute a drive against such an action, or if it develops into too blatant a breaking of the law, or if someone lays a complaint and information, the law will go into action and due penalty and punishment will be exacted. That was the position of the Christians in the empire all of whom were technically outlaws. In actual fact no action might be taken against them; but a kind of sword of Damocles was for ever suspended over them. None knew when information would be laid against him; none knew when a governor would take action; none knew when he might have to die. And that situation obtained consistently after the action of Nero. Up to that time the Roman authorities had not realized that Christianity was a new religion; but from then on the Christian was automatically an outlaw.

Let us, then, look at the situation as depicted in *First Peter*. Peter's people are undergoing various trials (1: 6). Their faith is liable to be tried as metal is tested with fire (1: 7). Clearly they are undergoing a campaign of slander in which ignorant and baseless charges are being maliciously directed against them (2: 12; 2: 15; 3: 16; 4: 4). At this very moment they are in the midst of an outbreak of persecution because they are Christians (4: 12, 14, 16; 5: 9). Such suffering is only to be expected and they must not be surprised at it (4: 12). In any event it gives them the happiness of suffering for righteousness' sake (3: 14, 17), and of being sharers in the sufferings of Christ (4: 13). There is no need to come down to the time of Trajan for this situation. It is one in which Christians daily found themselves in every part of the empire at any time after their true status had been disclosed by the action of Nero. The persecution situation in *First Peter* does not in any way compel us to date it after the lifetime of Peter.

HONOUR THE KING

But we must proceed with the arguments of those who cannot hold the Petrine authorship. It is argued that in the situation which obtained in the time of Nero, Peter could never have written: "Be subject for the Lord's sake to every human institution, whether it be to the emperor as supreme, or to governors as sent by him to punish those who do wrong and to praise those who do right. . . . Fear God. Honour the emperor." (2: 13–17). The fact is, however, that this is precisely the point of view expressed in *Romans* 13: 1–7. The whole teaching of the New Testament, except only in the *Revelation* in which Rome is damned, is that the Christian must be a loyal citizen and must demonstrate the falsity of the charges made against him by the excellence of his behaviour as such. (1 *Peter* 2: 15). Even in times of persecution the Christian fully acknowledged his obligation to be a good citizen; and his only defence against persecution was to show by the excellence of his citizenship that he did not deserve such treatment. It is by no means impossible that Peter should have written like that.

A SERMON AND A PASTORAL

What is the view of those who cannot believe that *First Peter* is the work of Peter himself?

First of all, it is suggested that the initial address (1: 1, 2), and the closing greetings and salutations (5: 12–14) are later additions and no part of the original letter.

It is then suggested that *First Peter* as it stands is composed of two separate and quite different works. In 4: 11 we find a doxology. The natural place for a doxology is at the end; and it is suggested that 1: 3—4: 11 is the first of the two works of which the letter is composed. It is further suggested that this part of *First Peter* was originally a baptismal sermon. There is indeed in it a reference to the baptism which saves us (3: 21); and the advice to slaves, wives and husbands (2: 18—3: 7) would be entirely relevant to those who were entering the Christian Church from paganism and setting out on the newness of the Christian life.

It is suggested that the second part of the letter, 4: 12—5: 11, contains the substance of a pastoral letter, written to strengthen and comfort during a time of persecution (4: 12–19). At such a time the elders were very important; on them the resistance power of the Church depended. The writer of this pastoral fears that greed and arrogance are creeping in (5: 1–3), and he urges them faithfully to perform their high task (5: 4).

On this view *First Peter* is composed of two separate works— a baptismal sermon, and a pastoral letter written in time of persecution and neither has anything to do with Peter.

ASIA MINOR, NOT ROME

If *First Peter* is a baptismal sermon and a pastoral letter in time of persecution, where is its place of origin? If the letter is not Peter's, there is no necessity to connect it with Rome; and, in any event, it appears that the Roman Church did not know or use *First Peter*. Let us put together certain facts.

(*a*) Pontus, Galatia, Cappadocia, Asia and Bithynia (1: 1) are all in *Asia Minor* and all centred in Sinope.

(*b*) The first extensive quoter of *First Peter* is Polycarp bishop of Smyrna, and Smyrna is in *Asia Minor*.

(*c*) Certain phrases in *First Peter* immediately turn our thoughts to parallel phrases in other parts of the New Testament. In 1 *Peter* 5: 13 the Church is called "she that is elect," and in 2 *John* 13 the Church is also described as an "elect sister." 1 *Peter* 1: 8 speaks of Jesus Christ, "without having seen him you love him; though you do not now see him you believe in him and rejoice with unutterable and exalted joy." This turns our thoughts very naturally to Jesus's saying to Thomas in the Fourth Gospel: "Blessed are those who have not seen, and believe" (*John* 20: 29). *First Peter* urges the elders to tend, that is, to shepherd, the flock of God (1 *Peter* 5: 2). That turns our thoughts to Jesus's injunction to Peter to feed his lambs and his sheep (*John* 21: 15–17), and to Paul's farewell injunction to the elders of Ephesus to take heed to the flock over which the Holy Spirit has made them guardians (*Acts* 20: 28). All this is to say that the memories *First Peter* awakens are of the Fourth Gospel, the Letters of John and of Paul at Ephesus. The Fourth Gospel and the Letters of John were most probably written at Ephesus, and Ephesus is in *Asia Minor*.

It seems that in the case of *First Peter* all roads lead to Asia Minor.

THE OCCASION OF THE PUBLICATION OF FIRST PETER

Assuming that *First Peter* has its origin in Asia Minor, can we suggest an occasion for its writing? It was written at a time of persecution. We know from Pliny's letters that in Bithynia about A.D. 112 there was a serious persecution of the Christians and Bithynia is one of the provinces named in the address. We may well conjecture that it was to give courage to the Christians then that *First Peter* was issued. It may be that at that time someone in a church in Asia Minor came upon these two documents and sent them out under the name of Peter. This would not be looked upon as forgery. Both in Jewish and in Greek practice it was the regular custom to attach books to the name of the great writers of the past.

THE AUTHOR OF FIRST PETER

If Peter did not write *First Peter,* is it possible to guess at the author? Let us reconstruct some of his essential qualifications. On our previous assumption, he must come from Asia Minor. On the basis of *First Peter* itself, he must be an *elder* and an *eye-witness* of the sufferings of Christ (1 *Peter* 5: 1). Is there anyone who fits these requirements? Papias,

Bishop of Hierapolis about A.D. 170, who spent his life collecting all the information he could about the early days of the Church, tells of his methods and his sources: "Nor shall I hesitate, along with my own interpretations, to set down for thee whatsoever I learned with care and remembered with care from the elders, guaranteeing its truth. . . . Furthermore, if anyone chanced to arrive who had been really a follower of the elders, I would enquire as to the sayings of the elders—as to what Andrew or Peter said, or Philip, or Thomas or James, or John or Matthew, or any other of the Lord's disciples, also as to what Aristion or the Presbyter John, the Lord's disciples say. For I supposed that things out of books would not be of such use to me as the utterances of a living voice which was still with us." Here we have an elder called Aristion who was a disciple of the Lord and, therefore, a witness of his sufferings. Is there anything to connect him with *First Peter*?

ARISTION OF SMYRNA

When we turn to the *Apostolic Constitutions* we find that one of the first bishops of Smyrna was called Ariston—which is the same name as Aristion. Now who is the great quoter of *First Peter*? None other than Polycarp, a later Bishop of Smyrna. What more natural than that Polycarp should quote what might well have been the devotional classic of his own Church?

Let us turn to the letters to the Seven Churches in the *Revelation* and read the letter to Smyrna: "Do not fear what you are about to suffer. Behold, the devil is about to throw some of you into prison, that you may be tested, and for ten days you will have tribulation. Be faithful unto death, and I will give you the crown of life" (*Revelation* 2: 10). Can this be the very same persecution as that which originally lay behind *First Peter*? And was it for this persecution that Aristion, the Bishop of Smyrna, first wrote the pastoral letter which was afterwards to become a part of *First Peter*?

Such is the suggestion of B. H. Streeter. He thinks that *First Peter* is composed of a baptismal sermon and a pastoral letter written by Aristion, Bishop of Smyrna. Originally the pastoral letter was written to comfort and strengthen the people of Smyrna in A.D. 90 when the persecution mentioned in the *Revelation* threatened the Church. These writings of Aristion became the devotional classics and the cherished possessions of the Church at Smyrna. Rather more than twenty years later a much wider and more far-reaching persecution broke out in Bithynia and spread throughout northern Asia Minor. Someone remembered the letter and the sermon of Aristion, felt that they were the very thing the Church needed in her time of trial, and sent them out under the name of Peter, the great apostle.

AN APOSTLE'S LETTER

We have stated in full both views of the origin, date and authorship of *First Peter*. There is no doubt of the ingenuity of the theory which B. H. Streeter has produced nor that those who favour a later date have produced arguments which have to be considered. For our own part, however, we see no reason to doubt that the letter is the work of Peter himself, and that it was written not long after the great fire of Rome and the first persecution of the Christians with the object of encouraging the Christians of Asia Minor to stand fast when the onrushing tide of persecution sought to engulf them and take their faith away.

1 PETER

THE GREAT INHERITANCE

1 *Peter* 1: 1, 2

> Peter, an apostle of Jesus Christ, to God's Chosen People, who
> are scattered as exiles throughout Pontus, Galatia, Cappadocia,
> Asia and Bithynia. I am an apostle, and you are chosen, according
> to the fore-knowledge of God, through the consecration of the
> Spirit, for obedience and to be sprinkled by the blood of Jesus
> Christ. May grace and peace be multiplied to you.

IT happens again and again in the New Testament that the
true greatness of a passage lies not only on the surface and
in what is actually said, but in the ideas and the convictions
which lie behind it. That is particularly so here.

It is clear that this letter was written to people who were
Gentiles. They have been released from the futile way of life
which they had learned from their fathers (1: 18). Those who
were once not a people had become nothing less than the
people of God (2: 10). In previous times they had walked
after the will and the lusts of the Gentiles (4: 3). But the
outstanding thing about this passage is that it takes words
and conceptions which had originally applied only to the Jews,
the Chosen Nation, and applies them to the Gentiles, who
had once been believed to be outside the mercy of God. Once
it had been said that "God created the Gentiles to be fuel for
the fires of Hell." Once it had been said that, just as the
best of the snakes must be crushed, so even the best of the
Gentiles must be destroyed. Once it had been said that God
loved only Israel of all nations upon the earth. But now the
mercy, the privileges, and the grace of God have gone out
to all the earth and to all men, even to those who could
never have expected them.

(i) Peter calls the people to whom he writes *the elect, God's*

Chosen People. Once that had been a title which belonged to Israel alone: "You are a people holy to the Lord your God; the Lord your God has chosen you to be a people for his own possession, out of all the peoples that are on the face of the earth" (*Deuteronomy* 7: 6; cp. 14: 2). The prophet speaks of "Israel, my chosen" (*Isaiah* 45: 4). The Psalmist speaks of "the sons of Jacob, his chosen ones" (*Psalm* 105: 6, 43).

But the nation of Israel failed in the purposes of God, for, when he sent his Son into the world, they rejected and crucified him. When Jesus spoke the Parable of the Wicked Husbandmen, he said that the inheritance of Israel was to be taken from them and given to others (*Matthew* 21: 41; *Mark* 12: 9; *Luke* 20: 16). That is the basis of the great New Testament conception of the Christian Church as the true Israel, the new Israel, the Israel of God (cp. *Galatians* 6: 16). All the privileges which had once belonged to Israel now belonged to the Christian Church. The mercy of God has gone out to the ends of the earth, and all nations have seen the glory and experienced the grace of God.

(ii) There is another word here which once belonged exclusively to Israel. The address literally reads: "To the elect strangers of the Diaspora throughout Pontus, Galatia, Cappadocia, Asia and Bithynia." *Diaspora*, literally the *dispersion*, was the technical name for the Jews scattered in exile in all the countries outside the bounds of Palestine. Sometimes in their troubled history the Jews had been forcibly deported from their native land; sometimes they had gone of their own free will to work, and often to prosper, in other lands. Those exiled Jews were called the *Diaspora*. But now the real Diaspora is not the Jewish nation; it is the Christian Church scattered abroad throughout the provinces of the Roman Empire and the nations of the world. Once the people who had been different from others were the Jews; now the people who are different are the Christians. They are the people whose King is God, whose home is eternity, and who are exiles in the world.

THE CHOSEN OF GOD AND THE EXILES OF ETERNITY

1 *Peter* 1: 1, 2 (*continued*)

WHAT we have just been saying means that the two great titles of which we have been thinking belong to us who are Christians.

(i) We are *the Chosen People of God*. There is *uplift* here. Surely there can be no greater compliment and privilege in all the world than to be chosen by God. The word *eklektos* can describe anything that is specially chosen; it can describe specially chosen fruit, articles specially chosen because they are so outstandingly well made, picked troops specially chosen for some great exploit. We have the honour of being specially chosen by God. But there is also *challenge* and *responsibility* here. God always chooses for service. The honour which he gives a man is that of being used for his purposes. It was precisely there that the Jews failed, and we have to see to it that the tragedy of a like failure does not mark our lives.

(ii) We are *the exiles of eternity*. This is never to say that we must withdraw from the world, but that in the realest sense we must be at the same time both in the world and not of it. It has been wisely said that the Christian must be *apart* from the world but never *aloof* from it. Wherever the exiled Jew settled, his eyes were towards Jerusalem. In foreign countries his synagogues were so built that, when the worshipper entered, he was facing towards Jerusalem. However useful a citizen of his adopted country the Jew was, his greatest loyalty was to Jerusalem.

The Greek word for such a sojourner in a strange land is *paroikos*. A *paroikos* was a man who was in a strange land and whose thoughts ever turned home. Such a sojourning was called a *paroikia*; and *paroikia* is the direct derivation of the English word *parish*. The Christians in any place are a group of people whose eyes are turned to God and whose loyalty is beyond. "Here," said the writer to the Hebrews, "we have no lasting city, but we seek the city which is to come" (*Hebrews* 13: 14).

We must repeat that this does not mean withdrawal from the world; but it does mean that the Christian sees all things in the light of eternity and life as a journey towards God. It is this which decides the importance which he attaches to anything; it is this which dictates his conduct. It is the touchstone and the dynamic of his life.

There is a famous unwritten saying of Jesus: "The world is a bridge. The wise man will pass over it, but he will not build his house upon it." This is the thought which is behind the famous passage in *The Epistle to Diognetus,* one of the best-known works of the post-apostolic age: "Christians are not marked out from the rest of mankind by their country or their speech or their customs. . . . They dwell in cities both Greek and barbarian, each as his lot is cast, following the customs of the region in clothing and in food and in the outward things of life generally; yet they manifest the wonderful and openly paradoxical character of their own state. They inhabit the lands of their birth, but as temporary residents thereof; they take their share of all responsibilities as citizens, and endure all disabilities as aliens. Every foreign land is their native land, and every native land a foreign land. . . . They pass their days upon earth, but their citizenship is in heaven."

It would be wrong to think that this makes the Christian a bad citizen of the land in which he lives. It is because he sees all things in the light of eternity that he is the best of all citizens, for it is only in the light of eternity that the true values of things can be seen.

We, as Christians, are the Chosen People of God; we are the exiles of eternity. Therein lie both our priceless privilege and our inescapable responsibility.

THE THREE GREAT FACTS OF THE CHRISTIAN LIFE

1 *Peter* 1 : 1, 2 (*continued*)

IN verse 2 we are confronted with the three great facts of the Christian life.

(i) The Christian is *chosen according to the foreknowledge of God*. C. E. B. Cranfield has a fine comment on this phrase: "If all our attention is concentrated on the hostility or indifference of the world or the exiguousness of our own progress in the Christian life, we may well be discouraged. At such times we need to be reminded that our election is *according to the foreknowledge of God the Father*. The Church is not just a human organization—though, of course, it is that. Its origin lies, not in the will of the flesh, in the idealism of men, in human aspirations and plans, but in the eternal purpose of God." When we are discouraged we may well remind ourselves that the Christian Church came into being according to the purpose and plan of God and, if it is true to him, it can never ultimately fail.

(ii) The Christian is chosen *to be consecrated by the Spirit*. Luther said: "I believe that I cannot by my own reason or strength believe in Jesus Christ my Lord, or come to him." For the Christian the Holy Spirit is essential to every part of the Christian life and every step in it. It is the Holy Spirit who awakens within us the first faint longings for God and goodness. It is the Holy Spirit who convicts us of our sin and leads us to the Cross where that sin is forgiven. It is the Holy Spirit who enables us to be freed from the sins which have us in their grip and to gain the virtues which are the fruit of the Spirit. It is the Holy Spirit who gives us the assurance that our sins are forgiven and that Jesus Christ is Lord. The beginning, the middle and the end of the Christian life are the work of the Holy Spirit.

(iii) The Christian is chosen *for obedience and for sprinkling by the blood of Jesus Christ*. In the Old Testament there are three occasions when sprinkling with blood is mentioned. It may well be that all three were present in Peter's mind and that all three have something to contribute to the thought behind these words.

(*a*) When a leper had been healed, he was sprinkled with the blood of a bird (*Leviticus* 14 : 1–7). Sprinkling with blood is, therefore, the symbol of *cleansing*. By the sacrifice of Christ, the Christian is cleansed from sin.

(*b*) Sprinkling with blood was part of the ritual of the setting apart of Aaron and the priests (*Exodus* 29 : 20–21 ; *Leviticus* 8 : 30). It was the sign of *setting apart* for the service of God. The Christian is specially set apart for the service of God, not only within the Temple, but also within the world.

(*c*) The great picture of the sprinkling comes from the covenant relationship between Israel and God. In the covenant, God, of his own gracious will, approached Israel that they might be his people and that he might be their God. But that relationship depended on the Israelites accepting the conditions of the covenant and obeying the law. Obedience was a necessary condition of the covenant, and failure in obedience meant failure of the covenant relationship between God and Israel. So the book of the covenant was read to Israel and the people pledged themselves : "All the words which the Lord has spoken we will do." As a token of this relationship of obedience between the people and God, Moses took half the blood of the sacrifice and sprinkled it on the altar, and half the blood of the sacrifice and sprinkled it on the people (*Exodus* 24 : 1–8). Sprinkling was for *obedience*.

Through the sacrifice of Jesus Christ the Christian is called into a new relationship with God, in which the sins of the past are forgiven and he is pledged to obedience in the time to come.

It is in the purpose of God that the Christian is called. It is by the work of the Holy Spirit that his life is hallowed towards God. It is by the sprinkling of the blood of Christ that he is cleansed from past sin and dedicated to future obedience to God.

THE REBIRTH OF THE CHRISTIAN

1 *Peter* 1: 3–5

Blessed be the God and Father of our Lord Jesus Christ, who, according to his great mercy, has brought about in us that rebirth which leads to a living hope through the resurrection of Jesus Christ from the dead, an inheritance imperishable, undefilable, and unfading, kept safe in heaven for us, who are protected by the power of God through faith, until there comes that deliverance which is ready to be revealed at the last time.

IT will take us a long time to appropriate the riches of this passage, for there are few passages in the New Testament where more of the great fundamental Christian ideas come together.

It begins with a doxology to God—but a doxology with a difference. For a Jew the commonest of all beginnings to prayer was, "Blessed art thou, O God." The Christian takes over that prayer—but with a difference. His prayer begins, "Blessed be the God and Father of our Lord Jesus Christ." He is not praying to a distant, unknown God; he is praying to the God who is like Jesus and to whom, through Jesus Christ, he may come with childlike confidence.

This passage begins with the idea of *rebirth*; the Christian is a man who has been reborn; begotten again by God to a new kind of life. Whatever else this means, it means that, when a man becomes a Christian, there comes into his life a change so radical that the only thing that can be said is that life has begun all over again for him. This idea of rebirth runs all through the New Testament. Let us try to collect what it says about it.

(i) The Christian rebirth happens by the will and by the act of God (*John* 1: 13; *James* 1: 18). It is not something which a man achieves any more than he achieves his physical birth.

(ii) Another way to put that is to say that this rebirth is the work of the Spirit (*John* 3: 1–15). It happens to a man, not by his own effort, but when he yields himself to be possessed and re-created by the Spirit within him.

(iii) It happens by the word of truth (*James* 1: 18; 1 *Peter* 1: 23). In the beginning it was the word of God which created heaven and earth and all that is in them. God spoke and the chaos became a world, and the world was equipped with and for life. It is the creative word of God in Jesus Christ which brings about this rebirth in a man's life.

(iv) The result of this rebirth is that the man who is reborn becomes the first fruits of a new creation (*James* 1: 18). It lifts him out of this world of space and time, of change and decay, of sin and defeat, and brings him here and now into touch with eternity and eternal life.

(v) When a man is reborn, it is to a living hope (1 *Peter* 1: 3). Paul describes the heathen world as being without hope (*Ephesians* 2: 12). Sophocles wrote: "Not to be born at all— that is by far the best fortune; the second best is as soon as one is born with all speed to return thither whence one has come." To the heathen the world was a place where all things faded and decayed; it might be pleasant enough in itself but it was leading out into nothing but an endless dark. To the ancient world the Christian characteristic was hope. That hope came from two things. (*a*) The Christian felt that he had been born, not of corruptible, but of incorruptible seed (1 *Peter* 1: 23). He had something of the very seed of God in him and, therefore, had in him a life which neither time nor eternity could destroy. (*b*) It came from the resurrection of Jesus Christ (1 *Peter* 1: 3). The Christian had for ever beside him—even more, was one with—this Jesus Christ who had conquered even death and, therefore, there was nothing of which he need be afraid.

(vi) The rebirth of the Christian is a rebirth to righteousness (1 *John* 2: 29; 3: 9; 5: 18). In this rebirth he is cleansed from himself, the sins which shackle him and the habits which bind him; and he is given a power which enables him to walk in righteousness. That is not to say that the man who is reborn will never sin; but it is to say that every time he falls he will be given the power and the grace to rise again.

(vii) The rebirth of the Christian is a rebirth to love

(1 *John* 4: 7). Because the life of God is in him, he is cleansed from the essential unforgiving bitterness of the self-centred life and there is in him something of the forgiving and sacrificial love of God.

(viii) Finally, the rebirth of the Christian is rebirth to victory (1 *John* 5: 4). Life ceases to be defeat and begins to be victory, over self and sin and circumstances. Because the life of God is in him, the Christian has learned the secret of victorious living.

THE GREAT INHERITANCE

1 *Peter* 1: 3–5 (*continued*)

FURTHER, the Christian has entered into a great *inheritance* (*klēronomia*). Here is a word with a great history; for it is the word which is regularly used in the Greek Old Testament for the inheritance of Canaan, the Promised Land. Again and again the Old Testament speaks of the land which God had given his people *for an inheritance to possess* (*Deuteronomy* 15: 4; 19: 10). To us *inheritance* tends to mean something which in the future we shall possess; as the Bible uses the word, it rather means a secure possession. To the Jew the great settled possession was the Promised Land.

But the Christian inheritance is even greater. Peter uses three words with three great pictures behind them to describe it. It is *imperishable* (*aphthartos*). The word does mean *imperishable* but it can also mean *unravaged by any invading army*. Many and many a time Palestine had been ravaged by the armies of the aliens; it had been fought over and blasted and destroyed. But the Christian possesses a peace and a joy, which no invading army can ravage and destroy. It is *undefilable*. The word is *amiantos*, and the verb *miainein*, from which this adjective comes, means to *pollute* with impious impurity. Many and many a time Palestine had been rendered impure by false worship of false gods (*Jeremiah* 2: 7, 23; 3: 2; *Ezekiel* 20: 43). The defiling things had often left their touch even on the Promised Land; but the Christian has a purity

which the sin of the world cannot infect. It is *unfading*
(*amarantos*). In the Promised Land, as in any land, even the
loveliest flower fades and the loveliest blossom dies. But the
Christian is lifted into a world where there is no change and
decay and where his peace and joy are untouched by the
chances and the changes of life.

What, then, is this wonderful inheritance which the reborn
Christian possesses? There may be many secondary answers
to that question but there is only one primary answer—the
inheritance of the Christian is God himself. The Psalmist said,
"The Lord is my chosen portion . . . I have a goodly
heritage" (*Psalm* 16: 5). God is his portion for ever (*Psalm*
73: 23–26). "The Lord," said the prophet, "is my portion;
therefore I will hope in him" (*Lamentations* 3: 24).

It is because the Christian possesses God and is possessed
by God that he has the inheritance which is imperishable,
undefilable and which can never fade away.

PROTECTED IN TIME AND SAFE IN ETERNITY

1 Peter 1: 3–5 (*continued*)

THE inheritance of the Christian, the full joy of God, is waiting
for him in heaven; and of that Peter has two great things to say.

(i) On our journey through this world to eternity we are
protected by the power of God through faith. The word which
Peter uses for *protect* (*phrourein*) is a military word. It means
that our life is garrisoned by God and that he stands sentinel
over us all our days. The man who has faith never doubts,
even when he cannot see him, that God is standing within
the shadows keeping watch upon his own. It is not that God
saves us from the troubles and the sorrows and the problems
of life; but he enables us to conquer them and march on.

(ii) The final salvation will be revealed at the last time.
Here we have two conceptions which are at the very basis of
New Testament thought.

The New Testament frequently speaks of the last day or days, or the last time. At the back of this is the way the Jews divided all time into two ages—the present age, which is wholly under the domination of evil and the age to come, which will be the golden age of God. In between came the day of the Lord during which the world would be destroyed and remade and judgment would come. It is this in between time which is the last days or the last time, that time when the world as we know it will come to an end.

It is not given to us to know when that time will come nor what will happen then. But we can gather together what the New Testament says about these last days.

(i) The Christians believed that they were already living in the last days. "It is the last hour," says John to his people (1 *John* 2: 18). The writer to the Hebrews speaks of the fullness of the revelation which has come to men in Christ in these last days (*Hebrews* 1: 2). As the first Christians saw it, God had already invaded time and the end was hastening on.

(ii) The last times were to be times of the pouring out of God's Spirit upon men (*Acts* 2: 17). The early Christians saw that being fulfilled in Pentecost and in the Spirit-filled Church.

(iii) It was the regular conviction of the early Christians that before the end the powers of evil would make a final assault and that all kinds of false teachers would arise (2 *Timothy* 3: 1; 1 *John* 2: 18; *Jude* 18).

(iv) The dead would be resurrected. It is Jesus's promise that at the last time he will raise up his own (*John* 6: 39, 40, 44, 54; 11: 24).

(v) Inevitably it would be a time of judgment when God's justice would be exercised and his enemies find their just condemnation and punishment (*John* 12: 48; *James* 5: 3).

Such are the ideas which are in the minds of the New Testament writers when they use this phrase *the last times* or *the last days*.

Clearly for many a man such a time will be a time of terror; but for the Christian there is, not terror, but deliverance. The word *sōzein* means *to save* in far more than a theological sense. It is the regular word for *to rescue from danger* and *to heal in sickness.* Charles Bigg in his commentary points out that in the New Testament *sōzein,* to save, and *sōtēria,* salvation, have four different, but closely related, spheres of meaning. (*a*) They describe deliverance from danger (*Matthew* 8: 25). (*b*) They describe deliverance from disease (*Matthew* 9: 21). (*c*) They describe deliverance from the condemnation of God (*Matthew* 10: 22; 24: 13). (*d*) They describe deliverance from the disease and power of sin (*Matthew* 1: 21). Salvation is a many-sided thing. In it there is deliverance from danger, deliverance from disease, deliverance from condemnation and deliverance from sin. And it is that, and nothing less than that, to which the Christian can look forward at the end.

THE SECRET OF ENDURANCE

1 *Peter* 1: 6, 7

> Herein you rejoice, even if it is at present necessary that for a brief time you should be grieved by all kinds of trials, for the object of these trials is that your tried and tested faith, more precious than gold which perishes though it is tested by the fire, may win praise and glory and honour when Jesus Christ shall appear.

PETER comes to the actual situation in life in which his readers found themselves. Their Christianity had always made them unpopular, but now they were facing almost certain persecution. Soon the storm was going to break and life was going to be an agonizing thing. In face of that threatening situation Peter in effect reminds them of three reasons why they can stand anything that may come upon them.

(i) They can stand anything because of what they are able to look forward to. At the end there is for them the magnificent inheritance, life with God. In fact this is how Westcott understands the phrase *in the last time* (*en kairō eschatō*). We have taken it to mean *in the time when the world as we know it will come to an end*; but the Greek can mean *when the worst comes to the worst*. It is then, says Westcott, when things have reached their limit, that the saving power of Christ will be displayed.

In any event, the ultimate meaning is the same. For the Christian persecution and trouble are not the end; beyond lies the glory; and in the hope of that glory he can endure anything that life brings to him. It sometimes happens that a man has to undergo a painful operation or course of treatment; but he gladly accepts the pain and the discomfort because of the renewed health and strength which lie beyond. It is one of the basic facts of life that a man can endure anything so long as he has something to look forward to—and the Christian can look forward to the ultimate joy.

(ii) They can stand anything that comes if they remember that every trial is, in fact, a test. Before gold is pure it has to be tested in the fire. The trials which come to a man test his faith and out of them that faith can emerge stronger than ever it was before. The rigours which the athlete has to undergo are not meant to make him collapse but to make him able to develop more strength and staying-power. In this world trials are not meant to take the strength out of us, but to put the strength into us.

In this connection there is something most suggestive in the language Peter uses. He says that the Christian for the moment may well have to undergo *various* trials. The Greek is *poikilos,* which literally means *many-coloured.* Peter uses that word only one other time and it is to describe the grace of God (1 *Peter* 4: 10). Our troubles may be many-coloured, but so is the grace of God; there is no colour in the human situation which that grace cannot match. There is a grace to match every trial and there is no trial without its grace.

(iii) They can stand anything, because at the end of it, when Jesus Christ appears, they will receive from him praise and glory and honour. Again and again in this life we make our biggest efforts and do our best work, not for pay or profit, but in order to see the light in someone's eyes and to hear his word of praise. These things mean more than anything else in the world. The Christian knows that, if he endures, he will in the end hear the Master's "Well done!"

Here is the recipe for endurance when life is hard and faith

is difficult. We can stand up to things because of the greatness
to which we can look forward, because every trial is another
test to strengthen and to purify our faith, and because at the
end of it Jesus Christ is waiting to say, "Well done!" to all
his faithful servants.

UNSEEN BUT NOT UNKNOWN

1 *Peter* 1: 8, 9

> Although you never knew him, you love him; although you do not
> see him, you believe in him. And you rejoice with unspeakable and
> glorious joy because you are receiving that which faith must end in—
> the salvation of your souls.

PETER is drawing an implicit contrast between himself and his
readers. It was his great privilege to have known Jesus in the
days of his flesh. His readers had not had that joy; but,
although they never knew Jesus in the flesh, they love him;
and although they do not see him with the bodily eye, they
believe. And that belief brings to them a joy beyond speech
and clad with glory, for even here and now it makes them
certain of the ultimate welfare of their souls.

E. G. Selwyn in his commentary distinguishes four stages in
man's apprehension of Christ.

(i) The first is the stage of hope and desire, the stage of
those who throughout the ages dreamed of the coming of the
King. As Jesus himself said to his disciples, "Many prophets
and kings desired to see what you see, and did not see it"
(*Luke* 10: 23, 24). There were the days of longings and
expectations which were never fully realized.

(ii) The second stage came to those who knew Christ in the
flesh. That is what Peter is thinking about here. That is what
he was thinking about when he said to Cornelius, "We are
witnesses to all that he did, both in the country of the Jews
and in Jerusalem" (*Acts* 10: 39). There were those who walked
with Jesus and on whose witness our knowledge of his life and
the words depends.

(iii) There are those in every nation and time who see Jesus with the eye of faith. Jesus said to Thomas, "Have you believed because you have seen me? Blessed are those who have not seen, and yet believe" (*John* 20: 29). This way of seeing Jesus is possible only because he is not someone who lived and died and exists now only as a figure in a book but someone who lived and died and is alive for evermore. It has been said that "no apostle ever *remembered* Jesus." That is to say, Jesus is not only a memory; he is a person whom we can meet.

(iv) There is the beatific vision. It was John's confidence that we shall see him as he is (1 *John* 3: 2). "Now," said Paul, "we see in a mirror dimly, but then face to face" (1 *Corinthians* 13: 12). If the eye of faith endures, the day will come when it will be the eye of sight, and we shall see face to face and know even as we are known.

> Jesus, these eyes have never seen
>   That radiant form of thine;
> The veil of sense hangs dark between
>   Thy blessed face and mine.
>
> I see thee not, I hear thee not,
>   Yet art thou oft with me;
> And earth hath ne'er so dear a spot
>   As where I meet with thee.
>
> Yet, though I have not seen, and still
>   Must rest in faith alone,
> I love thee, dearest Lord, and will,
>   Unseen but not unknown.
>
> When death these mortal eyes shall seal,
>   And still this throbbing heart,
> The rending veil shall thee reveal
>   All glorious as thou art.

THE FORETELLING OF THE GLORY

1 *Peter* 1: 10–12

> Prophets, who prophesied about the grace which was to come to you,
> enquired and searched concerning that salvation, seeking to find out
> when and how the Spirit of Christ within them, testifying in advance
> to the sufferings destined for Christ and to the glories which must
> follow them, was telling them that it would come. It was revealed to
> them that the ministry which they were exercising in these things
> was not for themselves but for you, things which have now been
> proclaimed to you through those who preached the gospel to you
> through the power of the Holy Spirit sent down from heaven, things
> of which the angels long to catch a glimpse.

HERE again we have a rich passage. The wonder of the salvation
which was to come to men in Christ was such that the prophets
searched and enquired about it; and even the angels were eager
to catch a glimpse of it. Few passages have more to tell us
about how the prophets wrote and about how they were
inspired.

(i) We are told two things about the prophets. First, they
searched and enquired about the salvation which was to come.
Second, the Spirit of Christ told them about Christ. Here we
have the great truth that inspiration depends on two things—
the searching mind of man and the revealing Spirit of God. It
used sometimes to be said that the men who wrote Scripture
were pens in the hands of God or flutes into which his Spirit
breathed or lyres across which his Spirit moved. That is to say,
they were held to be nothing more than almost unconscious
instruments in God's hands. But this passage tells us that God's
truth comes only to the man who searches for it. In inspiration
there is an element which is human and an element which is
divine; it is the product at one and the same time of the
search of man's mind and the revelation of God's Spirit.

Further, this passage tells us that the Holy Spirit, the Spirit
of Christ, was always operative in this world. Wherever men
have glimpsed beauty, wherever they have laid hold on truth,
wherever they have had longings for God, the Spirit of Christ

was there. Never has there been any time in any nation when the Spirit of Christ was not moving men to seek God and guiding them to find him. Sometimes they have been blind and deaf, sometimes they have misinterpreted that guidance, sometimes they have grasped but fragments of it, but always that revealing Spirit has been there to guide the searching mind.

(ii) This passage tells us that the prophets spoke of the sufferings and the glory of Christ. Such passages as *Psalm 22* and *Isaiah* 52: 13–53: 12 found their consummation and fulfilment in the sufferings of Christ. Such passages as *Psalm 2*, *Psalm* 16: 8–11, *Psalm* 110, found their fulfilment in the glory and the triumph of Christ. We need not think that the prophets foresaw the actual man Jesus. What they did foresee was that one would come some day in whom their dreams and visions would all be fulfilled.

(iii) This passage tells us for whom the prophets spoke. It was the message of the glorious deliverance of God that they brought to men. That was a deliverance which they themselves never experienced. Sometimes God gives a man a vision, but says to the man himself, "Not yet!" He took Moses to Pisgah and showed him the Promised Land and said to him, "I have let you see it with your eyes, but you shall not go over there" (*Deuteronomy* 34: 1–4). Someone tells of watching one night at dusk a blind lamplighter lighting the lamps. He tapped his way from lamp-post to lamp-post bringing to others a light which he himself would never see. As the prophets knew, it is a great gift to receive the vision, even if the consummation of the vision is for others still to come.

THE MESSAGE OF THE PREACHER

1 *Peter* 1: 10–12 (*continued*)

THIS passage tells us not only of the visions of the prophets but also of the message of the preacher. It was the preachers who brought the message of salvation to the readers of Peter's letter.

(i) It tells us that preaching is the announcement of salvation. Preaching may at different times have many notes and many aspects, but fundamentally it is the proclamation of the gospel, the good news. The preacher may at times have to warn, threaten and condemn; he may have to remind men of the judgment and the wrath of God; but basically, beyond all else, his message is the announcement of salvation.

(ii) It tells us that preaching is through the Holy Spirit sent down from heaven. The preacher's message is not his own; it is given to him. He brings, not his own opinions and even prejudices; he brings the truth as given him by the Holy Spirit. Like the prophet he will have to search and enquire; he will have to study and to learn; but he must then wait for the guidance of the Spirit to come to him.

(iii) It tells us that the preacher's message is of things of which the angels long to catch a glimpse. There is no excuse for triviality in preaching. There is no excuse for an earth-bound and unlovely message without interest or thrill. The salvation of God is a tremendous thing.

It is with the message of salvation and the inspiration of the Spirit of Christ that the preacher must ever appear before men.

THE NECESSARY VIRILITY
OF THE CHRISTIAN FAITH

1 *Peter* 1: 13

So, then, gird up the loins of your mind; be sober; come to a final decision to place your hope on the grace which is going to be brought to you at the revealing of Jesus Christ.

PETER has been talking about the greatness and the glory to which the Christian may look forward; but the Christian can never be lost in dreams of the future; he must always be virile in the battle of the present. So Peter sends out three challenges to his people.

(i) He tells them *to gird up the loins of their mind*. This is a deliberately vivid phrase. In the east men wore long flowing robes which hindered fast progress or strenuous action. Round the waist they wore a broad belt or girdle; and when strenuous action was necessary they shortened the long robe by pulling it up within the belt in order to give them freedom of movement. The English equivalent of the phrase would be to roll up one's sleeves or to take off one's jacket. Peter is telling his people that they must be ready for the most strenuous mental endeavour. They must never be content with a flabby and unexamined faith; they must set to and think things out and think them through. It may be that they will have to discard some things. It may be that they will make mistakes. But what they are left with will be theirs in such a way that nothing and nobody can ever take it away from them.

(ii) He tells them *to be sober*. The Greek word, like the English, can have two meanings. It can mean that they must refrain from drunkenness in the literal sense of the term; and it can also mean that they must be steady in their minds. They must become intoxicated neither with intoxicating liquor nor with intoxicating thoughts; they must preserve a balanced judgment. It is easy for the Christian to be carried away with this, that, or the next sudden enthusiasm and to become readily intoxicated with the latest fashion and the newest craze. Peter is appealing to them to maintain the essential steadiness of the man who knows what he believes.

(iii) He tells them *to set their hope on the grace which is going to be given to them when Jesus Christ comes*. It is the great characteristic of the Christian that he lives in hope; and because he lives in hope he can endure the trials of the present. Any man can endure struggle and effort and toil, if he is certain that it is all leading somewhere. That is why the athlete accepts his training and the student his study. For the Christian the best is always still to come. He can live with gratitude for all the mercies of the past, with resolution to meet the challenge of the present and with the certain hope that in Christ the best is yet to be.

THE CHRISTLESS LIFE
AND THE CHRIST-FILLED LIFE

1 *Peter* 1: 14–25

Be obedient children. Do not continue to live a life which matches the desires of the days of your former ignorance, but show yourselves holy in all your conduct of life as he who called you is holy, because it stands written: "You must be holy, because I am holy." If you address as Father him who judges each man according to his work with complete impartiality, conduct yourselves with reverence throughout the time of your sojourn in this world; for you know that it was not by perishable things, by silver or gold, that you were rescued from the futile way of life which you learned from your fathers, but it was by the precious blood of Christ, as of a lamb without blemish and without spot. It was before the creation of the world that he was predestined to his work; it is at the end of the ages that he has appeared, for the sake of you who through him believe in God, who raised him from the dead and gave him glory, so that your faith and hope might be in God. Now that you have purified your souls by obedience to the truth—a purification that must issue in a brotherly love that is sincere—love each other heartily and steadfastly, for you have been reborn, not of mortal but of immortal seed, through the living and abiding word of God, for, "All flesh is grass, and its beauty is like the flower of the field. The grass withers, the flower fades; but the word of our God will stand for ever." And that is the word, the good news of which was brought to you.

THERE are three great lines of approach in this passage and we look at them one by one.

1. JESUS CHRIST REDEEMER AND LORD

It has great things to say about Jesus Christ as Redeemer and Lord.

(i) Jesus Christ is the emancipator, through whom men are delivered from the bondage of sin and death; he is the lamb without blemish and without spot (verse 19). When Peter spoke like that of Jesus, his mind was going back to two Old

Testament pictures—to *Isaiah* 53, with its picture of the Suffering Servant, through whose suffering the people were saved and healed and above all to the picture of the Passover Lamb (*Exodus* 12: 5). On that memorable night when they left the slavery of Egypt, the children of Israel were bidden to take a lamb and slay it and mark their doorposts with its blood; and, when the angel of death went through the land slaying the first-born sons of the Egyptians, he passed over every house so marked. In that picture of the Passover Lamb there are the twin thoughts of emancipation from slavery and deliverance from death. No matter how we interpret it, it cost the life and death of Jesus Christ to liberate men from their bondage to sin and to death.

(ii) Jesus Christ is the eternal purpose of God. It was before the creation of the world that he was predestined for the work which was given him to do (verse 20). Here is a great thought. Sometimes we tend to think of God as first Creator and then Redeemer, as having created the world and then, when things went wrong, finding a way to rescue it through Jesus Christ. But here we have the vision of a God who was Redeemer *before* he was Creator. His redeeming purpose was not an emergency measure to which he was compelled when things went wrong. It goes back before creation.

(iii) Peter has a connection of thought which is universal in the New Testament. Jesus Christ is not only the lamb who was slain; he is the resurrected and triumphant one to whom God gave glory. The New Testament thinkers seldom separate the Cross and the Resurrection; they seldom think of the *sacrifice* of Christ without thinking of his *triumph*. Edward Rogers, in *That they might have Life,* tells us that on one occasion he went carefully through the whole story of the Passion and the Resurrection in order to find a way to represent it dramatically, and goes on, "I began to feel that there was something subtly and tragically wrong in any emphasis on the agony of the Cross which dimmed the brightness of the Resurrection, any suggestion that it was endured pain rather than overcoming love which secured man's salvation." He asks where the eyes of the

Christian turn at the beginning of Lent. What do we dominantly see? "Is it the darkness that covered the earth at noon, swirling round the pain and anguish of the Cross? Or is it the dazzling, mysterious early-morning brightness that shone from an empty tomb?" He continues, "There are forms of most earnest and devoted evangelical preaching and theological writing which convey the impression that somehow the Crucifixion has overshadowed the Resurrection and that the whole purpose of God in Christ was completed on Calvary. The truth, which is obscured only at grave spiritual peril, is that the Crucifixion cannot be interpreted and understood save in the light of the Resurrection."

Through his death Jesus emancipated men from their bondage to slavery and death; but through his Resurrection he gives them a life which is as glorious and indestructible as his own. Through this triumphant Resurrection we have faith and hope in God (verse 21).

In this passage we see Jesus the great emancipator at the cost of Calvary; we see Jesus the eternal redeeming purpose of God; we see Jesus the triumphant victor over death and the glorious Lord of life, the giver of life which death cannot touch and the bringer of hope which nothing can take away.

2. THE CHRISTLESS LIFE

Peter picks out three characteristics of the Christless life.

(i) It is the life of *ignorance* (verse 14). The pagan world was always haunted by the unknowability of God; at best men could but grope after his mystery. "It is hard," said Plato, "to investigate and to find the framer and the father of the universe; and, if one did find him, it would be impossible to express him in terms which all could understand." Even for the philosopher, to find God is difficult; and for the ordinary man, to understand him is impossible. Aristotle spoke of God as the supreme cause, by all men dreamed of and by no man known. The ancient world did not doubt that there was a God or gods but it believed that such gods as there were were quite unknowable and totally uninterested in men and the universe. In a world without Christ God was mystery and power but never love; there was no one to whom men could raise their hands for help or their eyes for hope.

(ii) It is the life *dominated by desire* (verse 14). As we read the records of that world into which Christianity came we cannot but be appalled at the sheer fleshliness of life within it. There was desperate poverty at the lower end of the social scale; but at the top we read of banquets which cost thousands of pounds, where peacocks' brains and nightingales' tongues were served and where the Emperor Vitellius set on the table at one banquet two thousand fish and seven thousand birds. Chastity was forgotten. Martial speaks of a woman who had reached her tenth husband; Juvenal of a woman who had eight husbands in five years; and Jerome tells us that in Rome there was one woman who was married to her twenty-third husband, she herself being his twenty-first wife. Both in Greece and in Rome homosexual practices were so common that they had come to be looked on as natural. It was a world mastered by desire, whose aim was to find newer and wilder ways of gratifying its lusts.

(iii) It was a life characterized by *futility*. Its basic trouble was that it was not going anywhere. Catullus· writes to his Lesbia pleading for the delights of love. He pleads with her to seize the moment with its fleeting joys. "Suns can rise and set again; but once our brief light is dead, there is nothing left but one long night from which we never shall awake." If a man was to die like a dog, why should he not live like a dog? Life was a futile business with a few brief years in the light of the sun and then an eternal nothingness. There was nothing for which to live and nothing for which to die. Life must always be futile when there is nothing on the other side of death.

3. The Christ-filled Life

Peter finds three characteristics of the Christ-filled life and for each he finds compelling reasons.

(i) The Christ-filled life is the life of *obedience and of holiness* (verses 14–16). To be chosen by God is to enter, not only into great privilege, but also into great responsibility. Peter remembers the ancient command at the very heart of all Hebrew religion. It was God's insistence to his people that they must be holy because he was holy (*Leviticus* 11: 44; 19: 2; 20: 7, 26). The word for *holy* is *hagios* whose root meaning is *different*. The Temple is *hagios* because it is different from other buildings; the Sabbath is *hagios* because it is different from other days; the Christian is *hagios* because he is different from other men. The Christian is God's man by God's choice. He is chosen for a task in the world and for a destiny in eternity. He is chosen to live for God in time and with him in eternity. In the world he must obey his law and reproduce his life. There is laid on the Christian the task of being different.

(ii) The Christ-filled life is the life of *reverence* (verses 17–21). Reverence is the attitude of mind of the man who is always aware that he is in the presence of God. In these five verses Peter picks out three reasons for this Christian reverence. (*a*) The Christian is a sojourner in this world. Life for him is lived in the shadow of eternity; he thinks all the time, not only of where he is but also of where he is going. (*b*) He is going to God; true, he can call God Father, but that very God whom he calls Father is also he who judges every man with strict impartiality. The Christian is a man for whom there is a day of reckoning. He is a man with a destiny to win or to lose. Life in this world becomes of tremendous importance because it is leading to the life beyond. (*c*) The Christian must live life in reverence, because it cost so much, nothing less than the life and death of Jesus Christ. Since, then, life is of such surpassing value, it cannot be wasted or thrown away. No honourable man squanders what is of infinite human worth.

(iii) The Christ-filled life is the life of *brotherly love*. It must issue in a love for the brethren which is sincere and hearty and steadfast. The Christian is a man who is reborn, not of mortal, but of immortal seed. That may mean either of two things. It may mean that the remaking of the Christian is due to no human agency but to the agency of God, another way of saying what John said when he spoke of those "who were born, not of blood, nor of the will of man, but of God" (*John* 1: 13). More probably it means that the Christian is remade by the entry into him of the seed of the word; and the picture is that of the Parable of the Sower (*Matthew* 13: 1–9). The quotation which Peter makes is from *Isaiah* 40: 6–8 and the second interpretation fits that better. However we take it, the meaning is that the Christian is remade. Because he is reborn, the life of God is in him. The great characteristic of the life of God is love, and so the Christian must show that divine love for men.

The Christian is the man who lives the Christ-filled life, the life that is different, never forgets the infinity of its obligation, and is made beautiful by the love of the God who gave it birth.

WHAT TO LOSE AND WHAT TO YEARN FOR

1 *Peter* 2: 1–3

> Strip off, therefore, all the evil of the heathen world and all deceitfulness, acts of hypocrisy and feelings of envy, and all gossiping disparagements of other people, and, like newly-born babes, yearn for the unadulterated milk of the word, so that by it you may grow up until you reach salvation. You are bound to do this if you have tasted that the Lord is kind.

No Christian can stay the way he is; and Peter urges his people to have done with evil things and to set their hearts on that which alone can nourish life.

There are things which must be *stripped off*. *Apothesthai* is the word for *stripping off* one's clothes. There are things of which the Christian must divest himself as he would strip off a soiled garment.

He must strip off *all the evil of the heathen world*. The word for evil is *kakia*; it is the most general word for wickedness and includes all the wicked ways of the Christless world. The other words are illustrations and manifestations of this *kakia*; and it is to be noted that they are all faults of character which hurt the great Christian virtue of brotherly love. There can be no brotherly love so long as these evil things exist.

There is *deceitfulness* (*dolos*). *Dolos* is the trickery of the man who is out to deceive others to attain his own ends, the vice of the man whose motives are never pure.

There is *hypocrisy* (*hupokrisis*). *Hupokritēs* (*hypocrite*) is a word with a curious history. It is the noun from the verb *hupokrinesthai* which means *to answer*; a *hupokritēs* begins by being an *answerer*. Then it comes to mean an *actor,* the man who takes part in the question and answer of the stage. Next it comes to mean a *hypocrite*, a man who all the time is acting a part and concealing his real motives. The hypocrite is the man whose alleged Christian profession is for his own profit and prestige and not for the service and glory of Christ.

There is *envy* (*phthonos*). It may well be said that envy is the last sin to die. It reared its ugly head even in the apostolic band. The other ten were envious of James and John, when they seemed to steal a march upon them in the matter of precedence in the coming Kingdom (*Mark* 10: 41). Even at the last supper the disciples were disputing about who should occupy the seats of greatest honour (*Luke* 22: 24). So long as self remains active within a man's heart there will be envy in his life. E. G. Selwyn calls envy "the constant plague of all voluntary organisations, not least religious organisations." C. E. B. Cranfield says that "we do not have to be engaged in what is called 'church work' very long to discover what a perennial source of trouble envy is."

There is *gossiping disparagement* (*katalalia*). *Katalalia* is a word with a definite flavour. It means *evil-speaking*; it is almost always the fruit of envy in the heart; and it usually takes place when its victim is not there to defend himself. Few things are so attractive as hearing or repeating spicy gossip. Disparaging gossip is something which everyone admits to be wrong and which at the same time almost everyone enjoys; and yet there is nothing more productive of heartbreak and nothing is so destructive of brotherly love and Christian unity.

These, then, are the things which the reborn man must strip off for, if he continues to allow them to have a grip upon his life, the unity of the brethren must be injured.

THAT ON WHICH TO SET THE HEART

1 *Peter* 2: 1–3 (*continued*)

BUT there is something on which the Christian must set his heart. He must yearn for *the unadulterated milk of the word*. This is a phrase about whose meaning there is some difficulty. The difficulty is with the word *logikos* which with the Authorized Version we have translated *of the word*. The Revised Version translates it *spiritual*, and in the margin gives the alternative translation *reasonable*. Moffatt has *spiritual*, as has the Revised Standard Version.

Logikos is the adjective from the noun *logos* and the difficulty is that it has three perfectly possible translations.

(*a*) *Logos* is the great Stoic word for the reason which guides the universe; *logikos* is a favourite Stoic word which describes what has to do with this divine reason which is the governor of all things. If this is the word's connection, clearly *spiritual* is the meaning.

(*b*) *Logos* is the normal Greek word for *mind* or *reason*; therefore, *logikos* often means *reasonable* or *intelligent*. It is in that way that the Authorized Version translates it in *Romans* 12: 1, where it speaks of our *reasonable* service.

(*c*) *Logos* is the Greek for *word,* and *logikos* means *belonging to the word*. This is the sense in which the Authorized Version takes it, and we think it is correct. Peter has just been talking about the word of God which abides for ever (1 *Peter* 1: 23–25). It is the word of God which is in his mind; and we think that what he means here is that the Christian must desire

with his whole heart the nourishment which comes from
the word of God, for by that nourishment he can grow
until he reaches salvation itself. In face of all the evil of the
heathen world the Christian must strengthen his soul with
the pure food of the word of God.

This food of the word is *unadulterated* (*adolos*). That is to
say, there is not the slightest admixture of anything evil in it.
Adolos is an almost technical word to describe corn that is
entirely free from chaff or dust or useless or harmful matter.
In all human wisdom there is some admixture of what is
either useless or harmful; the word of God alone is altogether
good.

The Christian is to yearn for this milk of the word; *yearn*
is *epipothein* which is a strong word. It is the word which
is used for the hart longing for the waterbrooks (*Psalm*
42: 1), and for the Psalmist *longing* for the salvation of the
Lord (*Psalm* 119: 174). For the sincere Christian, to study
God's word is not a labour but a delight, for he knows
that there his heart will find the nourishment for which it
longs.

The metaphor of the Christian as a baby and the word
of God as the milk whereby he is nourished is common in
the New Testament. Paul thinks of himself as the nurse who
cares for the infant Christians of Thessalonica (1 *Thessalonians*
2: 7). He thinks of himself as feeding the Corinthians with
milk for they are not yet at the stage of meat (1 *Corinthians*
3: 2); and the writer of the Letter to the Hebrews blames
his people for being still at the stage of milk when they
should have gone on to maturity (*Hebrews* 5: 12; 6: 2). To
symbolize the rebirth of baptism in the early church, the
newly baptized Christian was clothed in white robes, and
sometimes he was fed with milk as if he was a little child.
It is this nourishment with the milk of the word which makes
a Christian grow up and grow on until he reaches salvation.

Peter finishes this introduction with an allusion to *Psalm*
34: 8. "You are bound to do this," he writes, "if you have
tasted the kindness of God." Here is something of the

greatest significance. The fact that God is gracious is not an excuse for us to do as we like, depending on him to overlook it; it lays on us an obligation to toil towards deserving his graciousness and love. The kindness of God is not an excuse for laziness in the Christian life; it is the greatest of all incentives to effort.

THE NATURE AND FUNCTION OF THE CHURCH

1 *Peter* 2: 4–10

Come to him, the living stone, rejected by men but chosen and precious with God, and be yourselves, like living stones, built into a spiritual house until you become a holy priesthood to offer spiritual sacrifices, which are well-pleasing to God through Jesus Christ; for there is a passage in Scripture which says, "Behold, I place in Zion a stone, chosen, a cornerstone, precious, and he who believes in him shall not be put to shame." So, then, there is preciousness in that stone to you who believe; but, to those who disbelieve, the stone which the builders rejected has become the headstone of the corner, and a stone over which they will stumble, and a rock over which they will trip. They stumble because they disobey the word—a fate for which they were appointed. But you are a chosen race, a royal priesthood, a people dedicated to God, a nation for him specially to possess that you might tell forth the excellencies of him who called you out of darkness into his glorious light, you, who were once not a people and are now the people of the Lord, you who were once without mercy and have now found mercy.

PETER sets before us the nature and the function of the Church. There is so much in the passage that we divide it into four sections.

1. THE STONE WHICH THE BUILDERS REJECTED

Much is made of the idea of the *stone*. Three Old Testament passages are symbolically used; let us look at them one by one.

(i) The beginning of the whole matter goes back to the words

of Jesus himself. One of the most illuminating parables he
ever told was the Parable of the Wicked Husbandmen. In
it he told how the wicked husbandmen killed servant after
servant and in the end even murdered the son. He was
showing how the nation of Israel had again and again
refused to listen to the prophets and had persecuted them, and
how this refusal was to reach its climax with his own death.
But beyond the death he saw the triumph and he told of that
triumph in words taken from the *Psalms*: "The very stone
which the builders rejected has become the head of the corner;
this was the Lord's doing and it is marvellous in our eyes"
(*Matthew* 21: 42; *Mark* 12: 10; *Luke* 20: 17).

That is a quotation from *Psalm* 118: 22. In the original
it is a reference to the nation of Israel. A. K. Kirkpatrick
writes of it: "Israel is 'the head corner-stone.' The powers
of the world flung it aside as useless, but God destined it for
the most honourable and important place in the building of
his kingdom in the world. The words express Israel's consciousness of its mission and destiny in the purpose of God." Jesus
took these words and applied them to himself. It looked as if
he was utterly rejected by men; but in the purpose of God
he was the corner-stone of the edifice of the Kingdom,
honoured above all.

(ii) In the Old Testament there are other references to this
symbolic stone, and the early Christian writers used them
for their purposes. The first is in *Isaiah* 28: 16: "Therefore,
thus says the Lord God, Behold I am laying in Zion for a
foundation a stone, a tested stone, a precious cornerstone,
of a sure foundation; he who believes will not be in haste."
Again the reference is to Israel. The sure and precious stone
is God's unfailing relationship to his people, a relationship
which was to culminate in the coming of the Messiah. Once
again the early Christian writers took this passage and applied
it to Jesus Christ as the precious and immovable foundation
stone of God.

(iii) The second of these other passages is also from *Isaiah*:
"But the Lord of hosts, him you shall regard as holy; let him be

your fear, and let him be your dread. And he will become a sanctuary, and a stone of offence, and a rock of stumbling to both houses of Israel, a trap and a snare to the inhabitants of Jerusalem" (*Isaiah* 8: 13, 14). Its meaning is that God is offering his lordship to the people of Israel; that to those who accept him he will become a sanctuary and a salvation, but to those who reject him he will become a terror and a destruction. Again the early Christian writers took this passage and applied it to Jesus. To those who accept him Jesus is Saviour and Friend; to those who reject him he is judgment and condemnation.

(iv) For the understanding of this passage, we have to take in a New Testament reference to these Old Testament ones. It is hardly possible that Peter could speak of Jesus as the cornerstone and of Christians as being built into a spiritual house, united in him, without thinking of Jesus's own words to himself. When he made his great confession of faith at Caesarea Philippi, Jesus said to him, "You are Peter, and on this rock I will build my Church" (*Matthew* 16: 18). It is on the faith of the loyal believer that the Church is built.

These are the origins of the pictures in this passage.

2. THE NATURE OF THE CHURCH

From this passage we learn three things about the very nature of the Church.

(i) The Christian is likened to a living stone and the Church to a living edifice into which he is built (verse 5). Clearly that means that *Christianity is community*; the individual Christian finds his true place only when he is built into that edifice. "Solitary religion" is ruled out as an impossibility. C. E. B. Cranfield writes: "The free-lance Christian, who would be a Christian but is too superior to belong to the visible Church upon earth in one of its forms, is simply a contradiction in terms."

There is a famous story from Sparta. A Spartan king

boasted to a visiting monarch about the walls of Sparta. The visiting monarch looked around and could see no walls. He said to the Spartan king, "Where are these walls about which you boast so much?" His host pointed at his bodyguard of magnificent troops. "These," he said, "are the walls of Sparta, every man a brick."

The point is clear. So long as a brick lies by itself it is useless; it becomes of use only when it is incorporated into a building. So it is with the individual Christian. To realize his destiny he must not remain alone, but must be built into the fabric of the Church.

Suppose that in time of war a man says, "I wish to serve my country and to defend her from her enemies." If he tries to carry out that resolution alone, he can accomplish nothing. He can be effective in that purpose only by standing shoulder to shoulder with others of like mind. It is so with the Church. Individualistic Christianity is an absurdity; Christianity is community within the fellowship of the Church.

(ii) Christians are a holy priesthood (verse 5). There are two great characteristics of the priest.

(*a*) He is the man who himself has access to God and whose task it is to bring others to him. In the ancient world this access to God was the privilege of the professional priests, and in particular of the High Priest who alone could enter into the Holy of Holies. Through Jesus Christ, the new and living way, access to God becomes the privilege of every Christian, however simple he may be. Further, the Latin word for priest is *pontifex*, which means *bridge-builder*; the priest is the man who builds a bridge for others to come to God; and the Christian has the duty and the privilege of bringing others to that Saviour whom he himself has found and loves.

(*b*) The priest is the man who brings an offering to God. The Christian also must continuously bring his offerings to God. Under the old dispensation the offerings brought were animal sacrifices; but the sacrifices of the Christian are *spiritual* sacrifices. He makes his *work* an offering to God. Everything is done for God; and so even the meanest task is clad with glory. The Christian makes his *worship* an offering to God; and so the worship of God's house becomes, not a burden but a joy. The Christian makes *himself* an offering to God. "Present your bodies," said Paul, "as a living sacrifice to God" (*Romans* 12: 1). What God desires most of all is the love of our hearts and the service of our lives. That is the perfect sacrifice which every Christian must make.

(iii) The function of the Church is *to tell forth the excellencies* of God. That is to say, it is to witness to men concerning the mighty acts of God. By his very life, even more than by his words, the Christian is to be a witness of what God in Christ has done for him.

3. The Glory of the Church

In verse 9 we read of the things to which the Christian is a witness.

(i) God has called the Christian out of darkness into his glorious light. *The Christian is called out of darkness into light.* When a man comes to know Jesus Christ, he comes to know *God.* No longer does he need to guess and to grope. "He who has seen me," said Jesus, "has seen the Father" (*John* 14: 9). In Jesus is the light of the knowledge of God. When a man comes to know Jesus, he comes to know *goodness.* In Christ he has a standard by which all actions and motives may be tested. When a man comes to know Jesus Christ, he comes to know the *way.* Life is no longer a trackless road without a star to guide. In Christ the way becomes clear. When a man comes to know Jesus Christ, he comes to know *power.* It would be little use to know God without the power to serve him. It would be little use to know goodness and yet be helpless to attain to it. It would be little use to see the right way and be quite unable to take it. In Jesus Christ there is both the vision *and* the power.

(ii) God has made those who were not a people into the people of God. Here Peter is quoting from *Hosea* 1: 6, 9, 10; 2: 1, 23). This means that *the Christian is called out of*

insignificance into significance. It continually happens in this
world that a man's greatness lies not in himself but in what
has been given him to do. The Christian's greatness lies in the
fact that God has chosen him to be his man and to do his
work in the world. No Christian can be ordinary, for he is
a man of God.

(iii) *The Christian is called out of no mercy into mercy*. The
great characteristic of non-Christian religion is the fear of
God. The Christian has discovered the love of God and
knows that he need no longer fear him, because it is well
with his soul.

4. THE FUNCTION OF THE CHURCH

In verse 9 Peter uses a whole series of phrases which are
a summary of the functions of the Church. He calls the
Christians "a chosen race, a royal priesthood, a people
dedicated to God, a nation for him specially to possess."
Peter is steeped in the Old Testament and these phrases
are all great description of the people of Israel. They come
from two main sources. In *Isaiah* 43: 21 Isaiah hears God
say, "The people whom I formed for myself." But even
more in *Exodus* 19: 5, 6 the voice of God is heard: "Now,
therefore, if you will obey my voice and keep my covenant,
you shall be my own possession among all people; for all
the earth is mine: and you shall be to me a kingdom of priests,
and a holy nation." The great promises which God made
to his people Israel are being fulfilled to the Church, the new
Israel. Every one of these titles is full of meaning.

(i) Christians are *a chosen people*. Here we are back to the
covenant idea. *Exodus* 19: 5, 6 is from the passage which
describes how God entered into his covenant with Israel. In
the covenant he offered a special relationship with himself to
Israel; but it depended on the people of Israel accepting the
conditions of the covenant and keeping the law. That
relationship would hold only "if you will obey my voice, and
keep my covenant" (*Exodus* 19: 5).

From this we learn that the Christian is chosen for three things. (*a*) He is chosen for *privilege*. In Jesus Christ there is offered to him a new and intimate fellowship with God. God has become his friend and he has become God's friend. (*b*) He is chosen for *obedience*. Privilege brings with it responsibility. The Christian is chosen in order that he may become the obedient child of God. He is chosen not to do as he likes but to do as God likes. (*c*) He is chosen for *service*. His honour is that he is the servant of God. His privilege is that he will be used for the purposes of God. But he can be so used only when he brings to God the obedience he desires. Chosen for privilege, chosen for obedience, chosen for service—these three great facts go hand in hand.

(ii) Christians are *a royal priesthood*. We have already seen that this means that every Christian has the right of access to God; and that he must offer his work, his worship and himself to God.

(iii) Christians are what the Revised Standard Version calls *a holy nation*. We have already seen that the basic meaning of *hagios* (holy) is *different*. The Christian has been chosen that he may be different from other men. That difference lies in the fact that he is dedicated to God's will and to God's service. Other people may follow the standards of the world but for him the only standards are God's. A man need not even start on the Christian way unless he realizes that it will compel him to be different from other people.

(iv) Christians are *a people for God specially to possess*. It frequently happens that the value of a thing lies in the fact that some one has possessed it. A very ordinary thing acquires a new value, if it has been possessed by some famous person. In any museum we find quite ordinary things—clothes, a walking-stick, a pen, books, pieces of furniture—which are of value only because they were once possessed by some great person. It is so with the Christian. The Christian may be a very ordinary person but he acquires a new value because he belongs to God.

REASONS FOR RIGHT LIVING

1 *Peter* 2: 11, 12

> Beloved, I urge you, as strangers and sojourners, to abstain from
> the fleshly desires which carry on their campaign against the
> soul. Make your conduct amongst the Gentiles fine, so that in
> every matter in which they slander you as evil-doers, they may
> see from your fine deeds what you are really like and glorify God
> on the day when he will visit the earth.

THE basic commandment in this passage is that the Christian
should *abstain from fleshly desires*. It is of the greatest
importance that we should see what Peter means by this. The
phrases *sins of the flesh* and *fleshly desires* have become much
narrowed in meaning in modern usage. For us they usually
mean sexual sin; but in the New Testament they are much
wider than that. Paul's list of the sins of the flesh in *Galatians*
5: 19–21, includes "immorality, impurity, licentiousness,
idolatry, sorcery, enmity, strife, jealousy, anger, selfishness,
dissension, party spirit, envy, drunkenness, carousing, and the
like." There are far more than *bodily* sins here.

In the New Testament *flesh* stands for far more than the
physical nature of man. It stands for *human nature apart from
God;* it means unredeemed human nature; it means life
lived without the standards, the help, the grace and the
influence of Christ. *Fleshly desires* and *sins of the flesh,*
therefore, include not only the grosser sins but all that is
characteristic of fallen human nature. From these sins and
desires the Christian must abstain. As Peter sees it, there
are two reasons for this abstinence.

(i) The Christian must abstain from these sins because he
is a stranger and a pilgrim. The words are *paroikos* and
parepidēmos. They are quite common Greek words and
they describe someone who is only temporarily resident in a
place and whose home is somewhere else. They are used to
describe the patriarchs in their wanderings, and especially
Abraham who went out not knowing where he was to go
and whose search was for the city whose maker and builder

is God (*Hebrews* 11: 9, 13). They are used to describe the
children of Israel when they were slaves and strangers in the
land of Egypt before they entered into the Promised Land
(*Acts* 7: 6).

These words give us two great truths about the Christian.
(*a*) There is a real sense in which he is a stranger in the
world; and because of that he cannot accept the world's
laws and ways and standards. Others may accept them;
but the Christian is a citizen of the Kingdom of God and
it is by the laws of that Kingdom that he must direct his
life. He must take his full share of responsibility for living
upon earth, but his citizenship is in heaven and the laws of
heaven are paramount for him. (*b*) The Christian is not a
permanent resident upon earth; he is on the way to the country
which is beyond. He must therefore, do nothing which would
keep him from reaching his ultimate goal. He must never
become so entangled in the world that he cannot escape from
its grip; he must never so soil himself as to be unfit to enter
the presence of the holy God to whom he is going.

THE GREATEST ANSWER AND DEFENCE

1 *Peter* 2: 11, 12 (*continued*)

(ii) But there was for Peter another and even more
practical reason why the Christian must abstain from fleshly
desires. The early church was under fire. Slanderous charges
were continually being made against the Christians; and the
only effective way to refute them was to live lives so lovely
that the charges would be seen to be obviously untrue.

To modern ears the Authorized Version can be a little
misleading. It speaks about "having your conversation honest
among the Gentiles." That sounds to us as if it meant that
the Christian must always speak the truth, but the word
translated *conversation* is *anastrophē*, which means a man's
whole conduct, not simply his talk. That is, in fact, what
conversation did mean in the seventeenth century. The word

translated *honest* is *kalos*. In Greek there are two words for
good. There is *agathos,* which simply means good in quality;
and there is *kalos*, which means not only *good* but also
lovely—fine, attractive, winsome. That is what *honestus* means
in Latin. So, what Peter is saying is that the Christian must
make his whole way of life so lovely and so good to look
upon that the slanders of his heathen enemies may be
demonstrated to be false.

Here is timeless truth. Whether we like it or not, every
Christian is an advertisement for Christianity; by his life he
either commends it to others or makes them think less of it.
The strongest missionary force in the world is a Christian
life.

In the early church this demonstration of the loveliness
of the Christian life was supremely necessary, because of the
slanders the heathen deliberately cast on the Christian Church.
Let us see what some of these slanders were.

(i) In the beginning Christianity was closely connected
with the Jews. By race Jesus was a Jew; Paul was a Jew;
Christianity was cradled in Judaism; and inevitably many of
its early converts were Jews. For a time Christianity was
regarded merely as a sect of Judaism. Antisemitism is no new
thing. Friedlander gives a selection of the slanders which
were repeated against the Jews in his *Roman Life and Manners
under the Early Empire*. "According to Tacitus they (the
Jews) taught their proselytes above all to despise the gods,
to renounce their fatherland, to disregard parents, children,
brothers and sisters. According to Juvenal, Moses taught the
Jews not to show anyone the way, nor to guide the thirsty
traveller to the spring, except he were a Jew. Apion declares
that, in the reign of Antiochus Epiphanes, the Jews every
year fattened a Greek, and having solemnly offered him up
as a sacrifice on a fixed day in a certain forest, ate his
entrails and swore eternal hostility to the Greeks." These
were the things which the heathen had persuaded themselves
were true about the Jews, and inevitably the Christians
shared in this odium.

(ii) Apart from these slanders attached to the Jews, there were slanders directed particularly against the Christians themselves. They were accused of cannibalism. This accusation took its rise from a perversion of the words of the Last Supper, "This is my body," This cup is the new covenant in my blood." The Christians were accused of killing and eating a child at their feasts.

They were also accused of immorality and even of incest. This accusation took its rise from the fact that they called their meeting the *Agapē*, the Love Feast. The heathen perverted that name to mean that the Christian feasts were sensual orgies at which shameless deeds were done.

The Christians were accused of damaging trade. Such was the charge of the silversmiths of Ephesus (*Acts* 19: 21–41).

They were accused of "tampering with family relationships" because often homes were, in fact, broken up when some members of the family became Christians and others did not.

They were accused of turning slaves against their masters, and Christianity indeed did give to every man a new sense of worth and dignity.

They were accused of "hatred of mankind" and indeed the Christian did speak as if the world and the Church were entirely opposed to each other.

Above all they were accused of disloyalty to Caesar, for no Christian would worship the Emperor's godhead and burn his pinch of incense and declare that Caesar was Lord, for to him Jesus Christ and no other was Lord.

Such were the charges which were directed against the Christians. To Peter there was only one way to refute them and that was so to live that their Christian life demonstrated that they were unfounded. When Plato was told that a certain man had been making certain slanderous charges against him, his answer was: "I will live in such a way that no one will believe what he says." That was Peter's solution.

Jesus himself had said—and doubtless the saying was in Peter's mind: "Let your light so shine before men that they may see your good works and give glory to your Father who is in heaven" (*Matthew* 5: 16). This was a line of thought which the Jews knew well. In one of the books written between the Old and the New Testaments it says: "If ye work that which is good, my children, both men and angels shall bless you; and God shall be glorified among the Gentiles through you, and the devil shall flee from you" (*The Testament of Naphtali* 8: 4).

The striking fact of history is that by their lives the Christians actually did defeat the slanders of the heathen. In the early part of the third century Celsus made the most famous and the most systematic attack of all upon the Christians in which he accused them of ignorance and foolishness and superstition and all kinds of things—*but never of immorality*. In the first half of the fourth century, Eusebius, the great Church historian, could write: "But the splendour of the catholic and only true Church, which is always the same, grew in magnitude and power, and reflected its piety and simplicity and freedom, and the modesty and purity of its inspired life and philosophy to every nation both of Greeks and barbarians. At the same time the slanderous accusations which had been brought against the whole Church also vanished, and there remained our teaching alone, which has prevailed over all, and which is acknowledged to be superior to all in dignity and temperance, and in divine and philosophical doctrines. So that none of them now ventures to affix a base calumny upon our faith, or any such slander as our ancient enemies formerly delighted to utter" (Eusebius: *The Ecclesiastical History* 4.7.15). It is true that the terrors of persecution were not even then ended, for the Christians would never admit that Caesar was Lord; but the excellence of their lives had silenced the calumnies against the Church.

Here is our challenge and our inspiration. It is by the loveliness of our daily life and conduct that we must commend Christianity to those who do not believe.

THE DUTY OF THE CHRISTIAN

1 *Peter* 2: 13–15

Submit to every human institution for the Lord's sake, whether it be to the king, who has the first place, or to governors as sent by him for the punishment of those whose deeds are evil and the praise of those whose deeds are good, for it is the will of God that by so doing you should muzzle the ignorance of foolish men.

1. As a Citizen

PETER looks at the duty of the Christian within the different spheres of his life; and he begins with his duty as a citizen of the country in which he happens to live.

Nothing is further from the thought of the New Testament than any kind of anarchy. Jesus had said, "Render therefore to Caesar the things that are Caesar's; and to God the things that are God's" (*Matthew* 22: 21). Paul was certain that those who governed the nation were sent by God and held their responsibility from him, and were, therefore, no terror to the man who lived an honourable life (*Romans* 13: 1–7). In the Pastoral Epistles the Christian is instructed to pray for kings and all in authority (1 *Timothy* 2: 2). The instruction of the New Testament is that the Christian must be a good and useful citizen of the country in which his life is set.

It has been said that fear built the cities and that men huddled behind a wall in order to be safe. Men join themselves together and agree to live under certain laws, so that the good man may have peace to do his work and go about his business and the evil man may be restrained and kept from his evil-doing. According to the New Testament life is meant by God to be an ordered business and the state is divinely appointed to provide and to maintain that order.

The New Testament view is perfectly logical and just. It holds that a man cannot accept the privileges which the state provides without also accepting the responsibilities and the duties which it demands. He cannot in honour and decency take everything and give nothing.

How are we to translate this into modern terms? C. E. B. Cranfield has well pointed out that there is a fundamental difference between the state in New Testament times and the state as we in Britain know it. In New Testament times the state was *authoritarian*. The ruler was an absolute ruler; and the sole duty of the citizen was to render absolute obedience and to pay taxes (*Romans* 13: 6, 7). Under these conditions the keynote was bound to be *subjection to the state*. But we live in a *democracy*; and in a democracy something far more than unquestioning subjection becomes necessary. Government is not only government *of* the people; it is also *for* the people and *by* the people. The demand of the New Testament is that the Christian should fulfil his responsibility to the state. In the authoritarian state that consisted solely in submission. But what is that obligation in the very different circumstances of a democracy?

In any state there must be a certain subjection. As C. E. B. Cranfield puts it, there must be "a voluntary subordination of oneself to others, putting the interest and welfare of others above one's own, preferring to give rather than to get, to serve rather than to be served." But in a democratic state the keynote must be not *subjection* but *co-operation,* for the duty of the citizen is not only to submit to be ruled but to take a necessary share in ruling. Hence, if the Christian is to fulfil his duty to the state, he must take his part in its government. He must also take his part in local government and in the life of the trade union or association connected with his trade, craft, or profession. It is tragic that so few Christians really fulfil their obligation to the state and the society in which they live.

It remains to say that the Christian has a higher obligation than even his obligation to the state. While he must render to Caesar the things which are Caesar's, he must also render to God the things which are God's. He must on occasion make it quite clear that he must listen to God rather than to men (*Acts* 4: 19; 5: 29). There may be times, therefore, when the Christian will fulfil his highest duty to the state by refusing to obey it and by insisting on obeying God. By so doing, at least he will witness to the truth, and at best he may lead the state to take the Christian way.

THE DUTY OF THE CHRISTIAN

1 *Peter* 2: 16

> You must live as free men, yet not using your freedom as a cloak for evil, but as the slaves of God.

2. IN SOCIETY

ANY great Christian doctrine can be perverted into an excuse for evil. The doctrine of grace can be perverted into an excuse for sinning to one's heart's content. The doctrine of the love of God can be sentimentalized into an excuse for breaking his law. The doctrine of the life to come can be perverted into an excuse for neglecting life in this world. And there is no doctrine so easy to pervert as that of Christian freedom.

There are hints in the New Testament that it was frequently so perverted. Paul tells the Galatians that they have been called to liberty but they must not use that liberty as an occasion for the flesh to do as it wills (*Galatians* 5: 13). In *Second Peter* we read of those who promise others liberty and are themselves the slaves of corruption (2 *Peter* 2: 19). Even the great pagan thinkers saw quite clearly that perfect freedom is, in fact, the product of perfect obedience. Seneca said, "No one is free who is the slave of his body," and, "Liberty consists in obeying God." Cicero said, "We are the servants of the laws that we may be able to be free." Plutarch insisted that every bad man is a slave; and Epictetus declared that no bad man can ever be free.

We may put it this way. Christian freedom is always conditioned by Christian responsibility. Christian responsibility is always conditioned by Christian love. Christian love is the reflection of God's love. And, therefore, Christian liberty can rightly be summed up in Augustine's memorable phrase: "Love God, and do what you like."

The Christian is free because he is the slave of God. Christian freedom does not mean being free to do as we like; it means being free to do as we ought.

In this matter we have to return to the great central truth which we have already seen. *Christianity is community*. The Christian is not an isolated unit; he is a member of a community and within that community his freedom operates. Christian freedom therefore is the freedom to serve. Only in Christ is a man so freed from self and sin that he can become as good as he ought to be. Freedom comes when a man receives Christ as king of his heart and Lord of his life.

A SUMMARY OF CHRISTIAN DUTY

1 *Peter* 2: 17

Honour all men; love the brotherhood; fear God; honour the king.

HERE is what we might call a four-point summary of Christian duty.

(i) *Honour all men.* To us this may seem hardly needing to be said; but when Peter wrote this letter it was something quite new. There were 60,000,000 slaves in the Roman Empire, every one of whom was considered in law to be, not a person, but a thing, with no rights whatever. In effect, Peter is saying, "Remember the rights of human personality and the dignity of every man." It is still possible to treat people as things. An employer may treat his employees as so many human machines for producing so much work. Even in a welfare state, where the aim is to do so much for their physical welfare, there is a very real danger that people may be regarded as numbers on a form or as cards in a filing system.

John Lawrence in his book, *Hard Facts, A Christian Looks at the World,* says that one of the greatest needs in the welfare state is "to see through the files and forms in triplicate to God's creatures who are at the other end of the chain of organization." The danger is that we fail to see men and women as persons. This matter comes nearer home. When we regard anyone as existing solely to minister to our comfort or to further our plans, we are in effect regarding them, not as persons, but as things. The most tragic danger of all is that we may come to regard those who are nearest and dearest to us as existing for our convenience—and that is to treat them as things.

(ii) *Love the brotherhood.* Within the Christian community this respect for every man turns to something warmer and closer; it turns to love. The dominant atmosphere of the Church must always be love. One of the truest definitions of the Church is that it is "the extension of the family." The Church is the larger family of God and its bond must be love. As the Psalmist had it (*Psalm* 133: 1):

> Behold, how good a thing it is,
>   And how becoming well,
> Together such as brethren are
>   In unity to dwell!

(iii) *Fear God.* The writer of the proverbs has it: "The fear of the Lord is the beginning of knowledge" (*Proverbs* 1: 7). It may well be that the translation should be, not that the fear of the Lord is the *beginning* of knowledge but that the fear of the Lord is *the principal part,* the very *foundation* of knowledge. *Fear* here does not mean terror; it means awe and reverence. It is the simple fact of life that we will never reverence men until we reverence God. It is only when God is given his proper place in the centre that all other things take their proper place.

(iv) *Honour the king.* Of the four injunctions of this verse this is the most amazing, for, if it was really Peter who wrote this letter, the king in question is none other than Nero. It is the teaching of the New Testament that the ruler is sent by God to preserve order among men and that he must be respected, even when he is a Nero.

THE DUTY OF THE CHRISTIAN AS A SERVANT

1 *Peter* 2: 18–25

Servants, be subject to your masters with all respect, not only to those who are good and equitable, but also to those who are perverse, for it is a real sign of grace when a man bears pains in unjust suffering because of his consciousness of God. It is to live like this that you were called, because Christ too suffered for us, leaving behind him an example that we should follow in his steps. He did no sin nor was any guile found in his mouth. When he was insulted, he did not return insult for insult. When he suffered, he uttered no threats, but he committed himself to him who judges justly. He himself bore our sins in his body on the tree, that we might depart from sins and live to righteousness. With his stripes you have been healed, for you were straying away like sheep but now you have turned to the Shepherd and Watchman of your souls.

HERE is the passage which would be relevant to by far the greatest number of the readers of this letter, for Peter writes to servants and slaves, and they formed by far the greatest part of the early church. The word Peter uses for *servants* is not *douloi,* which is the commonest word for *slaves,* but *oiketai,* the word for the household and domestic slaves.

To understand the real meaning of what Peter is saying we must understand something of the nature of slavery in the time of the early church. In the Roman Empire there were as many as 60,000,000 slaves. Slavery began with Roman conquests, slaves being originally mainly prisoners taken in war, and in very early times Rome had few slaves but by New Testament times slaves were counted by the million.

It was by no means only menial tasks which were performed by slaves. Doctors, teachers, musicians, actors, secretaries, stewards were slaves. In fact, all the work of Rome was done by slaves. Roman attitude was that there was no point in being master of the world and doing one's own work. Let the slaves do that and let the citizens live in pampered idleness. The supply of slaves would never run out.

Slaves were not allowed to marry; but they cohabited; and the children born of such a partnership were the property of the master, not of the parents, just as the lambs born to the sheep belonged to the owner of the flock, and not to the sheep.

It would be wrong to think that the lot of slaves was always wretched and unhappy, and that they were always treated with cruelty. Many slaves were loved and trusted members of the family; but one great inescapable fact dominated the whole situation. In Roman law a slave was not a person but a thing; and he had absolutely no legal rights whatsoever. For that reason there could be no such thing as justice where a slave was concerned. Aristotle writes, "There can be no friendship nor justice towards inanimate things; indeed, not even towards a horse or an ox, nor yet towards a slave as a slave. For master and slave have nothing in common; a slave is a living tool, just as a tool is an inanimate slave." Varro divides the instruments of agriculture into three classes—the articulate, the inarticulate and the mute, "the articulate comprising the slaves, the inarticulate comprising the cattle, and the mute comprising the vehicles." The only difference between a slave and a beast or a farmyard cart was that a slave happened to be able to speak. Peter Chrysologus sums the matter up: "Whatever a master does to a slave, undeservedly, in anger, willingly, unwillingly, in forgetfulness, after careful thought, knowingly, unknowingly, is judgment, justice and law." In regard to a slave, his master's will, and even his master's caprice, was the only law.

The dominant fact in the life of a slave was that, even if he was well treated, he remained a thing. He did not possess even the elementary rights of a person and for him justice did not even exist.

THE PERIL OF THE NEW SITUATION

1 *Peter* 2: 18–25 (*continued*)

INTO this situation came Christianity with its message that every man was precious in the sight of God. The result was that within the Church the social barriers were broken down. Callistus, one of the earliest bishops of Rome, was a slave; and Perpetua, the aristocrat, and Felicitas, the slave-girl, met martyrdom hand in hand. The great majority of the early

Christians were humble folk and many of them were slaves. It was quite possible in the early days that the slave should be the president of the congregation and the master a member of it. This was a new and revolutionary situation. It had its glory and it had its dangers. In this passage Peter is urging the slave to be a good slave and a faithful workman; for he sees two dangers.

(i) Suppose both master and servant became Christians; there arose the danger that the slave might presume upon the new relationship and make an excuse for shirking his work, assuming that since he and his master were both Christians, he could get away with anything. That situation is by no means at an end. There are still people who trade on the goodwill of a Christian master and think that the fact that both they and their employers are Christians gives them a right to dispense with discipline and punishment. But Peter is quite clear. The relationship between Christian and Christian does not abolish the relationship between man and man. The Christian must, indeed, be a better workman than anyone else. His Christianity is not a reason for claiming exemption from discipline; it should bring him under self-discipline and make him more conscientious than anyone else.

(ii) There was the danger that the new dignity which Christianity brought him would make the slave rebel and seek to abolish slavery altogether. Some students are puzzled that no New Testament writer ever pleads for the abolition of slavery or even says in so many words that it is wrong. The reason was simple. To have encouraged the slaves to rise against their masters would have been the way to speedy disaster. There had been such revolts before and they had always been quickly and savagely crushed. In any event, such teaching would merely have gained for Christianity the reputation of being a subversionary religion. There are some things which cannot happen quickly; there are some situations in which the leaven has to work and in which haste is the surest way to delay the desired end. The leaven of Christianity had to work in the world for many generations before the abolition of slavery became a practical possibility. Peter was concerned that Christian slaves should demonstrate to the world that their Christianity did not make them disgruntled rebels but rather workmen who had found a new inspiration towards doing an honest day's work. It will still often happen that, when some situation cannot at the time be changed, the Christian duty is to be Christian within that situation and to accept what cannot be changed until the leaven has worked.

THE NEW ATTITUDE TO WORK

1 *Peter* 2: 18–25 (*continued*)

But Christianity did not leave the matter in that merely negative form. It introduced three great new principles into a man's attitude as a servant and a workman.

(i) Christianity introduced a new relationship between master and man. When Paul sent the runaway slave Onesimus back to Philemon, he did not for a moment suggest that Philemon should set Onesimus free. He did not suggest that Philemon should cease to be the master and that Onesimus should cease to be the slave. What he did say was that Philemon must receive Onesimus not now as a servant, but as a brother beloved (*Philemon* 16). Christianity did not abolish social differences; but it introduced a new relationship of brotherhood in which these other differences were overpassed and transformed. Where there is real brotherhood, it does not matter if you call one man master and the other servant. There is between them a bond which transforms the necessary differences which the circumstances of life make necessary. The solution of the world's problems lies in the new relationship between man and man.

(ii) Christianity introduced a new attitude to work. It is the conviction of the New Testament that all work must be done for Jesus Christ. Paul writes: "Whatever you do in word or deed, do everything in the name of the Lord Jesus" (*Colossians* 3: 17). "Whether you eat or drink, or whatever you do, do all to the glory of God" (1 *Corinthians* 10: 31). In the Christian ideal work is not done for an earthly master or for personal prestige or to make so much money; it is done for God. It is, of course, true that a man must work in order to earn a wage and he must work to satisfy a master; but beyond that there is for the Christian the conviction that his work must be done well enough to be able to show it to God without shame.

(iii) But when these great ideals were set against the situation in the early church—and the situation does not entirely change—one great question arose. Suppose a man has the Christian attitude to men and to work and is treated with injustice, insult and injury—what then? Peter's great answer is that this is exactly what happened to Jesus. He was none other than the *Suffering Servant*. Verses 21–25 are full of reminiscences and quotations of *Isaiah* 53, the supreme picture of the Suffering Servant of God, which came to life in Jesus. He was without sin and yet he was insulted and he suffered; but he accepted the insults and the suffering with serene love and bore them for the sins of mankind.

In so doing he left us an example that we should follow in his steps (verse 21). The word Peter uses for *example* is very vivid. It is *hupogrammos,* a word which comes from the way in which children were taught to write in the ancient world. *Hupogrammos* can mean two things—an *outline sketch* which the learner had to fill in or the *copyhead of copperplate handwriting* in a writing exercise book which the child had to copy out on the lines below. Jesus gave us the pattern which we have to follow. If we have to suffer insult and injustice and injury, we have only to go through what he has already gone through. It may be that at the back of Peter's mind there was a glimpse of a tremendous truth. That suffering of Jesus was for the sake of man's sin; he suffered in order to bring men back to God. And it may be that, when the Christian suffers insult and injury with uncomplaining steadfastness and unfailing love, he shows such a life to others as will lead them to God.

TWO PRECIOUS NAMES FOR GOD

1. The Shepherd of the Souls of Men

1 *Peter* 2: 18–25 (*continued*)

In the last verse of this chapter we come upon two of the great names for God—the Shepherd and Bishop of our souls—as the Authorized Version has it.

(i) God is *the Shepherd of the souls of men*. The Greek is *poimēn* and *shepherd* is one of the oldest descriptions of God. The Psalmist has it in the best-loved of all the Psalms: "The Lord is my shepherd" (*Psalm* 23: 1). Isaiah has it: "He will feed his flock like a shepherd: he will gather the lambs in his arms; he will carry them in his bosom, and gently lead those that are with young" (*Isaiah* 40: 11).

The great king whom God was going to send to Israel would be the shepherd of his people. Ezekiel hears the promise of God: "And I will set up over them one shepherd, my servant David, and he shall feed them; he shall feed them, and be their shepherd" (*Ezekiel* 34: 23; 37: 24).

This was the title which Jesus took to himself when he called himself the Good Shepherd and when he said that the Good Shepherd lays down his life for the sheep (*John* 10: 1–18). To Jesus the men and women who did not know God and who were waiting for what he could give them were like sheep without a shepherd (*Mark* 6: 34). The great privilege given to the servant and the minister of Christ is to shepherd the flock of God (*John* 21: 16; 1 *Peter* 5: 2).

It may be difficult for those of us who live in an industrial civilization to grasp the greatness of this picture; but in the East the picture would be very vivid, particularly in Judaea, where there was a narrow central plateau which held danger on either side. It was on this narrow tableland that the sheep grazed. Grass was sparse; there were no protecting walls; and the sheep wandered. The shepherd, therefore, had to be ceaselessly and sleeplessly on the watch lest harm should come to his flock.

In *The Historical Geography of the Holy Land* Sir George Adam Smith describes the shepherd of Judaea. "With us, sheep are often left to themselves; but I do not remember ever to have seen in the East a flock of sheep without a shepherd. In such a landscape as Judaea, where a day's pasture is thinly scattered over an unfenced track of country, covered with delusive paths, still frequented by wild beasts, and rolling off into the desert, the man and his character are indispensable. On some high moor, across which at night the hyenas howl, when you meet him, sleepless, far-sighted, weather-beaten, armed, leaning upon his staff, and looking out over his scattered sheep, everyone of them on his heart, you understand why the shepherd of Judaea sprang to the front in his people's history; why they gave his name to their king, and made him the symbol of providence; why Christ took him as the type of self-sacrifice."

This word *shepherd* tells us most vividly of the ceaseless vigilance and the self-sacrificing love of God for us who are his flock. "We are his people and the sheep of his pasture" (*Psalm* 100: 3).

TWO PRECIOUS NAMES FOR GOD

2. THE GUARDIAN OF OUR SOULS

1 *Peter* 2: 18–25 (*continued*)

(ii) The Authorized Version speaks of God as the Shepherd and *Bishop* of our souls; but nowadays *Bishop* is an inadequate and misleading translation of the Greek (*episkopos*).

Episkopos is a word with a great history. In Homer's *Iliad*, Hector, the great champion of the Trojans, is called the *episkopos* who, during his lifetime, guarded the city of Troy and kept safe its noble wives and infants. *Episkopos* is used of the gods who are the guardians of the treaties which men make and of the agreements to which men come, and who are the protectors of house and home. Justice, for instance, is the *episkopos,* who sees to it that a man shall pay the price for the wrong that he has done.

In Plato's *Laws* the Guardians of the state are those whose duty it is to oversee the games, the feeding and the education of the children that "they may be sound of hand and foot, and may in no wise, if possible, get their natures warped by their habits." The people whom Plato calls market-stewards are the *episkopoi* who "supervise personal conduct, keeping an eye on intemperate and outrageous behaviour, so as to punish him who needs punishment."

In Athenian law and administration the *episkopoi* were governors and administrators and inspectors sent out to subject states to see that law and order and loyalty were observed. In Rhodes the main magistrates were five *episkopoi* who presided over the good government and the law and order of the state.

Episkopos is, therefore, a many-sided but always a noble word. It means the protector of public safety; the guardian of honour and honesty; the overseer of right education and of public morals; the administrator of public law and order.

So, then, to call God the *episkopos* of our souls is to call him our Guardian, our Protector, our Guide, and our Director.

God is the Shepherd and the Guardian of our souls. In his love he cares for us; in his power he protects us; and in his wisdom he guides us in the right way.

THE SILENT PREACHING OF
A LOVELY LIFE

1 *Peter* 3: 1, 2

Likewise, you wives, be submissive to your husbands, so that, if there are any who refuse to believe the word, they may be won for Christ without a word because they have seen your pure and reverent behaviour.

PETER turns to the domestic problems which Christianity inevitably produced. It was inevitable that one marriage partner might be won for Christ, while the other remained untouched by the appeal of the gospel; and such a situation inevitably had difficulties.

It may seem strange that Peter's advice to wives is six times as long as that to husbands. This is because the wife's position was far more difficult than that of the husband. If a husband became a Christian, he would automatically bring his wife with him into the Church and there would be no problem. But if a wife became a Christian while her husband did not, she was taking a step which was unprecedented and which produced the most acute problems.

In every sphere of ancient civilization, women had no rights at all. Under Jewish law a woman was a thing; she was owned by her husband in exactly the same way as he owned his sheep and his goats; on no account could she leave him, although he could dismiss her at any moment. For a wife to change her religion while her husband did not was unthinkable.

In Greek civilization the duty of the woman was "to remain indoors and to be obedient to her husband." It was the sign of a good woman that she must see as little, hear as little and ask as little as possible. She had no kind of independent existence and no kind of mind of her own, and her husband could divorce her almost at caprice, so long as he returned her dowry.

Under Roman law a woman had no rights. In law she remained for ever a child. When she was under her father she was under the *patria potestas,* the father's power, which gave the father the right even of life and death over her; and when she married she passed equally into the power of her husband. She was entirely subject to her husband and completely at his mercy. Cato the Censor, the typical ancient Roman, wrote: "If you were to catch your wife in an act of infidelity, you can kill her with impunity without a trial." Roman matrons were prohibited from drinking wine, and Egnatius beat his wife to death when he found her doing so. Sulpicius Gallus dismissed his wife because she had once appeared in the streets without a veil. Antistius Vetus divorced his wife because he saw her secretly speaking to a freed woman in public. Publius Sempronius Sophus divorced his wife because once she went to the public games. The whole attitude of ancient civilization was that no woman could dare take any decision for herself.

What, then, must have been the problems of the wife who became a Christian while her husband remained faithful to the ancestral gods? It is almost impossible for us to realize what life must have been for the wife who was brave enough to become a Christian.

What, then, is Peter's advice in such a case? We must first note what he does *not* advise.

He does not advise the wife to leave her husband. In this he takes exactly the same attitude as Paul takes (1 *Corinthians* 7: 13–16). Both Paul and Peter are quite sure that the Christian wife must remain with the heathen husband so long as he does not send her away. Peter does not tell the wife to preach or to argue. He does not tell her to insist that there is no difference between slave and freeman, Gentile and Jew, male and female, but that all are the same in the presence of the Christ whom she has come to know.

He tells her something very simple—nothing else than to be a good wife. It is by the silent preaching of the loveliness of her life that she must break down the barriers of prejudice and hostility, and win her husband for her new Master.

She must be *submissive*. It is not a spineless submission that is meant but, as someone has finely put it, a "voluntary selflessness." It is the submission which is based on the death of pride and the desire to serve. It is the submission not of fear but of perfect love.

She must be *pure*. There must be in her life a lovely chastity and fidelity founded on love.

She must be *reverent*. She must live in the conviction that the whole world is the Temple of God and that all life is lived in the presence of Christ.

THE TRUE ADORNMENT

1 *Peter* 3: 3–6

> Let not your adornment be an outward thing of braided hair and
> ornaments of gold and wearing of robes, but let it be an adornment
> of the inward personality of the heart, wrought by the unfading
> loveliness of a gentle and quiet spirit, which is very precious in the
> sight of God. For it was thus in days of old the holy women, who
> placed their hopes in God, adorned themselves in submission to their
> husbands. It was thus that Sara obeyed Abraham calling him,
> "Lord." And you have become her children, if you do good, and if
> you do not become a prey to fluttering fears.

BENGEL speaks of "the labour bestowed on dress which
consumes much time." Such labour is no modern thing. We
have already seen that in the ancient world women had no
part in public life whatsoever; they had nothing to pass their
time; for that reason it was sometimes argued that they must
be allowed an interest in dress and adornment. Cato the Censor
insisted on simplicity; Lucius Valerius answered: "Why should
men grudge women their ornaments and their dress? Women
cannot hold public offices, or priesthoods, or gain triumphs;
they have no public occupations. What, then, can they do but
devote their time to adornment and to dress?" Undue interest
in self-adornment was then, as it still is, a sign that the person
who indulged in it had no greater things to occupy her mind.

The ancient moralists condemned undue luxury as much as
the Christian teachers did. Quintilian, the Roman master of
oratory, wrote: "A tasteful and magnificent dress, as the Greek
poet tells us, lends added dignity to the wearer: but effeminate
and luxurious apparel fails to adorn the body, and only reveals
the sordidness of the mind." Epictetus, the philosopher,
thinking of the narrow life to which women were condemned
in the ancient world, said, "Immediately after they are
fourteen, women are called 'ladies' by men. And so, when they
see that they have nothing else than to be bedfellows of men,
they begin to beautify themselves and put all their hopes on
that. It is, therefore, worthwhile for us to take pains to make
them understand that they are honoured for nothing else but

only for appearing modest and self-respecting." Epictetus and Peter agree.

There is at least one passage in the Old Testament which lists the various items of female adornment and threatens the day of judgment in which they will be destroyed. The passage is *Isaiah* 3: 18–24. It speaks of the "finery of the anklets, the headbands and the crescents; the pendants, the bracelets, and the scarfs; the headdresses, the armlets, the sashes, the perfume boxes and the amulets; the signet rings and nose rings; the festal robes, the mantles, the cloaks and the handbags; the garments of gauze, the linen garments, the turbans and the veils."

In the world of the Greeks and the Romans it is interesting to collect the references to personal adornments. There were as many ways of dressing the hair as there were bees in Hybca. Hair was waved and dyed, sometimes black, more often auburn. Wigs were worn, especially blonde wigs, which are found even in the Christian catacombs; and hair to manufacture them was imported from Germany, and even from as far away as India. Hairbands, pins and combs were made of ivory, and boxwood, and tortoiseshell; and sometimes of gold, studded with gems.

Purple was the favourite colour for clothes. One pound weight of the best Tyrian purple wool, strained twice through, cost 1,000 *denarii*, £43.50. A Tyrian cloak of the best purple cost well over £100. In one year silks, pearls, scents and jewellery were imported from India to the value of £1,000,000. Similar imports of luxury came from Arabia.

Diamonds, emeralds, topazes, opals and the sardonyx were favourite stones. Struma Nonius had a ring valued at £21,250. Pearls were loved most of all. Julius Caesar bought for Servilia a pearl which cost him £65,250. Earrings were made of pearls and Seneca spoke of women with two or three fortunes in their ears. Slippers were encrusted with them; Nero even had a room whose walls were covered with them. Pliny saw Lollia Paulina, wife of Caligula, wearing a dress so covered with pearls and emeralds that it had cost £450,000.

Christianity came into a world of luxury and decadence combined.

In face of all this Peter pleads for the graces which adorn the heart, which are precious in the sight of God. These were the jewels which adorned the holy women of old. Isaiah had called Sara the mother of God's faithful people (*Isaiah* 51: 2); and if Christian wives are adorned with the same graces of modesty, humility and chastity, they too will be her daughters and will be within the family of the faithful people of God.

A Christian wife of those times lived in a society where she would be tempted to senseless extravagance and where she might well go in fear of the caprices of her heathen husband; but she must live in selfless service, in goodness and in serene trust. That would be the best sermon she could preach to win her husband for Christ. There are few passages where the value of a lovely Christian life is so vividly stressed.

THE HUSBAND'S OBLIGATION

1 *Peter* 3: 7

> Likewise, you husbands, live understandingly with your wives, remembering that women are the weaker sex and assigning honour to them as fellow-heirs of the grace of life, so that there may be no barrier to your prayers.

SHORT as this passage is, it has in it much of the very essence of the Christian ethic. That ethic is what may be called a *reciprocal* ethic. It never places all the responsibility on one side. If it speaks of the duties of slaves, it speaks also of the obligations of masters. If it speaks of the duty of children, it speaks also of the obligations of parents (cp. *Ephesians* 6: 1–9; *Colossians* 3: 20–4: 1). Peter has just laid down the duty of wives; now he lays down the duty of husbands. A marriage must be based on reciprocal obligation. A marriage in which all the privileges are on one side and all the obligations on the other is bound to be imperfect with every chance of failure. This was a new conception in the ancient world. We have already noted the woman's total lack of rights then and quoted Cato's statement of the rights of the husband. But we did not finish that quotation and we do so now: "If you were to catch your wife in an act of infidelity, you can kill her with impunity without a trial; but, if she were to catch you, she would not venture to touch you with her finger and, indeed, she has no right." In the Roman moral code all the obligation was on the wife and all the privilege with the husband. The Christian ethic never grants a privilege without a corresponding obligation.

What are the obligations of the husband?

(i) He must be *understanding*. He must be considerate and sensitive to the feelings of his wife. Somerset Maugham's mother was a very beautiful woman with the world at her feet but his father was unhandsome. Someone once asked her: "Why do you remain faithful to that ugly little man you married?" Her answer was: "Because he never hurts me." Understanding and considerateness had forged an unbreakable bond. The cruelty which is hardest to bear is often not deliberate but the product of sheer thoughtlessness.

(ii) He must be *chivalrous*. He must remember that women are the weaker sex and treat them with courtesy. In the ancient world chivalry to women was well-nigh unknown. It was, and still is, no uncommon sight in the East to see the man riding on a donkey while the woman trudged by his side. It was Christianity which introduced chivalry into the relationship between men and women.

(iii) He must remember that the woman has *equal spiritual rights*. She is a fellow-heir of the grace of life. Women did not share in the worship of the Greeks and the Romans. Even in the Jewish synagogue they had no share in the service, and in the orthodox synagogue still have none. When they were admitted to the synagogue at all, they were segregated from the men and hidden behind a screen. Here in Christianity emerged the revolutionary principle that women had equal spiritual rights and with that the relationship between the sexes was changed.

(iv) Unless a man fulfils these obligations, there is a barrier between his prayers and God. As Bigg puts it: "The sighs of the injured wife come between the husband's prayers and God's hearing." Here is a great truth. Our relationships with God can never be right, if our relationships with our fellow-men are wrong. It is when we are at one with each other that we are at one with him.

THE MARKS OF THE CHRISTIAN LIFE (1)

1 *Peter* 3: 8–12

Finally, you must all be of one mind; you must have sympathy with each other and you must live in brotherly love; you must be compassionate and humble; you must not return evil for evil, nor insult for insult; on the contrary, you must return blessing; for it was to give and to inherit blessing that you were called.

> He that would love life,
>   And see good days,
> Let him keep his tongue from evil,
>   And his lips from speaking guile:
> Let him turn away from evil and do right;
>   Let him seek peace, and pursue it,
> For the eyes of the Lord are upon the righteous,
>   And his ears are open to their prayer;
> But the face of the Lord is against those that do evil.

PETER, as it were, gathers together the great qualities of the Christian life.

(i) Right in the forefront he sets *Christian unity*. It is worth while to collect together the great New Testament passages about unity, in order to see how great a place it occupies in New Testament thought. The basis of the whole matter is in the words of Jesus who prayed for his people that they might all be one, as he and his Father were one (*John* 17: 21–23). In the thrilling early days of the Church this prayer was fulfilled, for they were all of one heart and one soul (*Acts* 4: 32).

Over and over again Paul exhorts men to this unity and prays for it. He reminds the Christians of Rome that, though they are many, they are one body, and he pleads with them to be of one mind (*Romans* 12: 4, 16). In writing to the Christians of Corinth, he uses the same picture of the Christians as members of one body in spite of all their differing qualities and gifts (1 *Corinthians* 12: 12–31). He pleads with the quarrelling Corinthians that there should be no divisions among them and that they should be perfectly joined together in the same mind (1 *Corinthians* 1: 10). He tells them that strifes and divisions are fleshly things, marks that they are living on purely human standards, without the mind of Christ (1 *Corinthians* 3: 3). Because they have partaken of the one bread, they must be one body (1 *Corinthians* 10: 17). He tells them that they must be of one mind and must live in peace (2 *Corinthians* 13: 11). In Christ Jesus the dividing walls are down, and Jew and Greek are united into one (*Ephesians* 2: 13, 14). Christians must maintain the unity of the Spirit in the bond of peace, remembering that there is one Lord, one faith, one baptism, one God and Father of all (*Ephesians* 4: 3–6). The Philippians must stand fast in one spirit, striving together with one mind for the faith of the gospel; they will make Paul's happiness complete, if they have the same love and have one accord and one mind; the quarrelling Euodias and Syntyche are urged to be of one mind in the Lord (*Philippians* 1: 27; 2: 2; 4: 2).

All through the New Testament rings this plea for Christian unity. It is more than a plea; it is an announcement that no man can live the Christian life unless in his personal relationships he is at unity with his fellow-men; and that the Church cannot be truly Christian if there are divisions within it. It is tragic to realize how far men are from realizing this unity in their personal lives and how far the Church is from realizing it within herself. C. E. B. Cranfield writes so finely of this that we cannot do other than quote his whole comment in full, lengthy though it is: "The New Testament never treats this agreeing in Christ as an unnecessary though highly desirable spiritual luxury, but as something essential to the true being of the Church. Divisions, whether disagreements between individual members or the existence of factions and parties and—how much more!—our present-day denominations, constitute a calling in question of the Gospel itself and a sign that those who are involved are carnal. The more seriously we take the New Testament, the more urgent and painful becomes our sense of the sinfulness of the divisions, and the more earnest our prayers and strivings after the peace and unity of the Church on earth. That does not mean that the like-mindedness we are to strive for is to be a drab uniformity of the sort beloved of bureaucrats. Rather is it to be a unity in which powerful tensions are held together by an over-mastering loyalty, and strong antipathies of race and colour, temperament and taste, social position and economic interest, are overcome in common worship and common obedience. Such unity will only come when Christians are humble and bold enough to lay hold on the unity already given in Christ and to take it more seriously than their own self-importance and sin, and to make of these deep differences of doctrine, which originate in our imperfect understanding of the Gospel and which we dare not belittle, not an excuse for letting go of one another or staying apart, but rather an incentive for a more earnest seeking in fellowship together to hear and obey the voice of Christ.'' There speaks the prophetic voice to our modern condition.

THE MARKS OF THE CHRISTIAN LIFE (2)

1 *Peter* 3: 8–12 (*continued*)

(ii) Second Peter sets *sympathy*. Here again the whole New Testament urges this duty upon us. We are to rejoice with those who rejoice and to weep with those who weep (*Romans* 12: 15). When one member of the body suffers all the other members suffer with it; and when one member is honoured, all the members rejoice with it (1 *Corinthians* 12: 26), and it must be so with Christians, who are the body of Christ. One thing is clear, sympathy and selfishness cannot co-exist. So long as the self is the most important thing in the world, there can be no such thing as sympathy; sympathy depends on the willingness to forget self and to identify oneself with the pains and sorrows of others. Sympathy comes to the heart when Christ reigns there.

(iii) Third Peter sets *brotherly love*. Again the matter goes back to the words of Jesus. "A new commandment I give to you, that you love one another. . . . By this will all men know that you are my disciples, if you have love for one another" (*John* 13: 34, 35). Here the New Testament speaks with unmistakable definiteness and with almost frightening directness. "We know that we have passed out of death into life, because we love the brethren. He who does not love remains in death. Anyone who hates his brother is a murderer" (1 *John* 3: 14, 15). "If any one says, I love God, and hates his brother, he is a liar" (1 *John* 4: 20). The simple fact is that love of God and love of man go hand in hand; the one cannot exist without the other. The simplest test of the reality of the Christianity of a man or a Church is whether or not it makes them love their fellow-men.

(iv) Fourth Peter sets *compassion*. There is a sense in which pity is in danger of becoming a lost virtue. The conditions of our own age tend to blunt the edge of the mind to sensitiveness in pity. As C. E. B. Cranfield puts it: "We got used to hearing on the radio of a thousand-bomber raid as we ate our breakfast. We have got used to the idea of millions of people becoming refugees." We can read of the thousands of casualties on the roads with no reaction within our hearts, forgetting that each means a broken body or a broken heart for someone. It is easy to lose the sense of pity and still easier to be satisfied with a sentimentalism which feels a moment's comfortable sorrow and does nothing. Pity is of the very essence of God and compassion of the very being of Jesus Christ; a pity so great that God sent his only Son to die for men, a compassion so intense that it took Christ to the Cross. There can be no Christianity without compassion.

(v) Fifth Peter sets *humility*. Christian humility comes from two things. It comes, first, from the sense of creatureliness. The Christian is humble because he is constantly aware of his utter dependence on God and that of himself he can do nothing. It comes, second, from the fact that the Christian has a new standard of comparison. It may well be that when he compares himself with his fellow-men, he has nothing to fear from the comparison. But the Christian's standard of comparison is Christ, and, compared with his sinless perfection, he is ever in default. When the Christian remembers his dependence on God and keeps before him the standard of Christ, he must remain humble.

(vi) Lastly, and as a climax, Peter sets *forgiveness*. It is to receive forgiveness from God and to give forgiveness to men that the Christian is called. The one cannot exist without the other; it is only when we forgive others their sins against us that we are forgiven our sins against God (*Matthew* 6: 12, 14, 15). The mark of the Christian is that he forgives others as God has forgiven him (*Ephesians* 4: 32).

As was natural for him, Peter sums the matter up by quoting *Psalm* 34, with its picture of the man whom God receives and the man whom God rejects.

THE CHRISTIAN'S SECURITY IN A THREATENING WORLD

1 *Peter* 3: 13–15a

> Who will hurt you, if you are ardent lovers of goodness? Even if you do have to suffer for the sake of righteousness, you are blessed. Have no fear of them; do not be troubled; but in your hearts give Christ a unique place.

IN this passage we can see how Peter was soaked in the Old Testament; there are two Old Testament foundations for it. It is not so much that he actually quotes them, as that he could not have written the passage at all unless the Old Testament had been in his mind. The very first sentence is a reminiscence of *Isaiah* 50: 9: "Behold, the Lord God helps me; who will declare me guilty?" Again, when Peter is talking about the banishing of fear, he is thinking of *Isaiah* 8: 13, "But the Lord of hosts, him you shall regard as holy; let him be your fear, and let him be your dread."

There are three great conceptions in this passage.

(i) Peter begins by insisting on a passionate love of goodness. A man may have more than one attitude to goodness. It may be to him a burden or a bore or something which he vaguely desires but the price of which he is not willing to pay in terms of effort. The word we have translated an *ardent lover* is *zēlōtēs*; which is often translated *Zealot*. The Zealots were the fanatical patriots, who were pledged to liberate their native land by every possible means. They were prepared to take their lives in their hands, to sacrifice ease and comfort, home and loved ones, in their passionate love for their country. What Peter is saying is: "Love goodness with that passionate intensity with which the most fanatical patriot loves his country." Sir John Seeley said, "No heart is pure that is not passionate; no virtue safe which is not enthusiastic." It is only when a man falls in love with goodness that the wrong things lose their fascination and their power.

(ii) Peter goes on to speak about the Christian attitude to suffering. It has been well pointed out that we are involved in two kinds of suffering. There is the suffering in which we are involved because of our *humanity*. Because we are men, there come physical suffering, death, sorrow, distress of mind and weariness and pain of body. But there is also the suffering in which we may be involved because of our *Christianity*. There may be unpopularity, persecution, sacrifice for principle and the deliberate choosing of the difficult way, the necessary discipline and toil of the Christian life. Yet the Christian life has a certain blessedness which runs through it all. What is the reason for it?

(iii) Peter's answer is this. The Christian is the man to whom God and Jesus Christ are the supremacies in life; his relationship to God in Christ is life's greatest value. If a man's heart is set on earthly things, possessions, happiness, pleasure, ease and comfort, he is of all men most vulnerable. For, in the nature of things, he may lose these things at any moment. Such a man is desperately easily hurt. On the other hand, if he gives to Jesus Christ the unique place in his life, the most precious thing for him is his relationship to God and nothing can take that from him. Therefore, he is completely secure.

So, then, even in suffering the Christian is still blessed. When the suffering is for Christ, he is demonstrating his loyalty to Christ and is sharing his sufferings. When the suffering is part of the human situation, it still cannot despoil him of the most precious things in life. No man escapes suffering, but for the Christian suffering cannot touch the things which matter most of all.

THE CHRISTIAN ARGUMENT FOR CHRIST

1 *Peter* 3: 15b, 16

Always be prepared to make your defence to anyone who calls you to account concerning the hope that is in you; but do so with gentleness and reverence. Keep your conscience clear, so that, when you are abused, those who revile your good behaviour in Christ may be put to shame.

IN a hostile and suspicious world it was inevitable that the Christian would be called upon to defend the faith he held and the hope by which he lived. Here Peter has certain things to say about this Christian defence.

(i) It must be *reasonable*. It is a *logos* that the Christian must give, and a *logos* is a reasonable and intelligent statement of his position. A cultivated Greek believed that it was the mark of an intelligent man that he was able to give and to receive a *logos* concerning his actions and belief. As Bigg puts it, he was expected "intelligently and temperately to discuss matters of conduct." To do so we must know what we believe; we must have thought it out; we must be able to state it intelligently and intelligibly. Our faith must be a first-hand discovery and not a second-hand story. It is one of the tragedies of the modern situation that there are so many Church members who, if they were asked what they believe, could not tell, and who, if they were asked why they believe it, would be equally helpless. The Christian must go through the mental and spiritual toil of thinking out his faith, so that he can tell what he believes and why.

(ii) His defence must be given *with gentleness.* There are many people who state their beliefs with a kind of arrogant belligerence. Their attitude is that anyone who does not agree with them is either a fool or a knave and they seek to ram their beliefs down other people's throats. The case for Christianity must be presented with winsomeness and with love, and with that wise tolerance which realizes that it is not given to any man to possess the whole truth. "There are as many ways to the stars as there are men to climb them." Men may be wooed into the Christian faith when they cannot be bullied into it.

(iii) His defence must be given *with reverence.* That is to say, any argument in which the Christian is involved must be carried on in a tone which God can hear with joy. No debates have been so acrimonious as theological debates; no differences have caused such bitterness as religious differences. In any presentation of the Christian case and in any argument for the Christian faith, the accent should be the accent of love.

(iv) The only compelling argument is the argument of the Christian life. Let a man so act that his conscience is clear. Let him meet criticism with a life which is beyond reproach. Such conduct will silence slander and disarm criticism. "A saint," as someone has said, "is someone whose life makes it easier to believe in God."

THE SAVING WORK OF CHRIST

1 *Peter* 3: 17—4: 6

For it is better to suffer for doing right, if that should be the will of God, than to suffer for doing wrong. For Christ also died once and for all for sins, the just for the unjust, that he might bring us to God.

He was put to death in the flesh, but he was raised to life in the Spirit, in which also he went and preached to the spirits who are in prison, the spirits who were once upon a time disobedient, in the time when the patience of God waited in the days of Noah, while the ark was being built, in which some few—that is, eight souls—were brought in safety through the water. And water now saves you, who were symbolically represented in Noah and his company, I mean the water of baptism; and baptism is not merely the removal of dirt from the body, but the pledge to God of a good conscience, through the resurrection of Jesus Christ, who is at the right hand of God, because he went to heaven, after angels and authorities and power had been made subject to him.

Since, then, Christ suffered in the flesh, you too must arm your-selves with the same conviction that he who has suffered in the flesh has ceased from sin, and as a result of this the aim of such a man now is to spend the time that remains to him of life in the flesh no longer in obedience to human passions, but in obedience to the will of God. For the time that is past is sufficient to have done what the Gentiles will to do, to have lived a life of licentiousness, lust, drunkenness, revellings, carousings, and abominable idolatry. They think it strange when you do not rush to join them in the same flood of profligacy and they abuse you for not doing so. They will give account to him who is ready to judge the living and the dead. For this is why the gospel was preached even to the dead, so that, although they have already been judged in the flesh like men, they might live in the Spirit like God.

THIS is not only one of the most difficult passages in Peter's letter, it is one of the most difficult in the whole New Testament; and it is also the basis of one of the most difficult articles in the creed, "He descended into Hell." It is, therefore, better first of all to read it as a whole and then to study it in its various sections.

THE EXAMPLE OF THE WORK OF CHRIST

1 *Peter* 3: 17, 18a

For it is better to suffer for doing right, if that should be the will of God, than to suffer for doing wrong. For Christ also died once and for all for sins, the just for the unjust, that he might bring us to God.

ALTHOUGH this passage is one of the most difficult in the New Testament, it begins with something which anyone can understand. The point that Peter is making is that, even if the Christian is compelled to suffer unjustly for his faith, he is only walking the way that his Lord and Saviour has already walked. The suffering Christian must always remember that he has a suffering Lord. In the narrow compass of these two verses Peter has the greatest and the deepest things to say about the work of Christ.

(i) He lays it down that the work of Christ was *unique* and never need be repeated. Christ died *once and for all* for sins. The New Testament says this same thing often. When Christ died, he died once and for all (*Romans* 6: 10). The priestly sacrifices in the Temple have to be repeated daily but Christ made the perfect sacrifice once and for all when he offered himself up (*Hebrews* 7: 27). Christ was once and for all offered to bear the sin of many (*Hebrews* 9: 28). We are sanctified through the offering of the body of Christ once and for all (*Hebrews* 10: 10). The New Testament is completely sure that on the Cross something happened which never needs to happen again and that in that happening sin is finally defeated. On the Cross God dealt with man's sin in a way which is adequate for all sin, for all men, for all time.

(ii) He lays it down that that sacrifice was *for sin*. Christ died once and for all *for sins*. This again is frequently said in the New Testament. Christ died for our sins according to the scriptures (1 *Corinthians* 15: 3). Christ gave himself for our sins (*Galatians* 1: 4). The function of the High Priest, and Jesus Christ is the perfect High Priest, is to offer sacrifice for sins (*Hebrews* 5: 1, 3). He is the expiation for our sins (1 *John* 2: 2).

The Greek for *for sins* is either *huper* or *peri hamartiōn*. It so happens that in the Greek version of the Old Testament the regular phrase for a *sin-offering* is *peri hamartias* (*Hamartias* is the singular of *hamartiōn*), as, for instance, in *Leviticus* 5: 7 and 6: 30. That is to say, Peter is laying it down that the death of Christ is the sacrifice which atones for the sin of men.

We may put it this way. Sin is that which interrupts the

relationship which should exist between God and men. The object of sacrifice is to restore that lost relationship. The death of Christ upon the Cross, however we explain it, avails to restore the lost relationship between God and man. As Charles Wesley put it in verse:

> No condemnation now I dread:
>   Jesus, and all in him, is mine!
> Alive in him, my living Head,
>   And clothed in righteousness divine,
> Bold I approach the eternal throne,
> And claim the crown, through Christ my own.

It may be that we will never agree in our theories of what exactly happened on the Cross, for, indeed, as Charles Wesley said in that same hymn: " 'Tis mystery all!" But on one thing we can agree—through what happened there we may enter into a new relationship with God.

(iii) He lays it down that that sacrifice was *vicarious*. Christ died once and for all for sins, *the just for the unjust*. That the just should suffer for the unjust is an extraordinary thing. At first sight it looks like injustice. As Edwin H. Robertson put it: "Only forgiveness without reason can match sin without excuse." The suffering of Christ was for us; and the mystery is that he who deserved no suffering bore that suffering for us who deserved to suffer. He sacrificed himself to restore our lost relationship with God.

(iv) He lays it down that the work of Christ was *to bring us to God*. Christ died once and for all for sins, the just for the unjust, *that he might bring us to God*. The word for *to bring* is *prosagein*. It has two vivid backgrounds.

(*a*) It has a Jewish background. It is used in the Old Testament of bringing to God those who are to be priests. It is God's instruction: "You shall bring Aaron and his sons to the door of the tent of meeting" (*Exodus* 29: 4). The point is this—as the Jews saw it, only the priests had the right of close access to God. In the Temple the layman might come so far; he could pass through the Court of the Gentiles, the Court of the Women, the Court of the Israelites—but there he must stop. Into the Court of the Priests, into the nearer presence of God, he could not go; and of the priests, only the High Priest could enter into the Holy of Holies. But Jesus Christ brings *us* to God; he opens the way for *all* men to his nearer presence.

(*b*) It has a Greek background. In the New Testament the corresponding noun *prosagōgē* is three times used. *Prosagein* means *to bring in*; *prosagōgē* means the right of *access,* the result of the bringing in. Through Christ we have *access* to grace (*Romans* 5: 2). Through him we have *access* to God the Father (*Ephesians* 2: 18). Through him we have boldness and *access* and confidence to come to God (*Ephesians* 3: 12). In Greek this had a specialized meaning. At the court of kings there was an official called the *prosagōgeus,* the *introducer,* the *giver of access,* and it was his function to decide who should be admitted to the king's presence and who should be kept out. He, as it were, held the keys of access. It is Jesus Christ, through what he did, who gives men access to God.

(v) When we go beyond these two verses, further into the passage, we can add two more great truths to Peter's view of the work of Christ. In 3: 19 he says that Jesus preached to the spirits in prison; and in 4: 6 he says that the gospel was preached to them that are dead. As we shall go on to see, this most probably means that in the time between his death and his resurrection Jesus actually preached the gospel in the abode of the dead; that is to say, to those who in their lifetime had never had the opportunity to hear it. Here is a tremendous thought. It means that the work of Christ is infinite in its range. It means that no man who ever lived is outside the grace of God.

(vi) Peter sees the work of Christ in terms of *complete triumph.* He says that after his resurrection Jesus went into heaven and is at the right hand of God, angels and authorities and powers having been made subject to him (3: 22). The meaning is that there is nothing in earth and heaven outside the empire of Christ. To all men he brought the new relationship between man and God; in his death he even brought the good news to the dead; in his resurrection he conquered death; even the angelic and the demonic powers are subject to him; and he shares the very power and throne of God. Christ the sufferer has become Christ the victor; Christ the crucified has become Christ the crowned.

THE DESCENT INTO HELL (1)

1 *Peter* 3: 18b–20; 4: 6

> He was put to death in the flesh, but he was raised to life in the Spirit, in which also he went and preached to the spirits who are in prison, the spirits who were once upon a time disobedient in the time when the patience of God waited in the days of Noah, while the ark was being built. . . . For this is why the gospel was preached even to the dead, so that, although they have already been judged in the flesh like men, they might live in the spirit like God.

WE have already said that we are here face to face with one of the most difficult passages, not only in Peter's letter, but in the whole New Testament; and, if we are to grasp what it means, we must follow Peter's own advice and gird up the loins of our mind to study it.

This passage has lodged in the creed in the phrase: "He descended into hell." We must first note that this phrase is very misleading. The idea of the New Testament is not that Jesus descended into *hell* but that he descended into *Hades*. *Acts* 2: 27, as all the newer translations correctly show, should be translated not: "Thou wilt not leave my soul in hell," but, "Thou wilt not abandon my soul to Hades." The difference is this. Hell is the place of the punishment of the wicked; Hades was the place where all the dead went.

The Jews had a very shadowy conception of life beyond the grave. They did not think in terms of heaven and of hell but of a shadowy world, where the spirits of men moved like grey ghosts in an everlasting twilight and where there was neither strength nor joy. Such was Hades, into which the spirits of all men went after death. Isaiah writes: "For Sheol cannot thank thee, death cannot praise thee; those who go down to the pit cannot hope for thy faithfulness" (*Isaiah* 38: 18). The Psalmist wrote: "In death there is no remembrance of thee; in Sheol who can give thee praise?" (*Psalm* 6: 5). "What profit is there in my death if I go down to the pit? Will the dust praise thee? Will it tell of thy faithfulness?" (*Psalm* 30: 9). "Dost thou work wonders for the dead? Do the shades rise up to praise thee? Is thy steadfast love declared in the grave, or thy faithfulness in Abaddon? Are thy wonders known in the darkness, or thy saving help in the land of forgetfulness?" (*Psalm* 88: 10–12). "The dead do not praise the Lord, nor do any that go down into silence" (*Psalm* 115: 17). "Whatever your hand finds to do, do it with your might; for there is no work or thought or knowledge or wisdom in Sheol, to which you are going" (*Ecclesiastes* 9: 10). The Jewish conception of the world after death was of this grey world of shadows and forgetfulness, in which men were separated from life and light and God.

As time went on, there emerged the idea of stages and divisions in this shadow land. For some it was to last for ever; but for others it was a kind of prison-house in which they were held until the final judgment of God's wrath should blast them (*Isaiah* 24: 21, 22; *2 Peter* 2: 4; *Revelation* 20: 1–7). So, then, it must first of all be remembered that this whole matter is to be thought of, not in terms of hell, as we understand the word, but in terms of Christ's going to the dead in their shadowy world.

THE DESCENT INTO HELL (2)

1 *Peter* 3: 18b–20; 4: 6 (*continued*)

THIS doctrine of the descent into Hades, as we must now call it, is based on two phrases in our present passage. It says that Jesus went and preached to the spirits who are in prison (3: 19); and it speaks of the gospel being preached to the dead (4: 6).

In regard to this doctrine there have always been differing attitudes amongst thinkers.

(i) There are those who wish to eliminate it altogether. There is the attitude of *elimination*. Some wish to eliminate it altogether and attempt to do so along two lines.

(*a*) Peter says that in the Spirit Christ preached to the spirits in prison, who were disobedient in the time when the patience of God waited in the days of Noah, when the ark was being built. It is argued that what this means is that it was *in the time of Noah himself* that Christ did this preaching; that in the Spirit long ages before this he made his appeal to the wicked men of Noah's day. This would completely do away with the idea of the descent into Hades. Many great scholars have accepted that view; but we do not think it is the view which comes naturally from Peter's words.

(*b*) If we look at Moffatt's translation, we find something quite different. He translates: "In the flesh he (Christ) was put to death, but he came to life in the Spirit. It was in the Spirit that Enoch also went and preached to the imprisoned spirits who had disobeyed at the time when God's patience held out during the construction of the ark in the days of Noah." How does Moffatt arrive at this translation?

The name of Enoch does not appear in any Greek manuscript. But in the consideration of the text of any Greek author, scholars sometimes use a process called *emendation*. They think that there is something wrong with the text as it stands, that some scribe has perhaps copied it wrongly; and they, therefore, suggest that some word should be changed or added. In this passage Rendel Harris suggested that the word *Enoch* was missed out in the copying of Peter's writing and should be put back in.

(Although it involves the use of Greek some readers may be interested to see how Rendel Harris arrived at this famous emendation. In the top line in italic print, we have set down the Greek of the passage in English lettering and beneath each Greek word its English translation:

thanatōtheis	*men sarki*
having been put to death	in the flesh
zōopoiētheis	*de pneumati*
having been raised to life	in the Spirit

en	*hō*	*kai*	*tois*	*en*	*phulakē*	*pneumasi*
in	which	also	to the	in	prison	spirits

poreutheis	*ekēruxen*
having gone	he preached.

(*Men* and *de* are what are called particles; they are not translated but merely mark the contrast between *sarki* and *pneumati*). It was Rendel Harris's suggestion that between *kai* and *tois* the word *Enōch* had dropped out. His explanation was that, since most manuscript copying was done to dictation, scribes were very liable to miss out words which followed each other, if they sounded very similar. In this passage

en hō kai   and   *Enōch*

sound very much alike, and Rendel Harris thought it very likely that *Enōch* had for that reason been mistakenly omitted).

What reason is there for bringing *Enoch* into this passage at all? He has always been a fascinating and mysterious person. "And Enoch walked with God; and he was not; for God took him" (*Genesis* 5: 24). In between the Old and New Testaments many legends sprang up about Enoch and famous and important books were written under his name. One of the legends was that Enoch, though a man, acted as "God's envoy" to the angels who sinned by coming to earth and lustfully seducing mortal women (*Genesis* 6: 2). In the *Book of Enoch* it is said that he was sent down from heaven to announce to these angels their final doom (*Enoch* 12: 1) and that he proclaimed that for them, because of their sin, there was neither peace nor forgiveness ever (*Enoch* 12 and 13).

So then, according to Jewish legend, Enoch did go to Hades and preach doom to the fallen angels. And Rendel Harris thought that this passage referred, not to Jesus, but to Enoch, and Moffatt so far agreed with him as to put Enoch into his translation. That is an extremely interesting and ingenious suggestion but without doubt it must be rejected. There is no evidence for it at all; and it is not natural to bring in Enoch, for the whole picture is of the work of Christ.

THE DESCENT INTO HELL (3)

1 *Peter* 3: 18b–20; 4: 6 (*continued*)

WE have seen that the attempt at the *elimination* of this passage fails.

(ii) The second attitude is *limitation*. This attitude—and it is that of some very great New Testament interpreters—believes that Peter is indeed saying that Jesus went to Hades and preached, but that he by no means preached to all the inhabitants of Hades. Different interpreters limit that preaching in different ways.

(*a*) It is argued that Jesus preached in Hades *only* to the spirits of the men who were disobedient in the days of Noah. Those who hold this view often go on to argue that, since these sinners were desperately disobedient, so much so that God sent the flood and destroyed them (*Genesis* 6: 12, 13), we may believe that no man is outside the mercy of God. They were the worst of all sinners and yet they were given another chance of repentance; therefore, the worst of men still have a chance in Christ.

(*b*) It is argued that Jesus preached to the fallen angels, and preached, not salvation, but final and awful doom. We have already mentioned these angels. Their story is told in *Genesis* 6: 1–8. They were tempted by the beauty of mortal women; they came to earth, seduced them and begat children; and because of their action, it is inferred, the wickedness of man was great and his thoughts were always evil. 2 *Peter* 2: 4 speaks of these sinning angels as being imprisoned in hell, awaiting judgment. It was to them that Enoch did, in fact, preach; and there are those who think that what this passage means is not that Christ preached mercy and another chance;

but that, in token of his complete triumph, he preached terrible doom to those angels who had sinned.

(*c*) It is argued that Christ preached *only* to those who had been righteous and that he led them out of Hades into the paradise of God. We have seen how the Jews believed that all the dead went to Hades, the shadowy land of forgetfulness. The argument is that *before* Christ that was indeed so but he opened the gates of heaven to mankind; and, when he did so, he went to Hades and told the glad news to all the righteous men of all past generations and led them out to God. That is a magnificent picture. Those who hold this view often go on to say that, because of Christ, there is now no time spent in the shadows of Hades and the way to paradise is open as soon as this world closes on us.

THE DESCENT INTO HELL (4)

1 *Peter* 3: 18b–20; 4: 6 (*continued*)

(iii) There is the attitude that what Peter is saying is that Jesus Christ, between his death and resurrection, went to the world of the dead and preached the gospel there. Peter says that Jesus Christ was put to death in the flesh but raised to life in the Spirit, and that it was in the Spirit that he so preached. The meaning is that Jesus lived in a human body and was under all the limitations of time and space in the days of his flesh; and died with that body broken and bleeding upon the Cross. But when he rose again, he rose with a spiritual body, in which he was rid of the necessary weaknesses of humanity and liberated from the necessary limitations of time and space. It was in this spiritual condition of perfect freedom that the preaching to the dead took place.

As it stands this doctrine is stated in categories which are outworn. It speaks of the *descent* into Hades and the very word *descent* suggests a three-storey universe in which heaven is localized above the sky and Hades beneath the earth. But, laying aside the physical categories of this doctrine, we can find in it truths which are eternally valid and precious, three in particular.

(*a*) If Christ descended into Hades, then his death was no sham. It is not to be explained in terms of a swoon on the Cross, or anything like that. He really experienced death, and rose again. At its simplest, the doctrine of the descent into Hades lays down the complete identity of Christ with our human condition, even to the experience of death.

(*b*) If Christ descended into Hades, it means that his triumph is universal. This, in fact, is a truth which is ingrained into the New Testament. It is Paul's dream that at the name of Jesus every knee should bow, of things in heaven and things in earth and things under the earth (*Philippians* 2: 10). In the *Revelation* the song of praise comes from every creature which is in heaven, and on the earth and under the earth (*Revelation* 5: 13). He who ascended into Heaven is he who first descended into the lower parts of the earth (*Ephesians* 4: 9, 10). The total submission of the universe to Christ is woven into the thought of the New Testament.

(*c*) If Christ descended into Hades and preached there, there is no corner of the universe into which the message of grace has not come. There is in this passage the solution of one of the most haunting questions raised by the Christian faith— what is to happen to those who lived before Jesus Christ and to those to whom the gospel never came? There can be no salvation without repentance but how can repentance come to those who have never been confronted with the love and holiness of God? If there is no other name by which men may be saved, what is to happen to those who never heard it? This is the point that Justin Martyr fastened on long ago: "The Lord, the Holy God of Israel, remembered his dead, those sleeping in the earth, and came down to them to tell them the good news of salvation." The doctrine of the descent into Hades conserves the precious truth that no man who ever lived is left without a sight of Christ and without the offer of the salvation of God.

Many in repeating the creed have found the phrase "He descended into hell" either meaningless or bewildering, and have tacitly agreed to set it on one side and forget it. It may well be that we ought to think of this as a picture painted in terms of poetry rather than a doctrine stated in terms of theology. But it contains these three great truths—that Jesus Christ not only tasted death but drained the cup of death, that the triumph of Christ is universal and that there is no corner of the universe into which the grace of God has not reached.

THE BAPTISM OF THE CHRISTIAN

1 *Peter* 3: 18–22

> For Christ also died once and for all for our sins, the just for the unjust, that he might bring us to God. He was put to death in the flesh, but he was raised to life in the Spirit, in which also he went and preached to the spirits who are in prison, the spirits who were once upon a time disobedient in the time when the patience of God waited in the days of Noah, while the ark was being built, in which some few—that is, eight souls—were brought in safety through the water. And water now saves you, who were symbolically represented in Noah and his company, I mean the water of baptism; and baptism is not merely the removal of dirt from the body, but the pledge to God of a good conscience, through the resurrection of Jesus Christ, who is at the right hand of God, because he went to heaven, after angels and authorities and powers had been made subject to him.

PETER has been speaking about the wicked men who were disobedient and corrupt in the days of Noah; they were ultimately destroyed. But in the destruction by the flood eight people—Noah and his wife, his sons Shem, Ham and Japheth, and their wives—were brought to safety in the ark. Immediately the idea of being *brought to safety through the water* turns Peter's thoughts to Christian baptism, which is also a bringing to safety through the water. What Peter literally says is that baptism is an *antitype* of Noah and his people in the ark.

This word introduces us to a special way of looking at the Old Testament. There are two closely connected words. There is *tupos,* type, which means a *seal,* and there is *antitupos,* antitype, which means the *impression of the seal.* Clearly, between the seal and its impression there is the closest possible correspondence. So there are people and events and customs in the Old Testament which are types, and which find their antitypes in the New Testament. The Old Testament event or person is like the seal; the New Testament event or person is like the impression; the two answer to each other. We might put it that the Old Testament event symbolically represents and foreshadows the New Testament event. The science of finding types and antitypes in the Old and the New Testaments is very highly developed. But to take very simple and obvious examples, the Passover Lamb and the scape-goat, who bore the sins of the people, are types of Jesus; and the work of the High Priest in making sacrifice for the sins of the people is a type of his saving work. Here Peter sees the bringing safely through the waters of Noah and his family as a type of baptism.

In this passage Peter has three great things to say about baptism. It must be remembered that at this stage of the Church's history we are still dealing with adult baptism, the baptism of people who had come straight from heathenism into Christianity and who were taking upon themselves a new way of life.

(i) Baptism is not merely a physical cleansing; it is a spiritual cleansing of the whole heart and soul and life. Its effect must be on a man's very soul and on his whole life.

(ii) Peter calls baptism *the pledge of a good conscience to God* (verse 21). The word Peter uses for *pledge* is *eperōtēma.* In every business contract there was a definite question and answer which made the contract binding. The question was: "Do you accept the terms of this contract, and bind yourself to observe them?" And the answer, before witnesses was: "Yes." Without that question and answer the contract was not valid. The technical word for that question and answer clause is *eperōtēma* in Greek, *stipulatio* in Latin.

Peter is, in effect, saying that in baptism God said to the man coming direct from heathenism: "Do you accept the terms of my service? Do you accept its privileges and promises, and do you undertake its responsibilities and its demands?" And in the act of being baptized the man answered: "Yes."

We use the word *sacrament*. *Sacrament* is derived from the Latin *sacramentum,* which means *a soldier's oath of loyalty* on entering the army. Here we have basically the same picture. We cannot very well apply this question and answer in infant baptism, unless it be to the parents; but, as we have said, baptism in the very early church was of adult men and women coming spontaneously from heathenism into the Church. The modern parallel is entering upon full membership of the Church. When we enter upon Church membership, God asks us: "Do you accept the conditions of my service, with all privileges and all its responsibilities, with all its promises and all its demands?" and we answer; "Yes." It would be well if all were clearly to understand what they are doing when they take upon themselves membership of the Church.

(iii) The whole idea and effectiveness of baptism is dependent on the resurrection of Jesus Christ. It is the grace of the Risen Lord which cleanses us; it is to the Risen, Living Lord that we pledge ourselves; it is to the Risen, Living Lord that we look for strength to keep the pledge that we have given. Once again, where infant baptism is the practice, we must take these great conceptions and apply them to the time when we enter upon full membership of the Church.

THE OBLIGATION OF THE CHRISTIAN

1 *Peter* 4: 1–5

Since then, Christ suffered in the flesh, you too must arm yourselves with the same conviction, that he who has suffered in the flesh has ceased from sin, and as a result of this the aim of such a man now is to spend the time that remains to him of life in obedience to the will of God. For the time that is past is sufficient to have done what the Gentiles will to do, to have lived a life of licentiousness, lust, drunkenness, revellings, carousings, and abominable idolatry. They think it strange when you do not rush to join them in the same flood of profligacy, and they abuse you for not doing so. They will give account to him who is ready to judge the living and the dead.

THE Christian is committed to abandon the ways of heathenism and to live as God would have him to do.

Peter says, "He who has suffered in the flesh has ceased from sin." What exactly does he mean? There are three distinct possibilities.

(i) There is a strong line in Jewish thought that suffering is in itself a great purifier. In the *Apocalypse of Baruch* the writer, speaking of the experiences of the people of Israel, says, "Then, therefore, were they chastened that they might be sanctified" (13: 10). In regard to the purification of the spirits of men *Enoch* says, "And in proportion as the burning of their body becomes severe, a corresponding change will take place in their spirit for ever and ever; for before the Lord of spirits there will be none to utter a lying word" (67: 9). The terrible sufferings of the time are described in 2 *Maccabees,* and the writer says, "I beseech those that read this book that they be not discouraged, terrified or shaken for these calamities, but that they judge these punishments not to be for destruction but for chastening of our nation. For it is a token of his great goodness, when evil-doers are not suffered to go on in their ways any long time, but forthwith punished. For not as with other nations, whom the Lord patiently forbeareth to punish, till the day of judgment arrive, and they be come to the fullness of their sins, so dealeth he with us, lest that, being come to the height of sin, afterwards he should take vengeance on us. And though he punish sinners with adversity, yet doth he never forsake his people" (6: 12–16). The idea is that suffering sanctifies and that not to be punished is the greatest punishment which God can lay upon a man. "Blessed is the man whom thou dost chasten, O Lord," said the Psalmist (*Psalm* 94: 12). "Happy is the man whom God reproves," said Eliphaz (*Job* 5: 17). "For the Lord disciplines him whom he loves, and chastises every son whom he receives (*Hebrews* 12: 6).

If this is the idea, it means that he who has been disciplined by suffering has been cured of sin. That is a great thought. It enables us, as Browning said, "to welcome each rebuff that turns earth's smoothness rough." It enables us to thank God for the experiences which hurt but save the soul. But great as this thought is, it is not strictly relevant here.

(ii) Bigg thinks that Peter is speaking in terms of the experience which his people had of suffering for the Christian faith. He puts it this way: "He who has suffered in meekness and in fear, he who has endured all that persecution can do to him rather than join in wicked ways can be trusted to do right; temptation has manifestly no power over him." The idea is that if a man has come through persecution and not denied the name of Christ, he comes out on the other side with a character so tested and a faith so strengthened, that temptation cannot touch him any more.

Again there is a great thought here, the thought that every trial and every temptation are meant to make us stronger and better. Every temptation resisted makes the next easier to resist; and every temptation conquered makes us better able to overcome the next attack. But again it is doubtful if this thought comes in very relevantly here.

(iii) The third explanation is most probably the right one. Peter has just been talking about baptism. Now the great New Testament picture of baptism is in *Romans* 6. In that chapter Paul says that the experience of baptism is like being buried with Christ in death and raised with him to newness of life. We think that this is what Peter is thinking of here. He has spoken of baptism; and now he says, "He who in baptism has shared the sufferings and the death of Christ, is risen to such newness of life with him that sin has no more dominion over him" (*Romans* 6: 14). Again we must remember that this is the baptism of the man who is voluntarily coming over from paganism into Christianity. In that act of baptism he is identified with Christ; he shares his sufferings and even his death; and he shares his risen life and power, and is, therefore, victor over sin.

When that has happened, a man has said good-bye to his former way of life. The rule of pleasure, pride and passion is gone, and the rule of God has begun. This was by no means easy. A man's former associates would laugh at the new puritanism which had entered his life. But the Christian knows very well that the judgment of God will come, when the judgments of earth will be reversed and the pleasures that are eternal will compensate a thousandfold for the transitory pleasures which had to be abandoned in this life.

THE ULTIMATE CHANCE

1 *Peter* 4:6

> For this is the reason why the gospel was preached to the dead, so that, although they have been judged in the flesh like men, they may live in the Spirit like God.

THIS very difficult passage ends with a very difficult verse. Once again we have the idea of the gospel being preached to the dead. At least three different meanings have been attached to *dead*. (i) It has been taken to mean those who are *dead in sin*, not those who are physically dead. (ii) It has been taken to mean *those who died before the Second Coming of Christ*; but who heard the gospel before they died and so will not miss the glory. (iii) It has been taken to mean quite simply *all the dead*. There can be little doubt that this third meaning is correct; Peter has just been talking about the descent of Christ to the place of the dead, and here he comes back to the idea of Christ preaching to the dead.

No fully satisfactory meaning has ever been found for this verse; but we think that the best explanation is as follows. For mortal man, death is the penalty of sin. As Paul wrote: "Sin came into the world through one man and death through sin, and so death spread to all men because all men sinned" (*Romans* 5:12). Had there been no sin, there would have been no death; and, therefore, death in itself is a judgment. So Peter says, all men have already been judged when they die; in spite of that Christ descended to the world of the dead and preached the gospel there, giving them another chance to live in the Spirit of God.

In some ways this is one of the most wonderful verses in the Bible, for, if our explanation is anywhere near the truth, it gives a breath-taking glimpse of a gospel of a second chance.

THE APPROACHING END

1 *Peter* 4: 7a

The end of all things is near.

HERE is a note which is struck consistently all through the New Testament. It is the summons of Paul that it is time to wake out of sleep, for the night is far spent and the day is at hand (*Romans* 13: 12). "The Lord is at hand," he writes to the Philippians (*Philippians* 4: 5). "The coming of the Lord is at hand," writes James (*James* 5: 8). John says that the days in which his people are living are the last hour (1 *John* 2: 18). "The time is near," says the John of the *Revelation,* and he hears the Risen Christ testify: "Surely I am coming soon" (*Revelation* 1: 3; 22: 20).

There are many for whom all such passages are problems, for, if they are taken literally, the New Testament writers were mistaken; nineteen hundred years have passed and the end is not yet come. There are four ways of looking at the passages.

(i) We may hold that the New Testament writers were in fact mistaken. They looked for the return of Christ and the end of the world in their own day and generation; and these events did not take place. The curious thing is that the Christian Church allowed these words to stand although it would not have been difficult quietly to excise them from the New Testament documents. It was not until late in the second century that the New Testament began to be fixed in the form in which we have it today; and yet statements such as these became unquestioned parts of it. The clear conclusion is that the people of the early church still believed these words to be true.

(ii) There is a strong line of New Testament thought which, in effect, holds that the end *has* come. The consummation of history was the coming of Jesus Christ. In him time was invaded by eternity. In him God entered into the human situation. In him the prophecies were all fulfilled. In him the end has come. Paul speaks of himself and his people as those on whom the ends of the ages have come (1 *Corinthians* 10: 11). Peter in his first sermon speaks of Joel's prophecy of the outpouring of the Spirit and of all that should happen in the last days, and then says that at that very time men were actually living in those last days (*Acts* 2: 16–21).

If we accept that, it means that in Jesus Christ the end of history has come. The battle has been won; there remain only skirmishes with the last remnants of opposition. It means that at this very moment we are living in the "end time," in what someone has called "the epilogue to history." That is a very common point of view; but the trouble is that it flies in the face of facts. Evil is as rampant as ever; the world is still far from having accepted Christ as King. It may be the "end time," but the dawn seems as far distant as ever it was.

(iii) It may be that we have to interpret *near* in the light of history's being a process of almost unimaginable length. It has been put this way. Suppose all time to be represented by a column the height of Cleopatra's Needle with a single postage stamp on top, then the length of recorded history is represented by the thickness of the postage stamp and the unrecorded history which went before it by the height of the column. When we think of time in terms like that *near* becomes an entirely relative word. The Psalmist was literally right when he said that in God's sight a thousand years were just like a watch in the night (*Psalm* 90: 4). In that case *near* can cover centuries and still be correctly used. But it is quite certain that the Biblical writers did not take *near* in that sense, for they had no conception of history in terms like that.

(iv) The simple fact is that behind this there is one inescapable and most personal truth. *For everyone of us the time is near*. The one thing which can be said of every man is that he will die. For every one of us the Lord is at hand. We cannot tell the day and the hour when we shall go to meet him; and, therefore, all life is lived in the shadow of eternity.

"The end of all things is near," said Peter. The early thinkers may have been wrong if they thought that the end of the world was round the corner, but they have left us with the warning that for every one of us personally the end is near; and that warning is as valid today as ever it was.

THE LIFE LIVED IN THE SHADOW OF ETERNITY

1 *Peter* 4: 7b, 8

Be, therefore, steady and sober in mind so that you will really be able to pray as you ought. Above all cherish for each other a love that is constant and intense, because love hides a multitude of sins.

WHEN a man realizes the nearness of Jesus Christ, he is bound to commit himself to a certain kind of life. In view of that nearness Peter makes four demands.

(i) He says that we must be steady in mind. We might render it: "Preserve your sanity." The verb Peter uses is *sōphronein*; connected with that verb is the noun *sōphrosunē*, which the Greeks derived from the verb *sōzein, to keep safe*, and the noun *phronēsis, the mind. Sōphrosunē* is the wisdom which characterizes a man who is pre-eminently sane; and *sōphronein* means *to preserve one's sanity*. The great characteristic of sanity is that it sees things in their proper proportions; it sees what things are important and what are not; it is not swept away by sudden and transitory enthusiasms; it is prone neither to unbalanced fanaticism nor to unrealizing indifference. It is only when we see the affairs of earth in the light of eternity that we see them in their proper proportions; it is when God is given his proper place that everything takes its proper place.

(ii) He says that we must be sober in mind. We might render it: "Preserve your sobriety." The verb Peter uses is *nēphein* which originally meant *to be sober* in contradistinction to *being drunk* and then came to mean *to act soberly and sensibly*. This does not mean that the Christian is to be lost in a gloomy joylessness; but it does mean that his approach to life must not be frivolous and irresponsible. To take things seriously is to be aware of their real importance and to be ever mindful of their consequences in time and in eternity. It is to approach life, not as a jest, but as a serious matter for which we are answerable.

(iii) He says that we must do this in order to pray as we ought. We might render it: "Preserve your prayer life." When a man's mind is unbalanced and his approach to life is frivolous and irresponsible, he cannot pray as he ought. We learn to pray only when we take life so wisely and so seriously that we begin to say in all things: "Thy will be done." The first necessity of prayer is the earnest desire to discover the will of God for ourselves.

(iv) He says that we must cherish for each other a love that is constant and intense. We might render it: "Preserve your love." The word Peter uses to describe this love is *ektenēs* which has two meanings, both of which we have included in the translation. It means *outstretching* in the sense of *consistent*; our love must be the love that never fails. It also means stretching out as a runner stretches out. As C. E. B. Cranfield reminds us it describes a horse at full gallop and denotes "the taut muscle of strenuous and sustained effort, as of an athlete." Our love must be energetic. Here is a fundamental Christian truth. Christian love is not an easy, sentimental reaction. It demands everything a man has of mental and spiritual energy. It means loving the unlovely and the unlovable; it means loving in spite of insult and injury; it means loving when love is not returned. Bengel translates *ektenēs* by the Latin *vehemens, vehement*. Christian love is the love which never fails and into which every atom of man's strength is directed.

The Christian, in the light of eternity, must preserve his

sanity, preserve his sobriety, preserve his prayers and preserve his love.

THE POWER OF LOVE

1 *Peter* 4: 7b, 8 (*continued*)

"Love," says Peter, "hides a multitude of sins." There are three things which this saying may mean; and it is not necessary that we should choose between them, for they are all there.

(i) It may mean that *our* love can overlook many sins. "Love covers all offences," says the writer of the *Proverbs* (*Proverbs* 10: 12). If we love a person, it is easy to forgive. It is not that love is blind, but that it loves a person just as he is. Love makes patience easy. It is much easier to be patient with our own children than with the children of strangers. If we really love our fellow-men, we can accept their faults, and bear with their foolishness, and even endure their unkindness. Love indeed can cover a multitude of sins.

(ii) It may mean that, if we love others, God will overlook a multitude of sins in us. In life we meet two kinds of people. We meet those who have no faults at which the finger may be pointed; they are moral, orthodox, and supremely respectable; but they are hard and austere and unable to understand why others make mistakes and fall into sin. We also meet those who have all kinds of faults; but they are kind and sympathetic and they seldom or never condemn. It is the second kind of person to whom the heart more readily warms; and in all reverence we may say that it is so with God. He will forgive much to the man who loves his fellow-men.

(iii) It may mean that *God's* love covers the multitude of our sins. That is blessedly and profoundly true. It is the wonder of grace that, sinners as we are, God loves us; that is why he sent his Son.

CHRISTIAN RESPONSIBILITY

1 *Peter* 4: 9, 10

> Be hospitable to one another and never grudge it. As each has received a gift from God, so let all use such gifts in the service of one another, like good stewards of the grace of God.

PETER'S mind is dominated in this section by the conviction that the end of all things is near. It is of the greatest interest and significance to note that he does not use that conviction to urge men to withdraw from the world and to enter on a kind of private campaign to save their own souls; he uses it to urge them to go into the world and serve their fellow-men. As Peter sees it, a man will be happy if the end finds him, not living as a hermit, but out in the world serving his fellow-men.

(i) First, Peter urges upon his people the duty of hospitality. Without hospitality the early church could not have existed. The travelling missionaries who spread the good news of the gospel had to find somewhere to stay and there was no place for them to stay except in the homes of Christians. Such inns as there were were impossibly dear, impossibly filthy and notoriously immoral. Thus we find Peter lodging with one Simon a tanner (*Acts* 10: 6), and Paul and his company were to lodge with one Mnason of Cyprus, an early disciple (*Acts* 21: 16). Many a nameless one in the early church made Christian missionary work possible by opening the doors of his house and home.

Not only did the missionaries need hospitality; the local churches also needed it. For two hundred years there was no such thing as a church building. The church was compelled to meet in the houses of those who had bigger rooms and were prepared to lend them for the services of the congregation. Thus we read of the church which was in the house of Aquila and Priscilla (*Romans* 16: 5; 1 *Corinthians* 16: 19), and of the church which was in the house of Philemon (*Philemon* 2). Without those who were prepared to open their homes, the early church could not have met for worship at all.

It is little wonder that again and again in the New Testament the duty of hospitality is pressed upon the Christians. The Christian is to be given to hospitality (*Romans* 12: 13). A bishop is to be given to hospitality (1 *Timothy* 3: 2); the widows of the Church must have lodged strangers (1 *Timothy* 5: 10). The Christian must not forget to entertain strangers and must remember that some who have done so have entertained angels unawares. (*Hebrews* 13: 2). The bishop must be a lover of hospitality (*Titus* 1: 8). And it is ever to be remembered that it was said to those on the right hand: "I was a stranger, and you welcomed me" while the condemnation of those on the left hand was: "I was a stranger, and you did not welcome me" (*Matthew* 25: 35, 43).

In the early days the Church depended on the hospitality of its members; and to this day no greater gift can be offered than the welcome of a Christian home to the stranger in a strange place.

(ii) Such gifts as a man has he must place ungrudgingly at the service of the community. This again is a favourite New Testament idea which is expanded by Paul in *Romans* 12: 3–8 and 1 *Corinthians* 12. The Church needs every gift that a man has. It may be a gift of speaking, of music, of the ability to visit people. It may be a craft or skill which can be used in the practical service of the Church. It may be a house which a man possesses or money which he has inherited. There is no gift which cannot be placed at the service of Christ.

The Christian has to regard himself as a steward of God. In the ancient world the steward was very important. He might be a slave but his master's goods were in his hands. There were two main kinds of stewards, the *dispensator,* the dispenser, who was responsible for all the domestic arrangements of the household and laid in and divided out the household supplies; and the *vilicus,* the bailiff, who was in charge of his master's estates and acted as landlord to his master's tenants. The steward knew well that none of the things over which he had control belonged to him; they all belonged to his master. In everything he did he was answerable to his master and always it was his interests he must serve.

The Christian must always be under the conviction that nothing he possesses of material goods or personal qualities is his own; it all belongs to God and he must ever use what he has in the interests of God to whom he is always answerable.

THE SOURCE AND OBJECT OF ALL CHRISTIAN ENDEAVOUR

1 *Peter* 4: 11

If anyone speaks, let him speak as one uttering sayings sent from God. If anyone renders any service, let him do so as one whose service comes from the strength which God supplies, so that God may be glorified in all things through Jesus Christ to whom belong glory and power for ever and ever. Amen.

PETER is thinking of the two great activities of the Christian Church, preaching and practical service. The word he uses for *sayings* is *logia*. That is a word with a kind of divine background. The heathen used it for the oracles which came to them from their gods; the Christians used it for the words of scripture and the words of Christ. So Peter is saying, "If a man has the duty of preaching, let him preach not as one offering his own opinions or propagating his own prejudices, but as one with a message from God." It was said of one great preacher: "First he listened to God, and then he spoke to men." It was said of another that ever and again he paused, "as if listening for a voice." There lies the secret of preaching power.

Peter goes on to say that if a Christian is engaged in practical service, he must render that service in the strength which God supplies. It is as if he said, "When you are engaged in Christian service, you must not do it as if you were conferring a personal favour or distributing bounty from your own store, but in the consciousness that what you give you first received from God." Such an attitude preserves the giver from pride and the gift from humiliation.

The aim of everything is that God should be glorified. Preaching is not done to display the preacher but to bring men

face to face with God. Service is rendered not to bring prestige
to the giver but to turn men's thoughts to God. E. G. Selwyn
reminds us that the motto of the great Benedictine Order of
monks is four letters—IOGD—which stand for the Latin
words (*ut*) *in omnibus glorificetur Deus* (*in order that in all things
God may be glorified*). A new grace and glory would enter the
Church, if all church people ceased doing things for themselves
and did them for God.

THE INEVITABILITY OF PERSECUTION

1 *Peter* 4: 12, 13

> Beloved, do not regard the fiery ordeal through which you are
> passing and which has happened to you to test you, as something
> strange, as if some alien experience were happening to you, but
> rejoice in so far as you share the sufferings of Christ so that you
> may also rejoice with rapture when his glory shall be revealed.

In the nature of things persecution must have been a much
more daunting experience for Gentiles than it was for Jews.
The average Gentile had little experience of it; but the Jews
have always been the most persecuted people upon earth. Peter
was writing to Christians who were Gentiles and he had to try
to help them by showing them persecution in its true terms.
It is never easy to be a Christian. The Christian life brings its
own loneliness, its own unpopularity, its own problems, its own
sacrifices and its own persecutions. It is, therefore, well to have
certain great principles in our minds.

(i) It is Peter's view that persecution is inevitable. It is human
nature to dislike and to regard with suspicion anyone who is
different; the Christian is necessarily different from the man of
the world. The particular impact of the Christian difference
makes the matter more acute. To the world the Christian brings
the standards of Jesus Christ. That is another way of saying that
he inevitably is a kind of conscience to any society in which he
moves; and many a man would gladly eliminate the troublesome twinges of conscience. The very goodness of Christianity

can be an offence to a world in which goodness is regarded as
a handicap.

(ii) It is Peter's view that persecution is a test. It is a test
in a double sense. A man's devotion to a principle can be
measured by his willingness to suffer for it; therefore, any kind
of persecution is a test of a man's faith. But it is equally true
that it is only the real Christian who will be persecuted. The
Christian who compromises with the world will not be
persecuted. In a double sense persecution is the test of the
reality of a man's faith.

(iii) Now we come to the uplifting things. Persecution is a
sharing in the sufferings of Jesus Christ. When a man has to
suffer for his Christianity he is walking the way his Master
walked and sharing the Cross his Master carried. This is a
favourite New Testament thought. If we suffer with him, we
will be glorified with him (*Romans* 8: 17). It is Paul's desire to
enter into the fellowship of the sufferings of Christ (*Philippians*
3: 10). If we suffer with him, we shall reign with him
(2 *Timothy* 2: 12). If we remember that, anything we must
suffer for the sake of Christ becomes a privilege and not
a penalty.

(iv) Persecution is the way to glory. The Cross is the way to
the crown. Jesus Christ is no man's debtor and his joy and
crown await the man who, through thick and thin, remains
true to him.

THE BLESSEDNESS OF SUFFERING FOR CHRIST

1 *Peter* 4: 14–16

> If you are reproached for the name of Christ, you are blessed because
> the presence of the glory and the Spirit of God rest upon you. But let
> none of you suffer as a murderer, or a thief, or an evil-doer or a
> busybody. But if anyone suffers as a Christian, let him not be
> ashamed, but let him by this name bring glory to God.

HERE Peter says the greatest thing of all. If a man suffers for

Christ, *the presence of the glory* rests upon him. This is a very strange phrase. We think it can mean only one thing. The Jews had the conception of the *Shekinah,* the luminous glow of the very presence of God. This conception constantly recurs in the Old Testament. "In the morning," said Moses, "you shall see the *glory* of the Lord" (*Exodus* 16: 7). "The *glory* of the Lord settled upon Mount Sinai, and the cloud covered it six days," when the law was being delivered to Moses (*Exodus* 24: 16). In the tabernacle God was to meet with Israel and it was to be sanctified with his *glory* (*Exodus* 29: 43). When the tabernacle was completed, "then the cloud covered the tent of meeting, and the *glory* of the Lord filled the tabernacle" (*Exodus* 40: 34). When the ark of the covenant was brought into Solomon's temple, "a cloud filled the house of the Lord, so that the priests could not stand to minister because of the cloud; for the *glory* of the Lord filled the house of the Lord" (1 *Kings* 8: 10, 11). Repeatedly this idea of the *Shekinah,* the luminous glory of God, occurs in the Old Testament.

It is Peter's conviction that something of that glow of glory rests on the man who suffers for Christ. When Stephen was on trial for his life and it was certain that he would be condemned to death, to those who looked on him his face was as the face of an angel (*Acts* 6: 15).

Peter goes on to point out that it is as a Christian that a man must suffer and not as an evil-doer. The evils which he singles out are all clear enough until we come to the last. A Christian, Peter says, is not to suffer as an *allotriepiskopos.* The trouble is that there is no other instance of this word in Greek and Peter may well have invented it. It can have three possible meanings, all of which would be relevant. It comes from two words, *allotrios, belonging to another* and *episkopos, looking upon* or *looking into.* Therefore, it literally means *looking upon,* or *into, that which belongs to another.*

(i) To look on that which is someone else's might well be to cast covetous eyes upon it. That is how both the Latin Bible and Calvin take this word—to mean that the Christian must not be *covetous.*

(ii) To look upon that which belongs to another might well mean to be too interested in other people's affairs and to be a meddling busybody. That is by far the most probable meaning. There are Christians who do an infinite deal of harm with misguided interference and criticism. This would mean that the Christian must never be an *interfering busybody*. That gives good sense and, we believe, the best sense.

(iii) There is a third possibility. *Allotrios* means *that which belongs to someone else*; that is to say, *that which is foreign to oneself*. Along that line *allotriepiskopos* will mean *looking upon that which is foreign to oneself*. That would mean, of a Christian, entering upon undertakings which do not befit the Christian life. This would mean that a Christian must never interest himself in things which are alien to the life that a Christian should lead.

While all three meanings are possible, we think that the third is the right one.

It is Peter's injunction that, if a Christian has to suffer for Christ, he must do so in such a way that his suffering brings glory to God and to the name he bears. His life and conduct must be the best argument that he does not deserve the suffering which has come upon him and his attitude to it must commend the name he bears.

ENTRUSTING ALL LIFE TO GOD

1 *Peter* 4: 17–19

For the time has come for judgment to begin from the household of God. And, if it begins from us, what will be the end of those who disobey the good news which comes from God? And, if the righteous man is scarcely saved, where will the impious man and the sinner appear? So, then, let those who suffer in accordance with the will of God, entrust their souls to him who is a Creator·on whom you can rely, and continue to do right.

As Peter saw it, it was all the more necessary for the Christian to do right because judgment was about to begin.

It was to begin with the household of God. Ezekiel hears the voice of God proclaiming judgment upon his people, "Begin at my sanctuary" (*Ezekiel* 9: 6). Where the privilege has been greatest, there the judgment will be sternest.

If judgment is to fall upon the Church of God, what will be the fate of those who have been utterly disobedient to the invitation and command of God? Peter confirms his appeal with a quotation from *Proverbs* 11: 31: "If the righteous is requited on earth, how much more the wicked and the sinner!"

Finally, Peter exhorts his people to continue to do good and, whatever happens to them to entrust their lives to God, the Creator on whom they can rely. The word he uses for to entrust is *paratithesthai,* which is the technical word for *depositing money with a trusted friend.* In the ancient days there were no banks and few really safe places in which to deposit money. So, before a man went on a journey, he often left his money in the safe-keeping of a friend. Such a trust was regarded as one of the most sacred things in life. The friend was absolutely bound by all honour and all religion to return the money intact.

Herodotus (6: 86) has a story about such a trust. A certain Milesian came to Sparta, for he had heard of the strict honour of the Spartans, and entrusted his money to a certain Glaucus. He said that in due time his sons would reclaim the money and would bring tokens which would establish their identity beyond doubt. The time passed and the sons came. Glaucus treacherously said that he had no recollection of any money being entrusted to him and said that he wished four months to think about it. The Milesians departed sad and sorry. Glaucus consulted the gods as to what he ought to do, and they warned him that he must return the money. He did so, but before long he died and all his family followed him, and in the time of Herodotus there was not a single member of his family left alive because the gods were angry that he had even contemplated breaking the trust reposed in him. Even to think of evading such a trust was a mortal sin.

If a man entrusts himself to God, God will not fail him. If
such a trust is sacred to men, how much more is it sacred to
God? This is the very word used by Jesus, when he says
"Father, into thy hands I commit my spirit" (*Luke* 23: 46).
Jesus unhesitatingly entrusted his life to God, certain that he
would not fail him—and so may we. The old advice is still good
advice—trust in God and do the right.

THE ELDERS OF THE CHURCH

1 *Peter* 5: 1–4

> So, then, as your fellow-elder and a witness of the sufferings of
> Christ, as a sharer in the glory which is going to be revealed, I urge
> the elders who are among you, shepherd the flock of God which is
> in your charge, not because you are coerced into doing so, but of
> your own free-will as God would have you to do, not to make a
> shameful profit out of it, but with enthusiasm, not as if you aimed
> to be petty tyrants over those allotted to your care, but as being under
> the obligation to be examples to the flock; and when the Chief
> Shepherd appears, you will receive the unfading crown of glory.

FEW passages show more clearly the importance of the
eldership in the early church. It is to the elders that Peter
specially writes and he, who was the chief of the apostles, does
not hesitate to call himself a fellow-elder. It will be worth our
while to look at something of the background and history of
the eldership, the most ancient and the most important office
in the Church.

(i) It has a Jewish background. The Jews traced the
beginning of the eldership to the days when the children of
Israel were journeying through the wilderness to the Promised
Land. There came a time when Moses felt the burdens of
leadership too heavy for him to bear alone, and to help him
seventy elders were set apart and granted a share of the spirit
of God (*Numbers* 11: 16–30). Thereafter elders became a

permanent feature of Jewish life. We find them as the friends of the prophets (2 *Kings* 6: 32); as the advisers of kings (1 *Kings* 20: 8; 21: 11); as the colleagues of the princes in the administration of the affairs of the nation (*Ezra* 10: 8). Every village and city had its elders; they met at the gate and dispensed justice to the people (*Deuteronomy* 25: 7). The elders were the administrators of the synagogue; they did not preach, but they saw to the good government and order of the synagogue, and they exercised discipline over its members. The elders formed a large section of the Sanhedrin, the supreme court of the Jews, and they are regularly mentioned along with the Chief Priests and the rulers and the Scribes and the Pharisees (*Matthew* 16: 21; 21: 23; 26: 3, 57; 27: 1, 3; *Luke* 7: 3; *Acts* 4: 5; 6: 12; 24: 1). In the vision of the *Revelation* in the heavenly places there are twenty-four elders around the throne. The elders were woven into the very structure of Judaism, both in its civil and its religious affairs.

(ii) The eldership has a Greek background. Especially in Egyptian communities we find that elders are the leaders of the community and responsible for the conduct of public affairs, much as town councillors are today. We find a woman who had suffered an assault appealing to the elders for justice. When corn is being collected as tribute on the visit of a governor, we find that "the elders of the cultivators" are the officials concerned. We find them connected with the issuing of public edicts, the leasing of land for pasture, the ingathering of taxation. In Asia Minor, also, the members of councils were called elders. Even in the religious communities of the pagan world we find "elder priests" who were responsible for discipline. In the Socnopaeus temple we find the elder priests dealing with the case of a priest who is charged with allowing his hair to grow too long and with wearing woollen garments— an effeminacy and a luxury of which no priest should have been guilty.

We can see that long before Christianity took it over *elder* was a title of honour both in the Jewish and in the Graeco-Roman world.

THE CHRISTIAN ELDERSHIP

1 *Peter* 5: 1–4 (*continued*)

WHEN we turn to the Christian Church we find that the eldership is its basic office.

It was Paul's custom to ordain elders in every community to which he preached and in every church which he founded. On the first missionary journey elders were ordained in every church (*Acts* 14: 23). Titus is left in Crete to ordain elders in every city (*Titus* 1: 5). The elders had charge of the financial administration of the Church; it is to them that Paul and Barnabas delivered the money sent to relieve the poor of Jerusalem in the time of the famine (*Acts* 11: 30). The elders were the councillors and the administrators of the Church. We find them taking a leading part in the Council of Jerusalem at which it was decided to fling open the doors of the Church to the Gentiles. At that Council the elders and the apostles are spoken of together as the chief authorities of the Church (*Acts* 15: 2; 16: 4). When Paul came on his last visit to Jerusalem, it was to the elders that he reported and they suggested the course of action he should follow (*Acts* 21: 18–25). One of the most moving passages in the New Testament is Paul's farewell to the elders of Ephesus. We find there that the elders, as he sees them, are the overseers of the flock of God and the defenders of the faith (*Acts* 20: 28, 29). We learn from James that the elders had a healing function in the Church through prayers and anointing with oil (*James* 5: 14). From the Pastoral Epistles we learn that they were rulers and teachers, and by that time paid officials (1 *Timothy* 5: 17; the phrase *double honour* is better translated *double pay*).

When a man enters the eldership, no small honour is conferred upon him, for he is entering on the oldest religious office in the world, whose history can be traced through Christianity and Judaism for four thousand years; and no small responsibility falls upon him, for he has been ordained a shepherd of the flock of God and a defender of the faith.

THE PERILS AND PRIVILEGES OF
THE ELDERSHIP

1 *Peter* 5: 1–4 (*continued*)

PETER sets down in a series of contrasts the perils and the privileges of the eldership; and everything he says is applicable, not only to the eldership, but also to all Christian service inside and outside the Church.

The elder is to accept office, not under coercion, but willingly. This does not mean that a man is to grasp at office or to enter upon it without self-examining thought. Any Christian will have a certain reluctance to accept high office, because he knows only too well his unworthiness and inadequacy. There is a sense in which it is by compulsion that a man accepts office and enters upon Christian service. "Necessity," said Paul, "is laid upon me. Woe to me, if I do not preach the gospel" (1 *Corinthians* 9: 16). "The love of Christ controls us," he said (2 *Corinthians* 5: 14). But, on the other hand, there is a way of accepting office and of rendering service as if it was a grim and unpleasant duty. It is quite possible for a man to agree to a request in such an ungracious way that his whole action is spoiled. Peter does not say that a man should be conceitedly or irresponsibly eager for office; but that every Christian should be anxious to render such service as he can, although fully aware how unworthy he is to render it.

The elder is to accept office, not to make a shameful profit out of it, but eagerly. The word for *making a shameful profit* is the adverb *aischrokerdēs*. The noun from this is *aischrokerdeia,* and it was a characteristic which the Greek loathed. Theophrastus, the great Greek delineator of character, has a character sketch of this *aischrokerdeia. Meanness*— as it might be translated—is the desire for base gain. The mean man is he who never sets enough food before his guests and who gives himself a double portion when he is carving the joint. He waters the wine; he goes to the theatre only when he can get a free ticket. He never has enough money to pay the fare and always borrows from his fellow-passengers. When he is selling corn, he uses a measure in which the bottom is pushed up, and even then he carefully levels the top. He counts the half radishes left over from dinner in case the servants eat any. Rather than give a wedding present, he will go away from home when a wedding is in the offing.

Meanness is an ugly fault. It is quite clear that there were people in the early church who accused the preachers and missionaries of being in the job for what they could get out of it. Paul repeatedly declares that he coveted no man's goods and worked with his hands to meet his own needs so that he was burdensome to no man (*Acts* 20: 33; 1 *Thessalonians* 2: 9; 1 *Corinthians* 9: 12; 2 *Corinthians* 12: 14). It is certain that the payment any early office-bearer received was pitifully small and the repeated warnings that the office-bearers must not be greedy for gain shows that there were those who coveted more (1 *Timothy* 3: 3, 8; *Titus* 1: 7, 11). The point that Peter is making—and it is ever valid—is that no man dare accept office or render service for what he can get out of it. His desire must ever be to give and not to get.

The elder is to accept office, not to be a petty tyrant, but to be the shepherd and the example of the flock. Human nature is such that for many people prestige and power are even more attractive than money. There are those who love authority, even if it be exercised in a narrow sphere. Milton's Satan thought it better to reign in hell than to serve in heaven. Shakespeare spoke about proud man, dressed in a little brief authority, playing such fantastic tricks before high heaven as would make the angels weep. The great characteristic of the shepherd is his selfless care and his sacrificial love for the sheep. Any man who enters on office with the desire for pre-eminence, has got his whole point of view upside down. Jesus said to his ambitious disciples, "You know that those who are supposed to rule over the Gentiles lord it over them, and their great men exercise authority over them. But it shall not be so among you; but whoever would be great among you must be your servant,

and whoever would be first among you must be slave of all"
(*Mark* 10: 42–44).

THE IDEAL OF THE ELDERSHIP

1 *Peter* 5: 1–4 (*continued*)

ONE thing in this passage which defies translation and is yet
one of the most precious and significant things in it is what we
have translated "petty tyrants over those allotted to your care."
The phrase which we have translated *those allotted* is curious in
Greek; it is *tōn klēron,* the genitive plural of *klēros* which is a
word of extraordinary interest.

(i) It begins by meaning a *dice* or a *lot*. It is so used in
Matthew 27: 35 which tells how the soldiers beneath the Cross
were throwing dice (*klēroi*) to see who should possess the
seamless robe of Jesus.

(ii) Second, it means an office gained or assigned by *lot*. It is
the word used in *Acts* 1: 26 which tells how the disciples cast
lots to see who should inherit the office of Judas the traitor.

(iii) It then comes to mean an inheritance allotted to someone, as used in *Colossians* 1: 12 for the *inheritance* of the saints.

(iv) In classical Greek it very often means a public allotment
or estate of land. These allotments were distributed by the civic
authorities to the citizens; and very often the distribution was
made by drawing lots for the various pieces of land available
for distribution.

Even if we were to go no further than this, it would mean
that the office of the eldership and, indeed, any piece of service
offered to us is never *earned* by any merit of our own but
always *allotted* to us by God. It is never something that we
have deserved but always something given to us by the grace
of God.

But we *can* go further than this. *Klēros* means something
which is allotted to a man. In *Deuteronomy* 9: 29 we read
that Israel is the *heritage* (*klēros*) of God. That is to say,
Israel is the people specially assigned to God by his own choice.
Israel is the *klēros* of God; the congregation is the *klēros* of

the elder. Just as Israel is allotted to God, an elder's duties in the congregation are allotted to him. This must mean that the whole attitude of the elder to his people must be the same as the attitude of God to his people.

Here we have another great thought. In verse 2 there is a phrase in the best Greek manuscripts which is not in the Authorized or the Revised Standard Versions. We have translated it: "Shepherd the flock of God, which is in your charge, not because you are coerced into doing so, but of your own free-will *as God would have you to do.*" *As God would have you to do* is in Greek *kata theon,* and that could well mean quite simply *like God.* Peter says to the elders, "Shepherd your people *like God.*" Just as Israel is God's special allotment, the people we have to serve in the Church or anywhere else are our special allotment; and our attitude to them must be the attitude of God.

What an ideal! And what a condemnation! It is our task to show to people God's forbearance, his forgiveness, his seeking love, his illimitable service. God has allotted to us a task and we must do it as he himself would do it. That is the supreme ideal of service in the Christian Church.

MEMORIES OF JESUS

1 *Peter* 5: 1–4 (*continued*)

ONE of the lovely things about this passage is Peter's attitude throughout it. He begins by, as it were, taking his place beside those to whom he speaks. "Your fellow-elder" he calls himself. He does not separate himself from them but comes to share the Christian problems and the Christian experience with them. But in one thing he is different; he has memories of Jesus and these memories colour this whole passage. Even as he speaks, they are crowding into his mind.

(i) He describes himself as a witness of the sufferings of Christ. At first sight we might be inclined to question that statement, for we are told that, after the arrest in the garden, "All the disciples forsook him and fled" (*Matthew* 26: 56). But,

when we think a little further, we realise that it was given to
Peter to see the suffering of Jesus in a more poignant way than
was given to any other human being. He followed Jesus into
the courtyard of the High Priest's house and there in a time of
weakness he three times denied his Master. The trial came to
an end and Jesus was taken away; and there comes what may
well be the most tragic sentence in the New Testament: "And
the Lord turned and looked at Peter . . . and Peter went out
and wept bitterly" (*Luke* 22: 61, 62). In that look Peter saw the
suffering of the heart of a leader whose follower had failed him
in the hour of his bitterest need. Of a truth Peter was a witness
of the suffering that comes to Christ when men deny him; and
that is why he was so eager that his people might be staunch
in loyalty and faithful in service.

(ii) He describes himself as a sharer in the glory which is
going to be revealed. That statement has a backward and a
forward look. Peter had already had a glimpse of that glory on
the Mount of Transfiguration. There the sleeping three had
been awakened, and, as Luke puts it, "they kept awake and
they saw his glory" (*Luke* 9: 32). Peter had seen the glory. But
he also knew that there was glory to come, for Jesus had
promised to his disciples a share in the glory when the Son of
Man should come to sit on his glorious throne (*Matthew*
19: 28). Peter remembered both the experience and the promise
of glory.

(iii) There can surely be no doubt that, when Peter speaks of
shepherding the flock of God, he is remembering the task that
Jesus had given to him when he had bidden him feed his sheep
(*John* 21: 15–17). The reward of love was the appointment as
a shepherd; and Peter is remembering it.

(iv) When Peter speaks of Jesus as the Chief Shepherd, many
a memory must be in his mind. Jesus had likened himself to
the shepherd who sought at the peril of his life for the sheep
which was lost (*Matthew* 18: 12–14; *Luke* 15: 4–7). He had
sent out his disciples to gather in the lost sheep of the house of
Israel (*Matthew* 10: 6). He was moved with pity for the crowds,
for they were as sheep without a shepherd (*Matthew* 9: 36;

Mark 6:34). Above all, Jesus had likened himself to the Good Shepherd who was ready to lay down his life for the sheep (*John* 10:1–18). The picture of Jesus as the Shepherd was a precious one, and the privilege of being a shepherd of the flock of Christ was for Peter the greatest privilege that a servant of Christ could enjoy.

THE GARMENT OF HUMILITY

1 *Peter* 5:5

> In the same way, you younger people must be submissive to those who are older. In your relationships with one another you must clothe yourselves with the garment of humility, because God opposes the proud but gives grace to the humble.

PETER returns to the thought that the denial of self must be the mark of the Christian. He clinches his argument with a quotation from the Old Testament: "Toward the scorners God is scornful, but to the humble he shows favour" (*Proverbs* 3:34).

Here again it may well be that the memories of Jesus are in Peter's heart and are colouring all his thought and language. He tells his people that they must *clothe themselves* with the garment of humility. The word he uses for *to clothe oneself* is very unusual; it is *egkombousthai* which is derived from *kombos* which describes anything tied on with a knot. Connected with it is *egkombōma,* a garment tied on with a knot. It was commonly used for protective clothing; it was used for a pair of sleeves drawn over the sleeves of a robe and tied behind the neck. And it was used for a slave's apron. There was a time when Jesus had put upon himself just such an apron. At the Last Supper John says of him that he took a towel and girded himself, and took water and began to wash his disciples' feet (*John* 13:4, 5). Jesus girded himself with the apron of humility; and so must his followers.

It so happens that *egkombousthai* is used of another kind of garment. It is also used of putting on a long, stole-like garment which was the sign of honour and pre-eminence.

To complete the picture we must put both images together. Jesus once put on the slave's apron and undertook the humblest of all duties, washing his disciples' feet; so we must in all things put on the apron of humility in the service of Christ and of our fellow-men; but that very apron of humility will become the garment of honour for us, for it is he who is the servant of all who is greatest in the Kingdom of Heaven.

THE LAWS OF THE CHRISTIAN LIFE (1)

1 *Peter* 5: 6–11

So, then, humble yourselves under the mighty hand of God that in his good time he may exalt you.

Cast all your anxiety upon him because he cares for you.

Be sober; be watchful. Your adversary the devil prowls around like a roaring lion, seeking someone to devour. Stand up to him, staunch in the faith, knowing how to pay the same tax of suffering as your brethren in the world.

And after you have experienced suffering for a little while, the God of every grace, who called you to his eternal glory in Christ, will himself restore, establish, strengthen, settle you.

To him be dominion for ever and ever. Amen.

HERE Peter speaks in imperatives, laying down certain laws for the Christian life.

(i) There is the law of humility before God. The Christian must humble himself under his mighty hand. The phrase *the mighty hand of God* is common in the Old Testament; and it is most often used in connection with the deliverance which God wrought for his people when he brought them out of Egypt. "With a strong hand," said Moses, "the Lord has brought you out of Egypt" (*Exodus* 13: 9). "Thou hast only begun to show thy servant thy greatness, and thy mighty hand" (*Deuteronomy* 3: 24). God brought his people forth out of Egypt with a mighty hand (*Deuteronomy* 9: 26). The idea is that

God's mighty hand is on the destiny of his people, if they will humbly and faithfully accept his guidance. After all the varied experiences of life, Joseph could say to the brothers who had once sought to eliminate him: "As for you, you meant evil against me; but God meant it for good" (*Genesis* 50: 20). The Christian never resents the experiences of life and never rebels against them, because he knows that the mighty hand of God is on the tiller of his life and that he has a destiny for him.

(ii) There is the law of Christian serenity in God. The Christian must cast all his anxiety upon God. "Cast your burden on the Lord," said the Psalmist (*Psalm* 55: 22). "Do not be anxious about tomorrow," said Jesus (*Matthew* 6: 25–34). The reason we can do this with confidence is that we can be certain that God cares for us. As Paul had it, we can be certain that he who gave us his only Son will with him give us all things (*Romans* 8: 32). We can be certain that, since God cares for us, life is out not to break us but to make us; and, with that assurance, we can accept any experience which comes to us, knowing that in everything God works for good with those who love him (*Romans* 8: 28).

(iii) There is the law of Christian effort and of Christian vigilance. We must be sober and watchful. The fact that we cast everything upon God does not give us the right to sit back and to do nothing. Cromwell's advice to his troops was: "Trust in God, and keep your powder dry." Peter knew how hard this vigilance was, for he remembered how in Gethsemane he and his fellow-disciples slept when they should have been watching with Christ (*Matthew* 26: 38–46). The Christian is the man who trusts but at the same time puts all his effort and all his vigilance into the business of living for Christ.

(iv) There is the law of Christian resistance. The devil is ever out to see whom he can ruin. Again Peter must have been remembering how the devil had overcome him and he had denied his Lord. A man's faith must be like a solid wall against which the attacks of the devil exhaust themselves in vain. The devil is like any bully and retreats when he is bravely resisted in the strength of Jesus Christ.

THE LAWS OF THE CHRISTIAN LIFE (2)

1 *Peter* 5: 6–11 (*continued*)

(v) Finally, Peter speaks of the law of Christian suffering. He says that, after the Christian has gone through suffering, God will restore, establish, strengthen and settle him. Every one of the words which Peter uses has behind it a vivid picture. Each tells us something about what suffering is designed by God to do for a man.

(*a*) Through suffering God will *restore* a man. The word for *restore* is difficult in this case to translate. It is *kartarizein,* the word commonly used for setting a fracture, the word used in *Mark* 1: 19 for mending nets. It means to supply that which is missing, to mend that which is broken. So suffering, if accepted in humility and trust and love, can repair the weaknesses of a man's character and add the greatness which is not yet there. It is said that Sir Edward Elgar once listened to a young girl singing a solo from one of his own works. She had a voice of exceptional purity and clarity and range, and an almost perfect technique. When she had finished, Sir Edward said softly, "She will be really great when something happens to break her heart." Barrie tells how his mother lost her favourite son, and then says, "That is where my mother got her soft eyes, and that is why other mothers ran to her when they had lost a child." Suffering had done something for her that an easy way could never have done. Suffering is meant by God to add the grace notes to life.

(*b*) Through suffering God will *establish* a man. The word is *stērixein,* which means to make as solid as granite. Suffering of body and sorrow of heart do one of two things to a man. They either make him collapse or they leave him with a solidity of character which he could never have gained anywhere else. If he meets them with continuing trust in Christ, he emerges like toughened steel that has been tempered in the fire.

(*c*) Through suffering God will *strengthen* a man. The Greek is *sthenoun,* which means *to fill with strength*. Here is the same sense again. A life with no effort and no discipline almost inevitably becomes a flabby life. No one really knows what his faith means to him until it has been tried in the furnace of affliction. There is something doubly precious about a faith which has come victoriously through pain and sorrow and disappointment. The wind will extinguish a weak flame; but it will fan a strong flame into a still greater blaze. So it is with faith.

(*d*) Through suffering God will *settle* a man. The Greek is *themelioun,* which means *to lay the foundations.* When we have to meet sorrow and suffering we are driven down to the very bedrock of faith. It is then that we discover what are the things which cannot be shaken. It is in time of trial that we discover the great truths on which real life is founded.

Suffering is very far from doing these precious things for every man. It may well drive a man to bitterness and despair; and may well take away such faith as he has. But if it is accepted in the trusting certainty that a father's hand will never cause his child a needless tear, then out of suffering come things which the easy way may never bring.

A FAITHFUL HENCHMAN OF THE APOSTLES

1 *Peter* 5: 12

> I have written this brief letter to you through Silvanus, the faithful brother, as I reckon him to be, to encourage you and to testify that this is the true grace of God. Stand fast in it.

Peter bears witness that what he has written is indeed the grace of God, and he bids his people, amidst their difficulties, to stand fast in it.

He says that he has written *through Silvanus.* The Greek phrase (*dia Silouanou*) means that Silvanus was his agent in writing. Silvanus is the full form of the name Silas and he is almost certainly to be identified with the Silvanus of Paul's letters and the Silas of *Acts.* When we gather up the references to Silas or Silvanus, we find that he was one of the pillars of the early church.

Along with Judas Barsabas, Silvanus was sent to Antioch with the epoch-making decision of the Council of Jerusalem that the doors of the Church were to be opened to the Gentiles; and in the account of that mission Silvanus and Judas are called leading men among the brethren (*Acts* 15: 22, 27). Not only did he simply bear the message, he commended it in powerful words, for Silvanus was also a prophet (*Acts* 15: 32). During the first missionary journey Mark left Paul and Barnabas and returned home from Pamphylia (*Acts* 13: 13); in preparing for the second missionary journey Paul refused to have Mark with him again; the result was that Barnabas took Mark as his companion and Paul took Silvanus (*Acts* 15: 37–40). From that time forward Silvanus was for long Paul's right-hand man. He was with Paul in Philippi, where he was arrested and imprisoned with him (*Acts* 16: 19, 25, 29). He rejoined Paul in Corinth and with him preached the gospel there (*Acts* 18: 5; *2 Corinthians* 1: 19). So closely was he associated with Paul that in both the letters to the Thessalonians he is joined with Paul and Timothy as the senders of the letters (1 *Thessalonians* 1 : 1; 2 *Thessalonians* 1 : 1). It is clear that Silvanus was a most notable man in the early church.

As we saw in the introduction, it is most probable that Silvanus was far more than merely the scribe who wrote this letter for Peter and the bearer who delivered it. One of the difficulties of *First Peter* is the excellence of the Greek. It is Greek with such a classical tinge that it seems impossible that Peter the Galilaean fisherman should have written it for himself. Now Silvanus was not only a man of weight in the Church; he was also a Roman citizen (*Acts* 16: 37) and he would be much better educated than Peter was. Most probably he had a large share in the composition of this letter. We are told that in China, when a missionary wished to send a message to his people, he often wrote it in the best Chinese he could achieve, and then gave it to a Chinese Christian to correct and put into proper form; or, he might even just tell the Chinese Christian what he wished to say, leaving him to put it into literary form for his approval. That is most likely what Peter did. He either gave his letter to Silvanus to polish into excellent Greek or else he told Silvanus what he wished said and left him to say it, adding the last three verses as his personal greeting.

Silvanus was one of those men the Church can never do without. He was content to take the second place and to serve almost in the background so long as God's work was done. It was enough for him that he was Paul's assistant, even if Paul forever overshadowed him. It was enough for him to be Peter's penman, even if it meant only a bare mention of his name at the end of the letter. For all that, it is no little thing to go down in history as the faithful henchman on whom both Peter and Paul depended. The Church always has need of people like Silvanus and many who cannot be Peters or Pauls can still assist the Peters and Pauls to do their work.

GREETINGS

1 *Peter* 5: 13

> She who is at Babylon, and who has been chosen as you have been chosen, greets you, and so does Mark my son.

ALTHOUGH it sounds so simple, this is a troublesome verse. It presents us with certain questions difficult of solution.

(i) From whom are these greetings sent? The Authorized Version has "the Church that is at Babylon elected together with you, saluteth you." But "*the Church that is*" is in italics, which means that there is no equivalent in the Greek which simply says "*the one elected together with you at Babylon*" and the phrase is feminine. There are two possibilities.

(*a*) It is quite possible that the Authorized Version is correct. That is the way Moffatt takes it when he translates "your sister Church in Babylon." The phrase could well be explained as being based on the fact that the Church is the Bride of Christ and may be spoken of in this way. On the whole, the commonest view is that it is a Church which is meant.

(*b*) But it does have to be remembered that there is actually no word for *Church* in the Greek, and this feminine phrase might equally well refer to some well-known Christian lady. If it does, by far the best suggestion is that the reference is to Peter's wife. We know that she did actually accompany him on his preaching journeys (1 *Corinthians* 9: 5). Clement of Alexandria (*Stromateis* 7.11.63) tells us that she died a martyr, executed in Peter's own sight, while he encouraged her by saying, "Remember the Lord." She was clearly a well-known figure in the early church.

We would not wish to speak dogmatically on this question. It is perhaps more likely that the reference is to a Church; but it is not impossible that Peter is associating his wife and fellow-evangelist in the greetings which he sends.

(ii) From where was this letter written? The greetings are sent from *Babylon*. There are three possibilities.

(*a*) There was a Babylon in Egypt, near Cairo. It had been founded by Babylonian refugees from Assyria and was called by the name of their ancestral city. But by this time it was almost exclusively a great military camp; and in any event the name of Peter is never connected with Egypt. This Babylon may be disregarded.

(*b*) There was the Babylon in the east to which the Jews had been taken in captivity. Many had never come back and it was a centre of Jewish scholarship. The great commentary on the Jewish Law is called the *Babylonian Talmud*. So important were the Jews of Babylon that Josephus had issued a special edition of his histories for them. There is no doubt that there was a large and important colony of Jews there; and it would have been quite natural for Peter, the apostle of the Jews, to preach and to work there. But we do not find the name of Peter ever connected with Babylon and there is no trace of him having ever been there. Scholars so great as Calvin and Erasmus have taken Babylon to be this great eastern city but, on the whole, we think the probabilities are against it.

(*c*) Regularly Rome was called Babylon, both by the Jews and by the Christians. That is undoubtedly the case in the

Revelation where Babylon is the great harlot, drunk with the blood of the saints and the martyrs (*Revelation* 17 and 18). The godlessness, lust and luxury of ancient Babylon were, so to speak, reincarnated in Rome. Peter is definitely connected in tradition with Rome; and the likelihood is that it was from there that the letter was written.

(iii) Who is the Mark, whom Peter calls his son, and from whom he sends greetings? If we take the elect lady to be Peter's wife, Mark might quite well be literally Peter's son. But it is much more likely that he is the Mark who wrote the gospel. Tradition has always closely connected Peter with Mark, and has handed down the story that he was intimately involved with Mark's gospel. Papias, who lived towards the end of the second century and was a great collector of early traditions, describes Mark's gospel in this way: "Mark, who was Peter's interpreter, wrote down accurately though not in order, all that he recollected of what Christ had said or done. For he was not a hearer of the Lord or a follower of his; he followed Peter, as I have said, at a later date, and Peter adapted his instructions to practical needs, without any attempt to give the Lord's words systematically. So that Mark was not wrong in writing down some things in this way from memory, for his one concern was neither to omit nor to falsify anything he had heard." According to Papias, Mark's gospel is nothing other than the preaching material of Peter. In similar vein Irenaeus says that after the death of Peter and Paul at Rome, "Mark, the disciple and interpreter of Peter, also handed down to us in writing what had been preached by Peter." It is the consistent story of tradition that Mark, the evangelist, was indeed a son to Peter, and all the likelihood is that these greetings are from him.

So, then, we may gather up the possibilities. "She who is at Babylon, and who has been chosen, as you have been chosen," may either be the Church or the wife of Peter, herself a martyr. Babylon may be the Babylon of the east but is more likely to be the great and wicked city of Rome. Mark might possibly be the actual son of Peter, about whom we know nothing else, but is more likely to be Mark, the writer of the gospel, who was to Peter as a son.

AT PEACE WITH ONE ANOTHER

1 *Peter* 5 : 14

> Greet each other with a kiss of love. Peace be to you all that are in Christ.

THE most interesting thing here is the injunction to give each other the kiss of love. This was for centuries an integral and precious part of Christian fellowship and worship; and its history and gradual elimination, is of the greatest interest.

With the Jews it was the custom for a disciple to kiss his Rabbi on the cheek and to lay his hands upon his shoulder. That is what Judas did to Jesus (*Mark* 14: 44). The kiss was the greeting of welcome and respect, and we can see how much Jesus valued it, for he was grieved when it was not given to him (*Luke* 7: 45). Paul's letters frequently end with the injunction to salute each other with a holy kiss (*Romans* 16: 16; 1 *Corinthians* 16: 20; 2 *Corinthians* 13: 12; 1 *Thessalonians* 5: 26).

In the early church the kiss became an essential part of Christian worship. "What prayer is complete," asks Tertullian, "from which the holy kiss is divorced? What kind of sacrifice is that from which men depart without the peace?" (*Dex Oratione* 18). The kiss, we see here, was called *the peace*. It was specially a part of the communion service. Augustine says that, when Christians were about to communicate, "they demonstrated their inward peace by the outward kiss" (*De Amicitia* 6). It was usually given after the catechumens had been dismissed, when only members of the Church were present, and after the prayer before the elements were brought in. Justin Martyr says, "When we have ceased from prayer, we salute one another with a kiss. There is then brought to the president bread and a cup of wine" (1.65). The kiss was preceded by the prayer "for the gift of peace and of unfeigned love, undefiled by hypocrisy or deceit," and it was the sign that "our souls are mingled together, and have banished all remembrance of wrongs" (Cyril of Jerusalem, *Catechetical Lectures* 25.5.3). The kiss was the sign that all injuries were forgotten, all wrongs forgiven, and that those who sat at the Lord's Table were indeed one in the Lord.

This was a lovely custom and yet it is clear that it was sadly open to abuse. It is equally clear from the warnings so often given that abuses did creep in. Athenagoras insists that the kiss must be given with the greatest care, for "if there be mixed with it the least defilement of thought, it excludes us from eternal life" (*Legatio Christianis* 32). Origen insists that the kiss of peace must be "holy, chaste and sincere," not like the kiss of Judas (*Commentaria in Epistolam B. Pauli ad Romanos* 10: 33). Clement of Alexandria condemns the shameless use of the kiss, which ought to be mystic, for with the kiss "certain persons make the churches resound, and thereby occasion foul suspicions and evil reports" (*Paedagogus* 3: 11). Tertullian speaks of the natural reluctance of the heathen husband to think that his wife should be so greeted in the Christian Church (*Ad Uxorem* 2: 4).

In the Church of the west these inevitable problems gradually brought the end of this lovely custom. By the time of the *Apostolic Constitutions* in the fourth century, the kiss is confined to those of the same sex—the clergy are to salute the bishop, the men the men and the women the women. In this form the kiss of peace lasted in the Church of the west until the thirteenth century. Sometimes substitutes were introduced. In some places a little wooden or metal tablet, with a picture of the crucifixion on it, was used. It was kissed first by the priest, and then passed to the congregation, who each kissed it and handed it on, each man to his neighbour, in token of their mutual love for Christ and in Christ. In the oriental Churches the custom still obtains; it is not extinct in the Greek Church; the Armenian Church substituted a courteous bow.

We may note certain other uses of the kiss in the early church. At baptism the person baptized was kissed, first by the baptizer and then by the whole congregation, as a sign of his welcome into the household and family of Christ. A newly ordained bishop was given "the kiss in the Lord." The marriage ceremony was ratified by a kiss, a natural action taken over from paganism. Those who were dying first kissed the Cross and were then kissed by all present. The dead were kissed before burial.

To us the kiss of peace may seem very far away. It came from the day when the Church was a real family and fellowship, when Christians really did know and love one another. It is a tragedy that the modern Church, often with vast congregations who do not know each other and do not even wish to know each other, could not use the kiss of peace except as a formality. It was a lovely custom which was bound to cease when the reality of fellowship was lost within the Church.

"Peace to all of you that are in Christ," says Peter; and so he leaves his people to the peace of God which is greater than all the troubles and distresses the world can bring.

INTRODUCTION TO THE
SECOND LETTER OF PETER

THE NEGLECTED BOOK AND ITS CONTENTS

Second Peter is one of the neglected books of the New Testament. Very few people will claim to have read it, still less to have studied it in detail. E. F. Scott says "it is far inferior in every respect to *First Peter*"; and goes on "it is the least valuable of the New Testament writings." It was only with the greatest difficulty that *Second Peter* gained entry into the New Testament, and for many years the Christian Church seemed to be unaware of its existence. But, before we approach its history, let us look at its contents.

THE LAWLESS MEN

Second Peter was written to combat the beliefs and activities of certain men who were a threat to the Church. It begins by insisting that the Christian is a man who has escaped from the corruption of the world (1: 4) and must always remember that he has been purged of his old sins (1: 9). There is laid upon him the duty of moral goodness, which culminates in the great Christian virtue of love (1: 5–8).

Let us set out the characteristics of the men whom *Second Peter* rebukes. They twist Scripture to make it suit their own purpose (1: 20; 3: 16). They bring the Christian faith into disrepute (2: 2). They are covetous of gain and exploiters of their fellow-men (2: 3; 2: 14, 15). They are doomed and will share the fate of the sinning angels (2: 4), the men before the Flood (2: 5), the citizens of Sodom and Gomorrah (2: 6), and the false prophet Balaam (2: 15). They are bestial creatures, ruled by their brute instincts (2: 12), and dominated by their lusts (2: 10; 2: 18). Their eyes are full of adultery (2: 14). They are presumptuous, self-willed and arrogant (2: 10, 18). They spend even the daylight hours in unrestrained and luxurious revelry (2: 13). They speak of liberty but what they call liberty is unbridled licence and they themselves are the slaves of their own lusts (2: 19). Not only are they deluded, they also delude others and lead them astray (2: 14; 2: 18).

They are worse than those who never knew the right, because they knew what goodness is and have relapsed into evil, like a dog returning to its vomit and a sow returning to the mud after it has been washed (2: 20–22).

It is clear that Peter is describing Antinomians, men who used God's grace as a justification for sinning. In all probability they were Gnostics, who said that only spirit was good and that matter was essentially evil and that, therefore, it did not matter what we did with the body and that we could glut its appetites and it made no difference. They lived the most immoral lives and encouraged others to do so; and they justified their actions by perverting grace and interpreting Scripture to suit themselves.

THE DENIAL OF THE SECOND COMING

Further, these evil men denied the Second Coming (3: 3, 4). They argued that this was a stable world in which things remained unalterably the same, and that God was so dilatory that it was possible to assume that the Second Coming was never going to happen at all. The answer of *Second Peter* is that this is not a stable world; that it has, in fact, been destroyed by water in the Flood and that it will be destroyed by fire in the final conflagration (3: 5–7). What they regard as dilatoriness is in fact God withholding his hand in patience to give men still another chance to repent (3: 8, 9). But the day of destruction is coming (3: 10). A new heaven and a new earth are on the way; therefore, goodness is an absolute necessity if a man is to be saved in the day of judgment (3: 11–14). With this Paul agrees, however difficult his letters may be to understand, and however false teachers deliberately misinterpret them (3: 15, 16). The duty of the Christian is to stand fast, firmly founded in the faith, and to grow in grace and in the knowledge of Jesus Christ (3: 17, 18).

THE DOUBTS OF THE EARLY CHURCH

Such are the contents of the letter. For long it was regarded with doubt and with something very like misgiving. There is no trace of it until after A.D. 200. It is not included in the Muratorian Canon of A.D. 170 which was the first official list of New Testament books. It did not exist in the Old Latin Version of the Scriptures; nor in the New Testament of the early Syrian Church.

The great scholars of Alexandria either did not know it or were doubtful about it. Clement of Alexandria, who wrote outlines of the books of Scripture, does not appear to have included *Second Peter*. Origen says that Peter left behind one epistle which is generally acknowledged; "perhaps also a second, for it is a disputed question." Didymus commented on it, but concluded his work by saying: "It must not be forgotten that this letter is spurious; it may be read in public; but it is not part of the canon of Scripture."

Eusebius, the great scholar of Caesarea, who made a careful investigation of the Christian literature of his day, comes to the conclusion: "Of Peter, one Epistle, which is called his former Epistle, is acknowledged by all; of this the ancient presbyters have made frequent use in their writings as indisputably genuine; but that which is circulated as his second Epistle we have received to be not canonical although, since it appeared to be useful to many, it has been diligently read with the other Scriptures."

It was not until well into the fourth century that *Second Peter* came to rest in the canon of the New Testament.

THE OBJECTIONS

It is the well-nigh universal judgment of scholars, both ancient and modern, that Peter is not the author of *Second Peter*. Even John Calvin regarded it as impossible that Peter could have spoken of Paul as *Second Peter* speaks of him (3: 15, 16), although he was willing to believe that someone else wrote the letter at Peter's request. What, then, are the arguments against Peter's authorship?

(i) There is the extreme slowness, and even reluctance, of the early church to accept it. If it had been truly Peter's, there can be little doubt that the Church would have welcomed and honoured it from the first. But the case was very different. For the first two centuries the letter is never quoted at all in any certain instance; it is regarded with doubt and suspicion for more than another century; and only late in the fourth century is it accepted.

(ii) The contents make it difficult to believe that it is Peter's. There is no mention of the Passion, the Resurrection and the Ascension of Jesus Christ; no mention of the Church as the true Israel; no mention of that faith which is undefeatable hope and trust combined; no mention of the Holy Spirit, of prayer, of baptism; and no passionate desire to call men to the supreme example of Jesus Christ. If one took away these great verities from *First Peter* there would be little or nothing left, and yet none of them occurs in *Second Peter*.

(iii) It is wholly different in character and style from *First Peter*. This was realized as early as Jerome who wrote: "Simon Peter wrote two Epistles which are called Catholic, of which the authenticity of the second is denied by many because of the difference of the style from the first." The Greek style of this letter is very difficult. Clogg calls it ambitious, artificial and often obscure, and remarks that it is the only book in the New Testament which is improved by translation. Bishop Chase writes: "The Epistle does produce the impression of being a somewhat artificial piece of rhetoric. It shows throughout signs of self-conscious effort. The author appears to be ambitious of writing in a style which is beyond his literary power." He concludes that it is hard to reconcile the literary character of this letter with the supposition that Peter wrote it. Moffatt says: "*Second Peter* is more periodic and ambitious than *First Peter*, but its linguistic and its stylistic efforts only reveal by their cumbrous obscurity a decided inferiority of conception, which marks it off from *First Peter*."

It might be claimed, as Jerome claimed, that, while Peter used Silvanus for *First Peter*, he used a different amanuensis for *Second Peter* and that this explains the change in style. But J. B. Mayor compares the two letters. He quotes some of the great passages of *First Peter* and then says: "I think that none who read these words can help feeling that, not even in Paul, not even in John, is there to be found a more beautiful or a more living description of the secret of primitive Christianity, of the force that overcame the world, than in the perfect quaternion of faith and hope and love and joy, which pervades this short epistle (i.e. *First Peter*). No one could make the same assertion with regard to *Second Peter*: thoughtful and interesting as it is, it lacks that intense sympathy, that flame of love, which marks *First Peter*. . . . No change of circumstances can account for the change of tone of which we are conscious in passing from one epistle to the other." It is the conclusion of that great and conservative scholar that no explanation, other than difference of authorship, can explain, not so much the difference in style as the difference in atmosphere between *First* and *Second Peter*. It is true that from the purely linguistic point of view there are 369 words which occur in *First Peter* which do not occur in *Second Peter*; and there are 230 words which occur in *Second Peter* and not in *First Peter*. But there is more than a difference in style. A writer can change his style and his vocabulary to suit his audience and his occasion. But the difference between the two letters in atmosphere and attitude is so wide that it is hardly possible that the same person should have written both.

(iv) Certain things within *Second Peter* point well-nigh irresistibly to a late date. So much time has passed that men have begun to abandon hope of the Second Coming altogether (3: 4). The apostles are spoken of as figures of the past (3: 2). The fathers, that is the founders of the Christian faith, are now figures of the almost dim and distant past; there have been generations between this letter and the first coming of the Christian faith (3: 4).

There are references which require the passing of the years to explain them. The reference to Peter's approaching death looks very like a reference to Jesus's prophecy in *John* 21: 18, 19, and the Fourth Gospel was not written until about A.D. 100. The statement that Peter is going to leave something which will continue his teaching after he has gone looks very like a reference to Mark's Gospel (1: 12–14).

Above all there is the reference to the letters of Paul (3: 15, 16). From this it is quite certain that Paul's letters are known and used throughout all the Church; they are public property, and furthermore they are regarded as Scripture and on a level with "the other Scriptures" (3: 16). It was not until at least A.D. 90 that these letters were collected and published, and it would take many years for them to acquire the position of sacred Scripture. It is practically impossible that anyone should write like this until midway through the second century A.D.

All the evidence converges to prove that *Second Peter* is a late book. It is not until the third century that it is quoted. The great scholars of the early church did not regard it as Peter's although they did not question its usefulness. The letter has references which require the passing of the years to explain them. The great interest of *Second Peter* lies in the very fact that it was the last book in the New Testament to be written and the last to gain entry into the New Testament.

IN PETER'S NAME

How, then, did it become attached to the name of Peter? The answer is that it was *deliberately* attached. This may seem to us a strange proceeding but in the ancient world this was common practice. Plato's letters were written not by Plato but by a disciple in the master's name. The Jews repeatedly used this method of writing. Between the Old and the New Testament, books were written under the names of Solomon, Isaiah, Moses, Baruch, Ezra, Enoch and many another. And in New Testament times there is a whole literature around the name of Peter—The Gospel of Peter, The Preaching of Peter, The Apocalypse of Peter.

One salient fact makes this method of writing even more intelligible. The heretics used it. They issued misleading and pernicious books under the names of the great apostles, claiming that they were the secret teaching of the great founders of the Church handed down by word of mouth to them. Faced with this, the Church retaliated in kind and issued books in which men set down for their own generation the things they were quite sure that the apostles would have said had they been facing this new situation. There is nothing either unusual or discreditable in a book being issued under the name of Peter although Peter did not write it. The writer in humility was putting the message which the Holy Spirit had given him into the mouth of Peter because he felt his own name was unworthy to appear upon the book.

We will not find *Second Peter* easy to read; but it is a book of first-rate importance because it was written to men who were undermining the Christian ethic and the Christian doctrine and who had to be stopped before the Christian faith was wrecked by their perversion of the truth.

2 PETER

THE MAN WHO OPENED DOORS

2 *Peter* 1 : 1

> Symeon Peter, a servant and apostle of Jesus Christ, writes this
> letter to those to whom there has been allotted a faith equal in
> honour and privilege with our own, through the impartial justice of
> our God and Saviour Jesus Christ.

THE letter opens with a very subtle and beautiful allusion for
those who have eyes to see it and knowledge enough of the
New Testament to grasp it. Peter writes to "those to whom
there has been allotted a faith equal in honour and privilege
with our own"—and he calls himself *Symeon Peter*. Who were
these people? There can really be only one answer to that. They
must once have been Gentiles in contradistinction to the Jews
who were uniquely the chosen people of God. Those who had
once been no people are now the chosen people of God
(1 *Peter* 2: 10); those who were once aliens and strangers to
the commonwealth of Israel, and who were once far off, have
been brought nigh (*Ephesians* 2: 11–13).

Peter puts this very vividly, using a word which would at
once strike an answering chord in the minds of those who heard
it. Their faith is *equal in honour and privilege*. The Greek is
isotimos; *isos* means *equal* and *time* means *honour*. This word
was particularly used in connection with foreigners who were
given equal citizenship in a city with the natives. Josephus,
for instance, says that in Antioch the Jews were made *isotimoi,
equal in honour and privilege,* with the Macedonians and the
Greeks who lived there. So Peter addresses his letter to those
who had once been despised Gentiles but who had been given
equal rights of citizenship with the Jews and even with the
apostles themselves in the kingdom of God.

Two things have to be noted about this great privilege which had been extended to the Gentiles. (*a*) It had been *allotted* to them. That is to say, they had not earned it; it had fallen to them through no merit of their own, as some prize falls to a man by lot. In other words, their new citizenship was all of grace. (*b*) It came to them through the impartial justice of their God and Saviour Jesus Christ. It came to them because with God there is no "most favoured nation clause"; his grace and favour go out impartially to every nation upon earth.

What has this to do with the name *Symeon,* by which Peter is here called? In the New Testament, he is most often called Peter; he is fairly often called Simon, which was, indeed, his original name before Jesus gave him the name of Cephas or Peter (*John* 1: 41, 42); but only once in the rest of the New Testament is he called *Symeon.* It is in the story of that Council of Jerusalem in *Acts* 15 which decided that the door of the Church should be opened wide to the Gentiles. There James says, "Symeon has related how God first visited the Gentiles, to take out of them a people for his name" (*Acts* 15: 14). In this letter which begins with greetings to the Gentiles who have been granted by the grace of God privileges of equal citizenship in the kingdom with the Jews and with the apostles Peter is called by the name of *Symeon*; and the only other time he is called by that name is when he is the principal instrument whereby that privilege is granted.

Symeon has in it the memory that Peter is the man who opened doors. He opened the doors to Cornelius, the Gentile centurion (*Acts* 10); his great authority was thrown on the side of the open door at the Council of Jerusalem (*Acts* 15).

THE GLORIOUS SERVITUDE

2 *Peter* 1: 1 (*continued*)

PETER calls himself the *servant* of Jesus Christ. The word is *doulos* which really means *slave.* Strange as it may seem, here is a title, apparently one of humiliation, which the greatest of men took as a title of greatest honour. Moses the great leader and lawgiver was the *doulos* of God (*Deuteronomy* 34: 5; *Psalm* 105: 26; *Malachi* 4: 4). Joshua the great commander was the *doulos* of God (*Joshua* 24: 29). David the greatest of the kings was the *doulos* of God (2 *Samuel* 3: 18; *Psalm* 78: 70). In the New Testament Paul is the *doulos* of Jesus Christ (*Romans*1: 1; *Philippians* 1: 1; *Titus* 1: 1), a title which James (*James* 1: 1), and Jude (*Jude* 1) both proudly claim. In the Old Testament the prophets are the *douloi* of God (*Amos* 3: 7; *Isaiah* 20: 3). And in the New Testament the Christian man frequently is Christ's *doulos* (*Acts* 2: 18; 1 *Corinthians* 7: 22; *Ephesians* 6: 6; *Colossians* 4: 12; 2 *Timothy* 2: 24). There is deep meaning here.

(i) To call the Christian the *doulos* of God means that he is inalienably possessed by God. In the ancient world a master possessed his slaves in the same sense as he possessed his tools. A servant can change his master; but a slave cannot. The Christian inalienably belongs to God.

(ii) To call the Christian the *doulos* of God means that he is unqualifiedly at the disposal of God. In the ancient world the master could do what he liked with his slave; he had even the power of life and death over him. The Christian has no rights of his own, for all his rights are surrendered to God.

(iii) To call the Christian the *doulos* of God means that he owes an unquestioning obedience to God. A master's command was a slave's only law in ancient times. In any situation the Christian has but one question to ask: "Lord, what will *you* have me do?" The command of God is *his* only law.

(iv) To call the Christian the *doulos* of God means that he must be constantly in the service of God. In the ancient world the slave had literally no time of his own, no holidays, no leisure. All his time belonged to his master. The Christian cannot, either deliberately or unconsciously, compartmentalize life into the time and activities which belong to God, and the time and activities in which he does what he likes. The Christian is necessarily the man every moment of whose time is spent in the service of God.

We note one further point. Peter speaks of the impartial justice of *our God and Saviour Jesus Christ*. The Authorized Version translates, "the righteousness of God and our Saviour Jesus Christ," as if this referred to two persons, God and Jesus; but, as Moffatt and the Revised Standard Version both show, in the Greek there is only one person involved and the phrase is correctly rendered *our God and Saviour Jesus Christ*. Its great interest is that it does what the New Testament very, very seldom does. It calls Jesus God. The only real parallel to this is the adoring cry of Thomas: "My Lord and my God." (*John* 20: 28). This is not a matter to argue about; it is not even a matter of theology; for Peter and Thomas to call Jesus God was not a matter of theology but an outrush of adoration. It was simply that they felt human terms could not contain this person they knew as Lord.

THE ALL-IMPORTANT KNOWLEDGE

2 *Peter* 1: 2

> May grace and peace be multiplied to you by the knowledge of God, and of Jesus, our Lord.

PETER puts this in an unusual way. Grace and peace are to come from *knowledge,* the knowledge of God and of Jesus Christ, our Lord. Is he turning Christian experience into something dependent on knowledge? Or is there some other meaning here? First, let us look at the word which he uses for knowledge (*epignōsis*). It can be interpreted in two directions.

(*a*) It can mean *increasing knowledge. Gnōsis,* the normal Greek word for *knowledge,* is here preceded by the preposition *epi* which means *towards*, *in the direction of. Epignōsis* then could be interpreted as knowledge which is always moving further in the direction of that which it seeks to know. Grace and peace are multiplied to the Christian as he comes to know Jesus Christ better and better. As it has been put: "The more Christians realize the meaning of Jesus Christ, the more they realize the meaning of grace and the experience of peace."

(*b*) *Epignōsis* has a second meaning. Often in Greek it means *full knowledge*. Plutarch, for instance, uses it of the scientific knowledge of music as opposed to the knowledge of the mere amateur. So it may be that the implication here is that knowledge of Jesus Christ is what we might call "the master-science of life." The other sciences may bring new skill, new knowledge, new abilities, but the master-science, the knowledge of Jesus Christ, alone brings the grace men need and the peace for which their hearts crave.

There is still more. Peter has a way of using words which were commonly on the lips of the pagans of his day and charging them with a new meaning. Knowledge was a much used word in pagan religious thought in the days when this letter was written. To take but one example, the Greeks defined *sophia, wisdom,* as knowledge of things both human and divine. The Greek seekers after God sought that knowledge in two main ways.

(*a*) They sought it by philosophic speculation. They sought to reach God by the sheer power of human thought. There are obvious troubles there. For one thing, God is infinite; the mind of man is finite; and the finite can never grasp the infinite. Long ago Zophar had asked: "Can you (by searching) find out the deep things of God?" (*Job* 11 : 7). If God is ever to be known, he must be known, not because man's mind discovers him but because he chooses to reveal himself. For another thing, if religion is based on philosophic speculation, at its highest it can be the preserve of only the few, for it is not given to every man to be a philosopher. Whatever Peter meant by *knowledge,* he did not mean that.

(*b*) They sought it by mystical experience of the divine, until they could say, "I am thou, and thou art I." This was the way of the Mystery Religions. They were all passion plays; the dramatically acted story of some god who suffered and died and rose again. The initiate was carefully prepared by instruction in the inner meaning of the story, by long fasting and continence, and by the deliberate building up of psychological tension. The play was then played out with a magnificent liturgy, sensuous music, carefully calculated lighting and the burning of incense. The aim was that, as the initiate watched, he should so enter into this experience that he became actually one with the suffering, dying, rising, and eternally triumphant God. Again there are troubles here. For one thing, not every one is capable of mystical experience. For another thing, any such experience is necessarily transient; it may leave an effect, but it cannot be a continual experience. Mystical experience is the privilege of the few.

(*c*) If this knowledge of Jesus Christ does not come by philosophic speculation or by mystical experience, what is it and how does it come? In the New Testament knowledge is characteristically *personal* knowledge. Paul does not say, "I know *what* I have believed"; he says, "I know *whom* I have believed" (2 *Timothy* 1: 12). Christian knowledge of Christ is personal acquaintance with him; it is knowing him as a person and entering day by day into a more intimate relationship with him.

When Peter speaks of grace and peace coming through the knowledge of God and of Jesus Christ, he is not intel-lectualizing religion; he is saying that Christianity means an ever-deepening personal relationship with Jesus Christ.

THE GREATNESS OF JESUS CHRIST FOR MEN

2 *Peter* 1: 3–7

Since his divine power has bestowed upon us all things that are necessary for true life and true religion, through the knowledge of him who called us to his own glory and excellence, and since through these gifts there have been bestowed upon us precious and very great promises, that through them we might escape the world's corruption caused by lust and become sharers in the divine nature—since all this is so, bend all your energy to the task of equipping your faith with courage, your courage with knowledge, your knowledge with self-control, your self-control with steadfastness, your steadfastness with piety, your piety with brotherly affection, your brotherly affection with Christian love.

IN verses 3 and 4 there is a tremendous and comprehensive picture of Jesus Christ.

(i) He is the *Christ of power*. In him there is the divine power which cannot be ultimately defeated or frustrated. In this world one of the tragedies of life is that love is so often frustrated because it cannot give what it wants to give, cannot do what it wants to do and must so often stand helpless while the loved one meets disaster. But always Christ's love is backed by his power and is, therefore, a victorious love.

(ii) He is the *Christ of generosity*. He bestows on us all things necessary for true life and true religion. The word Peter uses for religion is *eusebeia,* the characteristic meaning of which is *practical religion*. Peter is saying that Jesus Christ tells us what life is and then enables us to live it as it ought to be lived. He gives us a religion which is not withdrawal from life but triumphant involvement in it.

(iii) He is the *Christ of the precious and great promises*. That does not so much mean that he brings us the great and precious promises as that in him these promises come true. Paul put the same thing in a different way when he said that all the promises of God are Yes and Amen in Christ (2 *Corinthians* 1: 20). That is to say Christ says, "Yes. So let it be," to these promises; he confirms and guarantees them. It has been put this way— once we know Jesus Christ, every time we meet a promise in Scripture which begins with the word "Whosoever," we can immediately say to ourselves, "That means me."

(iv) He is the *Christ by whom we escape the world's corruption*. Peter had to meet the Antinomians, the people who used the grace of God as an excuse for sin. They declared that grace was wide enough to cover every sin; therefore, sin does not matter any more, the grace of Christ will win forgiveness for it. For any man to speak like that is simply to show that he *wants* to sin. But Jesus Christ is the person who can help us overcome the fascination of the world's lust and cleanse us by his presence and his power. So long as we live in this world sin will never completely lose its fascination for us; but in the presence of Christ we have our defence against that fascination.

(v) He is the *Christ who makes us sharers in the divine nature*. Here again Peter is using an expression which the pagan thinkers well knew. They spoke much about sharing in the divine nature. But there was this difference—they believed that man had a share in the divine nature by virtue of being man. All men had to do was to live in accordance with the divine nature already in them. The trouble about that is that life flatly contradicts it. On every side we see bitterness, hatred, lust, crime; on every side we see moral failure, helplessness and frustration. Christianity says that men are *capable of becoming* sharers in the divine nature. It realistically faces man's actuality but at the same time sets no limit to his potentiality. "I am come," said Jesus, "that they may have life, and have it abundantly" (*John* 10: 10). As one of the great early fathers said, "He became what we are to make us what he is." Man has it in him to share the nature of God—but only in Jesus Christ can that potentiality be realized.

EQUIPMENT FOR THE WAY

2 *Peter* 1: 3–7 (*continued*)

PETER says that we must bend all our energies *to equip* ourselves with a series of great qualities. The word he uses for *to equip* is *epichorēgein* which he uses again in verse 11 when he speaks of us being *richly gifted* with the right of entry into the eternal kingdom.

This is one of the many Greek words which have a pictorial background. The verb *epichorēgein* comes from the noun *chorēgos,* which literally means *the leader of a chorus*. Perhaps the greatest gift that Greece, and especially Athens, gave to the world was the great works of men like Aeschylus, Sophocles and Euripides, which are still among its most cherished possessions. All these plays needed large choruses and were, therefore, very expensive to produce. In the great days of Athens there were public-spirited citizens who voluntarily took on the duty, at their own expense, of collecting, maintaining, training and equipping such choruses. It was at the great religious festivals that these plays were produced. For instance, at the city Dionysia there were produced three tragedies, five comedies and five dithyrambs. Men had to be found to provide the choruses for them all, a duty which could cost as much as 3,000 drachmae. The men who undertook these duties out of their own pocket and out of love for their city were called *chorēgoi,* and *chorēgein* was the verb used for undertaking such a duty. The word has a certain lavishness in it. It never means to equip in any cheese-paring and miserly way; it means lavishly to pour out everything that is necessary for a noble performance. *Epichorēgein* went out into a larger world and it grew to mean not only to equip a chorus but to be responsible for any kind of equipment. It can mean to equip an army with all necessary provisions; it can mean to equip the soul with all the necessary virtues for life. But always at the back of it there is this idea of a lavish generosity in the equipment.

So Peter urges his people to equip their lives with every virtue; and that equipment must not be simply a necessary minimum, but lavish and generous. The very word is an incitement to be content with nothing less than the loveliest and the most splendid life.

But there is something else at the back of this. In verses 5 and 6 Peter goes on that we must, as the Revised Standard Version has it, *add* virtue to virtue, until the whole culminates in Christian love. Behind this is a Stoic idea. The Stoics insisted that in life there must continuously be what they called *prokopē, moral progress. Prokopē* can be used for *the advance of an army towards its objective.* In the Christian life there must be steady moral advance. Moffatt quotes a saying that, "the Christian life must not be an initial spasm followed by a chronic inertia." It is very apt to be just that; a moment of enthusiasm, when the wonder of Christianity is realized, and then a failure to work out the Christian life in continuous progress.

That brings us to still another basic idea here. Peter bids his people *bend every energy* to do this. That is to say, in the Christian life the supreme effort of man must co-operate with the grace of God. As Paul has it: "Work out your own salvation with fear and trembling; for God is at work in you, both to will and to work his good pleasure" (*Philippians* 2: 12, 13). It is true that everything is of faith; but a faith which does not issue in life is not faith at all, as Paul would heartily have agreed. Faith is not only commitment to the promises of Christ; it is also commitment to his demands.

Bigg well points out that Aristotle, in the *Nicomachean Ethics,* says that there are three theories of the source of happiness. (i) It is something which can come by training, by learning and by the formation of right habits. (ii) It is a matter of divine allotment, the gift of God. (iii) It is all a matter of chance.

The truth is that, as the Christian sees it, happiness depends *both* on God's gift and on our effort. We do not earn salvation but at the same time we have to bend every energy towards the Christian objective of a lovely life. Bengel, in commenting on this passage, asks us to compare the Parable of the Ten Virgins, five of whom were wise and five of whom were foolish. He writes: "The flame is that which is imparted to us by God and from God without our own labour; but the oil is that which a man must pour into life by his own study and his own faithful effort, so that the flame may be fed and increased."

Faith does not exempt a man from works; the generosity of God does not absolve a man from effort. Life is at its noblest and its best when our effort co-operates with God's grace to produce the necessary loveliness.

THE LADDER OF VIRTUES (1)

2 Peter 1: 3–7 (*continued*)

LET us then look at the list of virtues which have to be added one to another. It is worth noting that in the ancient world such lists were common. It was a world in which books were not nearly so cheap and so readily available as they are today. Instruction, therefore, had for the most part to be carried in the pupil's head; and easily memorized lists were one of the commonest ways of inculcating instruction. One ingenious way of teaching the child the names of the virtues was by means of a game played with counters which could be won or lost, each of which bore the name of one of the virtues. Lists of virtues were common in the early Christian writings. Paul gives us the fruit of the Spirit—love, joy, peace, patience, kindness, goodness, faithfulness, gentleness, self-control (*Galatians* 5: 22, 23). In the Pastoral Epistles the man of God is bidden to follow after righteousness, godliness, faith, love, steadfastness, gentleness (1 *Timothy* 6: 11). In *The Shepherd of Hermas* (*Visions* 3.8.1–7), faith, self-control, simplicity, innocence and reverence, understanding and love are daughters one of another. In the *Epistle of Barnabas* (2) fear and endurance are the helpers of faith; patience and self-control are our allies; and when these are present a man can develop and possess wisdom, prudence, understanding and knowledge. Let us look one by one at the stages in the list which this letter gives us.

(i) It begins with *faith* (*pistis*); everything goes back to that. For Peter faith is the conviction that what Jesus Christ says is true and that we can commit ourselves to his promises and launch ourselves on his demands. It is the unquestioning certainty that the way to happiness and peace and strength on earth and in heaven is to accept him at his word.

(ii) To faith must be added what the Revised Standard Version calls *virtue* and we have called *courage*. The word is *aretē*; it is very rare in the New Testament but it is the supreme Greek word for virtue in every sense of the term. It means *excellence*. It has two special directions in which its meaning moves. (*a*) *Aretē* is what we might call *operative*, or *efficient*, *excellence*. To take two examples of its usage from widely differing spheres—it can be used of land which is fertile; and it can be used of the mighty deeds of the gods. *Aretē* is that virtue which makes a man a good citizen and friend; it is that virtue which makes him an expert in the technique of living well. (*b*) *Aretē* often means *courage*. Plutarch says that God is a hope of *aretē,* not an excuse for cowardice. In 2 *Maccabees* we read of how Eleazar died rather than be false to the laws of God and his fathers; and the story ends by saying that he left his death for an example of noble courage (*aretē*) and a memorial of virtue, not only to young men, but also to all the nation (2 *Maccabees* 6: 31).

In this passage it is not necessary to choose between these two meanings; they are both there. Faith must issue, not in the retirement of the cloister and the cell, but in a life effective in the service of God and man; and it must issue in the courage always to show whose it is and whom it serves.

(iii) To courage must be added *knowledge*. The word is *gnōsis*. In ethical Greek language there are two words which have a similar meaning with a very significant difference. *Sophia* is wisdom, in the sense of "knowledge of things both human and divine, and of their causes." It is knowledge of first causes and of deep and ultimate things. *Gnōsis* is *practical knowledge*; it is the ability to apply to particular situations the ultimate knowledge which *sophia* gives. *Gnōsis* is that knowledge which enables a man to decide rightly and to act honourably and efficiently in the day to day circumstances of life. So, then, to faith must be added courage and effectiveness; to courage and effectiveness must be added the practical wisdom to deal with life.

THE LADDER OF VIRTUES (2)

2 *Peter* 1: 3–7 (*continued*)

(iv) To this practical knowledge must be added *self-control,* or *self-mastery*. The word is *egkrateia,* and it means literally *the ability to take a grip of oneself*. This is a virtue of which the great Greeks spoke and wrote and thought much. In regard to a man and his passions Aristotle distinguishes four states in life. There is *sōphrosunē,* in which passion has been entirely subjugated to reason; we might call it *perfect temperance*.

There is *akolasia,* which is the precise opposite; it is the state
in which reason is entirely subjugated to passion; we might
call it *unbridled lust.* In between these two states there is
akrasia, in which reason fights but passion prevails; we might
call it *incontinence.* There is *egkrateia,* in which reason fights
against passion and prevails; we call it *self-control,* or
self-mastery.

Egkrateia is one of the great Christian virtues; and the place
it holds is an example of the realism of the Christian ethic. That
ethic does not contemplate a situation in which a man is
emasculated of all passion; it envisages a situation in which
his passions remain, but are under perfect control and so
become his servants, not his tyrants.

(v) To this self-control must be added *steadfastness.* The
word is *hupomonē.* Chrysostom called *hupomonē* "The Queen
of the Virtues." In the Authorized Version it is usually translated *patience*; but *patience* is too passive a word. *Hupomonē*
has always a background of courage. Cicero defines *patientia,*
its Latin equivalent, as: "The voluntary and daily suffering of
hard and difficult things, for the sake of honour and usefulness." Didymus of Alexandria writes on the temper of Job:"It
is not that the righteous man must be without feeling, although he must patiently bear the things which afflict him;
but it is true virtue when a man deeply feels the things he
toils against, but nevertheless despises sorrows for the sake of
God." *Hupomonē* does not simply accept and endure; there is
always a forward look in it. It is said of Jesus, by the writer
to the Hebrews, that for the joy that was set before him,
he *endured* the Cross, despising the shame (*Hebrews* 12: 2).
That is *hupomonē,* Christian steadfastness. It is the courageous
acceptance of everything that life can do to us and the trans-
muting of even the worst event into another step on the upward
way.

(vi) To this steadfastness must be added *piety.* The word is
eusebeia and is quite untranslatable. Even *piety* is inadequate,
carrying as it does a suggestion sometimes of something not
altogether attractive. The great characteristic of *eusebeia* is that

it looks in two directions. The man who has *eusebeia* always correctly worships God and gives him his due; but he always correctly serves his fellow-men and gives them their due. The man who is *eusebēs* (the corresponding adjective) is in a right relationship both with God and his fellow-men. *Eusebeia* is piety but in its most practical aspect.

We may best see the meaning of this word by looking at the man whom the Greeks held to be its finest example. That man was Socrates whom Xenophon describes as follows: "He was so pious and devoutly religious that he would take no step apart from the will of heaven; so just and upright that he never did even a trifling injury to any living soul; so self-controlled, so temperate, that he never at any time chose the sweeter instead of the better; so sensible, so wise, and so prudent that in distinguishing the better from the worse he never erred" (Xenophon: *Memorabilia* 1.5.8–11).

In Latin the word is *pietas*; and Warde Fowler describes the Roman idea of the man who possesses that quality: "He is superior to the enticements of individual passion and of selfish ease; (*pietas* is) a sense of duty which never left a man, of duty first to the gods, then to father and to family, to son and to daughter, to his people and to his nation."

Eusebeia is the nearest Greek word for *religion*; and, when we begin to define it, we see the intensely practical character of the Christian religion. When a man becomes a Christian, he acknowledges a double duty, to God and to his fellow-men.

(vii) To this piety must be added *brotherly affection*. The word is *philadelphia*, which literally means *love of the brethren*. The point is this—there is a kind of religious devotion which separates a man from his fellow-men. The claims of his fellow-men become an intrusion on his prayers, his study of God's word and his meditation. The ordinary demands of human relationships become a nuisance. Epictetus, the great Stoic philosopher, never married. Half-jestingly he said that he was doing far more for the world by being an unfettered philosopher than if he had produced "two or three dirty-nosed children." "How can he who has to teach mankind run to get something in which to heat the water to give the baby his bath?" What Peter is saying is that there is something wrong with the religion which finds the claims of personal relationships a nuisance.

(viii) The ladder of Christian virtue must end in Christian love. Not even affection for the brethren is enough; the Christian must end with a love which is as wide as that love of God which causes his sun to rise on the just and on the unjust, and sends his rain on the evil and the good. The Christian must show to all men the love which God has shown to him.

ON THE WAY

2 Peter 1: 8–11

> For, if these things exist and increase within you, they will make you not ineffective and not unfruitful in your progress towards the knowledge of our Lord Jesus Christ. For whoever does not possess these things is blind, short-sighted, and has lapsed into forgetfulness that the sins of his old way of life have been cleansed away. So, brothers, be the more eager to confirm your calling and your choice. For, if you do practise these virtues, you will never slip; for you will be richly gifted with the right of entry into the eternal kingdom of our Lord Jesus Christ.

PETER strongly urges his people to keep climbing up this ladder of virtues which he has set before them. The more we know of any subject the more we are fit to know. It is always true that "to him that hath it shall be given." Progress is the way to more progress. Moffatt says of ourselves and Jesus Christ: "We learn him as we live with him and for him." As the hymn has it:

> May every heart confess thy name,
>   And ever thee adore,
> And, seeking thee, itself inflame
>   To seek thee more and more.

To keep climbing up the ladder of the virtues is to come ever nearer to knowing Jesus Christ; and the further we climb, the further we are able to climb.

On the other hand, if we refuse to make the effort of the upward climb, certain things happen. (*a*) We grow blind; we are left without the guiding light that the knowledge of Jesus Christ brings. As Peter sees it, to walk without Christ is to walk in the dark and not to be able to see the way. (*b*) We grow what Peter calls *muōpazōn*. This word can have either of two meanings. It can mean *short-sighted*. It is easy to become short-sighted in life, to see things only as they appear at the moment and to be unable to take the long view of things, to have our eyes so fixed upon earth that we never think of the things beyond. It can also mean *blinking, shutting the eyes*. Again, it is easy in life to shut our eyes to what we do not wish to see, and to walk, as it were, in blinkers. To walk without Christ is to be in danger of taking the short-sighted or the blinkered view of life.

Further, to fail to climb the ladder of virtue is to forget that the sins of the old way of life have been cleansed away. Peter is thinking of baptism. At that time baptism was adult baptism; it was a deliberate act of decision to leave the old way and to enter upon the new. The man who, after baptism, does not begin upon the upward climb has forgotten, or never realized, the meaning of the experience through which he has passed. For many of us the parallel to baptism in this sense is entry into the membership of the Christian Church. To make our commitment and then to remain exactly the same, is to fail to understand what church membership means, for our entry into it should be the beginning of a climb upon the upward way.

In view of all this, Peter urges his people to make every effort to confirm their calling by God. Here is a most significant demand. In one way all is of God; it is God's call which gives us entry into the fellowship of his people; without his grace and his mercy we could do nothing and could expect nothing. But that does not absolve us from every possible effort.

Let us take an analogy, which, although not perfect, may

help us to understand. Suppose a man who is wealthy and kind picks out a poor lad, who would never otherwise have had the chance, and offers him the privilege of a university education. The benefactor is giving the lad something which he could never have achieved for himself; but the lad cannot make use of that privilege unless he is prepared to work, and the harder he works the more he will enter into the privilege offered to him. The gracious free offer and the personal hard work have to combine before the privilege becomes fully effective.

It is so with us and God. God has called us in his free mercy and his unmerited grace; but at the same time we have to bend every effort to toil upwards and onwards on the way.

If we follow this upward way, Peter says, we shall in the end be richly gifted with the right of entry into his eternal kingdom; and we shall not slip upon the way. By this Peter does not mean that we will never sin. The picture in his mind is of a march and he means that we will never fall out upon the march and be left behind. If we set out upon this upward and onward way, the effort will be great but God's help will also be great; and in spite of all the toil, he will enable us to keep going until we reach our journey's end.

THE PASTOR'S CARE

2 *Peter* 1: 12–15

It is for this reason that I intend constantly to remind you of these things, although you already know them, and although you are already firmly established in the truth which you possess. I think it is right, so long as I am in this tent, to rouse you by reminding you, for I know that the time to put off my tent is coming soon, as indeed our Lord Jesus Christ has told me. Yes, and I will make it my endeavour to see to it that after my departure you will constantly remember these things.

HERE speaks the pastor's care. In this passage Peter shows us two things about preaching and teaching. First, preaching is very often reminding a man of what he already knows. It is bringing back to his memory that truth which he has forgotten, or at which he refuses to look, or whose meaning he has not fully appreciated. Second, Peter is going to go on to uncompromising rebuke and warning, but he begins with something very like a compliment. He says that his people already possess the truth and are firmly established in it. Always a preacher, a teacher or a parent will achieve more by encouragement than by scolding. We do more to reform people and to keep them safe by, as it were, putting them on their honour than by flaying them with invective. Peter was wise enough to know that the first essential to make men listen is to show that we believe in them.

Peter looks forward to his early death. He talks of his body as his tent, as Paul does (2 *Corinthians* 5: 4). This was a favourite picture with the early Christian writers. *The Epistle to Diognetus* says, "The immortal soul dwells in a mortal tent." The picture comes from the journeyings of the patriarchs in the Old Testament. They had no abiding residence but lived in tents because they were on the way to the Promised Land. The Christian knows well that his life in this world is not a permanent residence but a journey towards the world beyond. We get the same idea in verse 15. There Peter speaks of his approaching death as his *exodos*, his departure. *Exodos* is, of course, the word which is used for the departure of the children of Israel from Egypt, and their setting out to the Promised Land. Peter sees death, not as the end but as the going out into the Promised Land of God.

Peter says that Jesus Christ has told him that for him the end will soon be coming. This may be a reference to the prophecy in *John* 21: 18, 19, when Jesus foretells that there will come a day when Peter also will be stretched out upon a cross. That time is about to come.

Peter says that he will take steps to see that what he has got to say to them will be held before their memory even when he is gone from this earth. That may well be a reference to the Gospel according to St. Mark. The consistent tradition is that it is the preaching material of Peter. Irenaeus says that, after the death of Peter and Paul, Mark, who had been his disciple and interpreter, handed on in writing the things which it had been Peter's custom to preach. Papias, who lived towards the end of the second century and collected many traditions about the early days of the Church, hands down the same tradition about Mark's gospel: "Mark, who was Peter's interpreter, wrote down accurately, though not in order, all that he recollected of what Christ had said or done. For he was not a hearer of the Lord, or a follower of his; he followed Peter, as I have said, at a later date and Peter adapted his instruction to practical needs, without any attempt to give the Lord's words systematically. So that Mark was not wrong in writing down some things in this way from memory, for his one concern was neither to omit nor to falsify anything that he had heard." It may well be that the reference here means that Peter's teaching was made still available to his people in Mark's Gospel after his death.

In any event, the pastor's aim was to bring to his people God's truth while he was still alive and to take steps to keep it in their memories after he was dead. He wrote, not to preserve his own name, but the name of Jesus Christ.

THE MESSAGE AND THE RIGHT TO GIVE IT

2 Peter 1: 16–18

For it was not cleverly invented fables that we followed when we made known to you the power and the coming of our Lord Jesus Christ; it was because we were made eye-witnesses of his majesty. This happened to us on that occasion when he received honour and glory from God the Father, when this voice was borne to him by the majestic glory—"This is my Son, the Beloved, in whom I am well pleased." It was this voice that we heard, borne from heaven, when we were with him in the sacred mountain.

PETER comes to the message which it was his great aim to bring to his people, concerning "the power and the coming of our Lord Jesus Christ." As we shall see quite clearly as we go on, the great aim of this letter is to recall men to certainty in regard to the Second Coming of Jesus Christ. The heretics whom Peter is attacking no longer believed in it; it was so long delayed that people had begun to think it would never happen at all.

Such, then, was Peter's message. Having stated it, he goes on to speak of his right to state it; and does something which is, at least at first sight, surprising. His right to speak is that he was with Jesus on the Mount of Transfiguration and that there he saw the glory and the honour which were given to him and heard the voice of God speak to him. That is to say, Peter uses the transfiguration story, not as a foretaste of the Resurrection of Jesus, as it is commonly regarded, but as a foretaste of the triumphant glory of the Second Coming. The transfiguration story is told in *Matthew* 17: 1–8; *Mark* 9: 2–8; *Luke* 9: 28–36. Was Peter right in seeing in it a foretaste of the Second Coming rather than a prefiguring of the Resurrection?

There is one particularly significant thing about the transfiguration story. In all three gospels, it immediately follows the prophecy of Jesus which said that there were some standing there who would not pass from the world until they had seen the Son of Man coming in his kingdom (*Matthew* 16: 29; *Mark* 9: 1; *Luke* 9: 27). That would certainly seem to indicate that the transfiguration and the Second Coming were in some way linked together.

Whatever we may say, this much is certain, that Peter's great aim in this letter is to recall his people to a living belief in the Second Coming of Christ and he bases his right to do so on what he saw on the Mount of Transfiguration.

In verse 16 there is a very interesting word. Peter says, "We were made *eye-witnesses* of his majesty." The word he uses for *eye-witness* is *epoptēs*. In the Greek usage of Peter's day this was a technical word. We have already spoken about the Mystery Religions. They were all of the nature of passion plays, in which the story of a god who lived, suffered, died, and rose again was played out. It was only after a long course of instruction and preparation that the worshipper was finally allowed to be present at the passion play, and to be offered the experience of becoming one with the dying and rising God. When he reached this stage, he was an initiate and the technical word to describe him was *epoptēs*; he was a privileged eye-witness of the experiences of God. So Peter says that the Christian is an eye-witness of the sufferings of Christ. With the eye of faith he sees the Cross; in the experience of faith he dies with Christ to sin and rises to righteousness. His faith has made him one with Jesus Christ in his death and in his risen life and power.

THE WORDS OF THE PROPHETS

2 *Peter* 1: 19–21

So this makes the word of the prophets still more certain for us; and you will do well to pay attention to it, as it shines like a lamp in a dingy place, until the day dawns and the Morning Star rises within your hearts. For you must first and foremost realize that no prophecy in Scripture permits of private interpretation; for no prophecy was ever borne to us by the will of man, but men spoke from God, when they were carried away by the Holy Spirit.

THIS is a particularly difficult passage, because in both halves of it the Greek can mean quite different things. We look at these different possibilities and in each case we take the less probable first.

(i) The first sentence can well mean: "In prophecy we have an even surer guarantee, that is, of the Second Coming." If Peter did say this, he means that the words of the prophets are an even surer guarantee of the reality of the Second Coming than his own experience on the Mount of Transfiguration.

However unlikely it may seem, it is by no means impossible that he did say just that. When he was writing there was a tremendous interest in the words of prophecy whose fulfilment in Christianity was seen to prove its truth. We get case after case of people converted in the days of the early church by reading the Old Testament books and seeing their prophecies fulfilled in Jesus. It would be quite in line with that to declare that the strongest argument for the Second Coming is that the prophets foretold it.

(ii) But we think that the second possibility is to be preferred: "What we saw on the Mount of Transfiguration makes it even more certain that what is foretold in the prophets about the Second Coming must be true."

However we take it, the meaning is that the glory of Jesus on the mountain top and the visions of the prophets combine to make it certain that the Second Coming is a living reality which all men must expect and for which all men must prepare.

There is also a double possibility about the second part of this passage. "No prophecy of the Scripture," as the Revised Standard Version has it, "is a matter of one's own interpretation."

(i) Many of the early scholars took this to mean: "When any of the prophets interpreted any situation in history or told how history was going to unfold itself, they were not expressing a private opinion of their own; they were passing on a revelation which God had given them." This is a perfectly possible meaning. In the Old Testament the mark of a false prophet was that he was speaking *of himself,* as it were, *privately,* and not saying what God had told him to say. Jeremiah condemns the false prophets: "They speak visions of their own minds, not from the mouth of the Lord" (*Jeremiah* 23: 16). Ezekiel says, "Woe to the foolish prophets who follow their own spirit, and have seen nothing" (*Ezekiel* 13: 3). Hippolytus describes the way in which the words of the true prophets came: "They did not speak of their own power, nor did they proclaim what they themselves wished, but first they were given right wisdom by the word, and were then instructed by visions."

On this view the passage means that, when the prophets spoke, it was no private opinion they were giving; it was a revelation from God and, therefore, their words must be carefully heeded.

(ii) The second way to take this passage is as referring to *our* interpretation of the prophets. A situation was confronting Peter in which the heretics and the evil men were interpreting the prophets to suit themselves. On this view, which we support, Peter is saying: "No man can go to Scripture and interpret it as it suits himself."

This is of first-rate practical importance. Peter is saying that no man has the right to interpret Scripture, to use his own word, *privately*. How then must it be interpreted? To answer that question we must ask another. How did the prophets receive their message? They received it from the Spirit. It was sometimes even said that the Spirit of God used the prophets as a writer uses a pen or as a musician uses a musical instrument. In any event the Spirit gave the prophet his message. The obvious conclusion is that it is only through the help of that same Spirit that the prophetic message can be understood. As Paul had already said, spiritual things are spiritually discerned (1 *Corinthians* 2: 14, 15). As the Jews viewed the Holy Spirit, he has two functions—he brings God's truth to men *and* he enables men to understand that truth when it is brought. So, then, Scripture is not to be interpreted by private cleverness or private prejudice; it is to be interpreted by the help of the Holy Spirit by whom it was first given.

Practically that means two things.

(*a*) Throughout all the ages the Spirit has been working in devoted scholars who under the guidance of God have opened the Scriptures to men. If, then, we wish to interpret Scripture, we must never arrogantly insist that our own interpretation must be correct; we must humbly go to the works of the scholars to learn what they have to teach us because of what the Spirit taught them.

(*b*) There is more than that. The one place in which the Spirit specially resides and is specially operative is the Church; and, therefore, Scripture must be interpreted in the light of the teaching, the belief and the tradition of the Church. God is our Father in the faith, but the Church is our mother in the faith. If a man finds that his interpretation of Scripture is at variance with the teaching of the Church, he must humbly examine himself and ask whether his guide has not been his own private wishes rather than the Holy Spirit.

It is Peter's insistence that Scripture does not consist of any man's private opinions but is the revelation of God to men through his Spirit; and that, therefore, its interpretation must not depend on any man's private opinions but must ever be guided by that same Spirit who is still specially operative within the Church.

FALSE PROPHETS

2 *Peter* 2: 1

> There were times when false prophets arose among the people, even as amongst you too there will be false teachers, men who will insidiously introduce destructive heresies and deny the Lord who bought them; and by so doing they will bring swift destruction on themselves.

THAT there should arise false prophets within the Church was something only to be expected, for in every generation false prophets had been responsible for leading God's people astray and for bringing disaster on the nation. It is worth while looking at the false prophets in the Old Testament story for their characteristics were recurring in the time of Peter and are still recurring today.

(i) The false prophets were more interested in gaining popularity than in telling the truth. Their policy was to tell people what they wanted to hear. The false prophets said, "Peace, peace, when there is no peace" (*Jeremiah* 6: 14). They saw visions of peace, when the Lord God was saying that there was no peace (*Ezekiel* 13: 16). In the days of Jehosaphat, Zedekiah, the false prophet, donned his horns of iron and said that Israel would push the Syrians out of the way as he pushed with these horns; Micaiah the true prophet foretold disaster if Jehosaphat went to war. Of course, Zedekiah was popular and his message was accepted; but Jehosaphat went forth to war with the Syrians and perished tragically (1 *Kings* 22). In the days of Jeremiah, Hananiah prophesied the swift end of the power of Babylon, while Jeremiah prophesied the servitude of the nation to her; and again the prophet who told people what they wished to hear was the popular one (*Jeremiah* 28). Diogenes, the great cynic philosopher, spoke of the false teachers of his day whose method was to follow wherever the applause of the crowd led. One of the first characteristics of the false prophet is that he tells men what they want to hear and not the truth they need to hear.

(ii) The false prophets were interested in personal gain. As Micah said, "Its priests teach for hire, and its prophets divine for money" (*Micah* 3: 11). They teach for filthy lucre's sake (*Titus* 1: 11), and they identify godliness and gain, making their religion a money-making thing (1 *Timothy* 6: 5). We can see these exploiters at work in the early church. In *The Didachē, The Teaching of the Twelve Apostles,* which is what might be called the first service-order book, it is laid down that a prophet who asks for money or for a table to be spread in front of him, is a false prophet. "Traffickers in Christ" *The Didachē* calls such men (*The Didachē* II). The false prophet is a covetous creature who regards men as dupes to be exploited for his own ends.

(iii) The false prophets were dissolute in their personal life. Isaiah writes: "The priest and the prophet reel with strong drink; they are confused with wine" (*Isaiah* 28: 7). Jeremiah says, "In the prophets of Jerusalem I have seen a horrible thing; they commit adultery and walk in lies; they strengthen the hands of evil-doers. . : . They lead my people astray by their lies and their recklessness" (*Jeremiah* 23: 14, 32). The false prophet in himself is a seduction to evil rather than an attraction to good.

(iv) The false prophet was above all a man who led other men further away from God instead of closer to him. The prophet who invites the people: "Let us go after other gods," must be mercilessly destroyed (*Deuteronomy* 13: 1–5; 18: 20). The false prophet takes men in the wrong direction.

These were the characteristics of the false prophets in the ancient days and in Peter's time; and they are their characteristics still.

THE SINS OF THE FALSE PROPHETS
AND THEIR END

2 *Peter* 2: 1 (*continued*)

IN this verse Peter has certain things to say about these false prophets and their actions.

(i) They insidiously introduce destructive heresies. The Greek for *heresy* is *hairesis*. It comes from the verb *haireisthai*, which means *to choose*; and originally it was a perfectly honourable word. It simply meant a line of belief and action which a man had chosen for himself. In the New Testament we read of the *hairesis* of the Sadducees, the Pharisees, and the Nazarenes (*Acts* 5: 17; 15: 5; 24: 5). It was perfectly possible to speak of the *hairesis* of Plato and to mean nothing more than those who were Platonist in their thought. It was perfectly possible to speak of a group of doctors who practised a certain method of treatment as a *hairesis*. But very soon in the Christian Church *hairesis* changed its complexion. In Paul's thought heresies and schisms go together as things to be condemned (1 *Corinthians* 11: 18, 19); *haireseis* (the plural form of the word) are part of the works of the flesh; a man that is a heretic is to be warned and even given a second chance, and then rejected (*Titus* 3: 10).

Why the change? The point is that before the coming of Jesus, who is the way, the truth, and the life, there was no such thing as definite, God-given truth. A man was presented with a number of alternatives any one of which he was perfectly free to choose to believe. But with the coming of Jesus, God's truth came to men and they had either to accept or to reject it. A heretic then became a man who believed what *he* wished to believe instead of accepting the truth of God which he ought to believe.

What was happening in the case of Peter's people was that certain self-styled prophets were insidiously persuading men to believe the things they wished to be true rather than the things which God had revealed to be true. They did not set themselves up as opponents of Christianity. Far from it. They set themselves up as the finest fruits of Christian thinking; and so it was gradually and subtly that people were being lured away from God's truth to other men's private opinions, which is what heresy is.

(ii) These men denied the Lord who had bought them. This idea of Christ buying men for himself is one which runs through the whole New Testament. It comes from his own word that he had come to give his life a ransom for many (*Mark* 10: 45). The idea was that men were slaves to sin and Jesus purchased them at the cost of his life for himself, and, therefore, for freedom. "You were bought with a price," says Paul (1 *Corinthians* 7: 23). "Christ redeemed us (bought us out) from the curse of the law" (*Galatians* 3: 13). In the new song in the *Revelation* the hosts of heaven tell how Jesus Christ bought them with his blood out of every kindred and tongue and people and nation (*Revelation* 5: 9). This clearly means two things. It means that the Christian by right of purchase belongs absolutely to Christ; and it means that a life which cost so much cannot be squandered on sin or on cheap things.

The heretics in Peter's letter were *denying* the Lord who bought them. That could mean that they were saying that they did not know Christ; and it could mean that they were denying his authority. But it is not as simple as that; one might say that it is not as honest as that. We have seen that these men claimed to be Christians; more, they claimed to be the wisest and the most advanced of Christians. Let us take a human analogy. Suppose a man says that he loves his wife and yet is consistently unfaithful to her. By his acts of infidelity he denies, gives the lie to, his words of love. Suppose a man protests eternal friendship to someone, and yet is consistently disloyal to him. His actions deny, give the lie to, his protestations of friendship. What these evil men, who were troubling Peter's people, were doing, was to say that they loved and served Christ, while the things they taught and did were a complete denial of him.

(iii) The end of these evil men was destruction. They were insidiously introducing destructive heresies, but these heresies would in the end destroy themselves. There is no more certain way to ultimate condemnation than to teach another to sin.

THE WORK OF FALSEHOOD

2 Peter 2: 2, 3

And many will follow the way of their blatant immoralities and through them the true way will be brought into disrepute. In their evil ambition they will exploit you with cunningly forged arguments. Their sentence was settled long ago, and now it is not inactive, and their destruction is not asleep.

IN this short passage we see four things about the false teachers and their teaching.

(i) We see the *cause* of false teaching. It is *evil ambition*. The word is *pleonexia*; *pleon* means *more* and *exia* comes from the verb *echein,* which means *to have*. *Pleonexia* is *the desire to possess more* but it acquires a certain flavour. It is by no means always a sin to desire to possess more; there are many cases in which that is a perfectly honourable desire, as in the case of virtue, or knowledge, or skill. But *pleonexia* comes to mean the desire to possess that which a man has no right to desire, still less to take. So it can mean covetous desire for money and for other people's goods; lustful desire for someone's person; unholy ambition for prestige and power. False teaching comes from the desire to put its own ideas in the place of the truth of Jesus Christ; the false teacher is guilty of nothing less than of usurping the place of Christ.

(ii) We see the *method* of false teaching. It is the use of cunningly forged arguments. Falsehood is easily resisted when it is presented as falsehood; it is when it is disguised as truth that it becomes menacing. There is only one touchstone. Any teacher's teaching must be tested by the words and presence of Jesus Christ himself.

(iii) We see the *effect* of the false teaching. It was twofold. It encouraged men to take the way of blatant immorality. The word is *aselgeia* which describes the attitude of the man who is lost to shame and cares for the judgment of neither man nor God. We must remember what was at the back of this false teaching. It was perverting the grace of God into a justification for sin. The false teachers were telling men that grace was inexhaustible and that, therefore, they were free to sin as they liked for grace would forgive.

This false teaching had a second effect. It brought Christianity into disrepute. In the early days, just as now, every Christian was a good or bad advertisement for Christianity and the Christian Church. It is Paul's accusation to the Jews that through them the name of God has been brought into disrepute (*Romans* 2: 24). In the Pastoral Epistles the younger women are urged to behave with such modesty and chastity that the Church will never be brought into disrepute (*Titus* 2: 5). Any teaching which produces a person who repels men from Christianity instead of attracting them to it is false teaching, and the work of those who are enemies of Christ.

(iv) We see the *ultimate end* of false teaching and that is destruction. Sentence was passed on the false prophets long ago; the Old Testament pronounced their doom (*Deuteronomy* 13: 1–5). It might look as if that sentence had become inoperative or was slumbering, but it was still valid, and the day would come when the false teachers would pay the terrible price of their falsehood. No man who leads another astray will ever escape his own judgment.

THE FATE OF THE WICKED AND THE RESCUE OF
THE RIGHTEOUS

2 Peter 2: 4–11

If God did not spare even angels who had sinned, but condemned them to the lowest hell and committed them to the pits
of darkness, where they remain kept for judgment; if he did not
spare the ancient world, but preserved in safety Noah, the preacher
of righteousness, with seven others, when he despatched the
flood on a world of impious men; if he reduced the cities of
Sodom and Gomorrah to ashes, when he sentenced them to
destruction and so gave an example of what would happen to
those who would one day act with impiety, but rescued righteous
Lot, who was distressed by the blatantly immoral conduct of
lawless men, for, to such a man, righteous in his looking and
in his hearing, it was torture for his righteous soul to live his
daily life amidst such people and amidst such lawless deeds—
if all this is so, you can be sure that the Lord knows how to rescue
truly religious men from trial and how to preserve the unrighteous
under punishment, until the day of judgment comes, especially
those whose lives are dominated by the polluting lusts of the flesh
and who despise the celestial powers. Audacious, self-willed men
they are; they do not shrink from speaking evil of the angelic
glories, whereas angels who are greater in strength and power do
not bring an accusation of evil against them in the presence of the
Lord.

HERE is a passage which for us combines undoubted power
and equally undoubted obscurity. The white heat of its
rhetorical intensity glows through it to this day; but it
moves in allusions which would be terrifyingly effective to
those who heard it for the first time, but which have become
unfamiliar to us today. It cites three notorious examples of sin
and its destruction; and in two of the cases it shows how,
when sin was obliterated, righteousness was rescued and
preserved by the mercy and the grace of God. Let us look
at these examples one by one.

1. THE SIN OF THE ANGELS

Before we retell the story which lies behind this in Jewish legend, there are two separate words at which we must look.

Peter says that God condemned the sinning angels to the lowest depths of hell. Literally the Greek says that God condemned the angels to *Tartarus* (*tartaroun*). Tartarus was not a Hebrew conception but Greek. In Greek mythology Tartarus was the lowest hell; it was as far beneath Hades as the heaven is high above the earth. In particular it was the place into which there had been cast the Titans who had rebelled against Zeus, the Father of gods and men.

The second word is that which speaks of the *pits* of darkness. Here there is a doubt. There are two Greek words, both rather uncommon, which are confused in this passage. One is *siros* or *seiros* which originally meant a great earthenware jar for the storing of grain. Then it came to mean the great underground pits in which grain was stored and which served as granaries. *Siros* has come into English *via* Provençal in the form of *silo,* which still describes the towers in which grain is stored. Still later the word went on to mean a pit in which a wolf or other wild animal was trapped. If we think that this is the word which Peter uses, and according to the best manuscripts it is, it will mean that the wicked angels were cast into great subterranean pits and kept there in darkness and in punishment. This well suits the idea of a Tartarus beneath the lowest depths of Hades.

But there is a very similar word *seira*, which means a *chain*. This is the word which the Authorized Version translates when it speaks of *chains of darkness* (verse 4). The Greek manuscripts of *Second Peter* vary between *seiroi,* pits, and *seirai,* chains. But the better manuscripts have *seiroi,* and *pits of darkness* makes better sense than *chains of darkness*; so we may take *seiros* as right, and assume that here the Authorized Version is in error.

The story of the fall of the angels is one which rooted itself deeply in Hebrew thought and which underwent much

development as the years went on. The original story is in
Genesis 6: 1–5. There the angels are called *the sons of God,*
as they commonly are in the Old Testament. In *Job, the sons
of God* come to present themselves before the Lord, and Satan
comes amongst them (*Job* 1: 6; cp. 2: 1; 38: 7). The Psalmist
speaks of the sons of gods (*Psalm* 89: 6). These angels came
to earth and seduced mortal women. The result of this lustful
union was the race of giants; and through them wickedness
came upon the earth. Clearly this is an old, old story
belonging to the childhood of the race.

This story was much developed in the *Book of Enoch*, and
it is from it that Peter is drawing his allusions, for in his day
that was a book which everyone would know. In *Enoch* the
angels are called *The Watchers*. Their leader in rebellion was
Semjaza or Azazel. At his instigation they descended to
Mount Hermon in the days of Jared, the father of Enoch.
They took mortal wives and instructed them in magic and
in arts which gave them power. They produced the race of the
giants, and the giants produced the *nephillim*, the giants who
inhabited the land of Canaan and of whom the people were
afraid (*Numbers* 13: 33).

These giants became cannibals and were guilty of every
kind of lust and crime, and especially of insolent arrogance
to God and man. The apocryphal literature has many
references to them and their pride. *Wisdom* (14: 6) tells how
the proud giants perished. *Ecclesiasticus* (16: 7) tells how
the ancient giants fell away in the strength of their foolishness.
They had no wisdom and they perished in their folly (*Baruch*
3: 26–28). Josephus says that they were arrogant and
contemptuous of all that was good and trusted in their own
strength (*Antiquities* 1.3.1). Job says that God charged his
angels with folly (*Job* 4: 18).

This old story makes a strange and fleeting appearance in the
letters of Paul. In 1 *Corinthians* 11: 10 Paul says that women
must have their hair covered in the Church *because of the
angels*. Behind that strange saying lies the old belief that it
was the loveliness of the long hair of the women of the

olden times which moved the angels to desire; and Paul wishes to see that the angels are not tempted again.

In the end even men complained of the sorrow and misery brought into the world by these giants through the sin of the angels. The result was that God sent out his archangels. Raphael bound Azazel hand and foot and shut him up in darkness; Gabriel slew the giants; and the Watchers, the sinning angels, were shut up in the abysses of darkness under the mountains for seventy generations and then confined for ever in everlasting fire. Here is the story which is in Peter's mind; and which his readers well knew. The angels had sinned and God had sent his destruction, and they were shut up for ever in the pits of darkness and the depths of hell. That is what happens to rebellious sin.

The story does not stop there; and it reappears in another of its forms in this passage of *Second Peter*. In verse 10 Peter speaks of those who live lives dominated by the polluting lusts of the flesh and who despise the *celestial powers*. The word is *kuriotēs*, which is the name of one of the ranks of angels. They speak evil of the *angelic glories*. The word is *doxai,* which also is a word for one of the ranks of angels. They slander the angels and bring them into disrepute.

Here is where the second turn of the story comes in. Obviously this story of the angels is very primitive and, as time went on, it became rather an awkward and embarrassing story because of its ascription of lust to angels. So in later Jewish and Christian thought two lines of thought developed. First, it was denied that the story involved angels at all. The sons of God were said to be good men who were the descendants of Seth, and the daughters of men were said to be evil women who were the daughters of Cain and corrupted the good men. There is no scriptural evidence for this distinction and this way of escape. Second, the whole story was allegorised. It was claimed, for instance by Philo, that it was never meant to be taken literally and described the fall of the human soul under the attack of the seductions of lustful pleasures. Augustine declared that no man could take this story literally and talk of the angels like that. Cyril of Alexandria said that it could not be taken literally, for did not Jesus say that in the after-life men would be like angels and there would be no marrying or giving in marriage (*Matthew* 22: 30)? Chrysostom said that, if the story was taken literally, it was nothing short of blasphemy. And Cyril went on to say that the story was nothing other than an incentive to sin, if it was taken as literally true.

It is clear that men began to see that this was indeed a dangerous story. Here we get our clue as to what Peter means when he speaks of men who despise the celestial powers and bring the angelic glories into disrepute by speaking slanderously of them. The men whom Peter was opposing were turning their religion into an excuse for blatant immorality. Cyril of Alexandria makes it clear that in his day the story could be used as an incentive to sin. Most probably what was happening was that the wicked men of Peter's time were citing the example of the angels as a justification for their own sin. They were saying, "If angels came from heaven and took mortal women, why should not we?" They were making the conduct of the angels an excuse for their own sin.

We have to go still further with this passage. In verse 11 it finishes very obscurely. It says that angels who are greater in strength and in power do not bring a slanderous charge against them in the presence of God. Once again Peter is speaking allusively, in a way that would be clear enough to the people of his day but which is obscure to us. His reference may be to either of two stories.

(*a*) He may be referring to the story to which Jude refers in *Jude* 9; that the archangel Michael was entrusted with the burying of the body of Moses. Satan claimed the body on the grounds that all matter belonged to him and that once Moses had murdered an Egyptian. Michael did not bring a railing charge against Satan; all he said was: "The Lord rebuke you." The point is that even an angel so great as Michael would not bring an evil charge against an angel so dark as Satan. He left the matter to God. If Michael refrained from slandering an evil angel, how can men bring slanderous charges against the angels of God?

(*b*) He may be referring to a further development of the *Enoch* story. *Enoch* tells that when the conduct of the giants on earth became intolerable, men made their complaint to the archangels Michael, Uriel, Gabriel and Raphael. The archangels took this complaint to God; but they did not rail against the evil angels who were responsible for it all; they simply took the story to God, for him to deal with (*Enoch* 9).

As far as we can see today, the situation behind Peter's allusions is that the wicked men who were the slaves of lust claimed that the angels were their examples and their justification and so slandered them; Peter reminds them that not even archangels dared slander other angels and demands how men can dare to do so.

This is a strange and difficult passage; but the meaning is clear. Even angels, when they sinned, were punished. How much more shall men be punished? Angels could not rebel against God and escape the consequences. How shall men escape? And men need not seek to put the blame on others, not even on angels; nothing but their own rebelliousness is responsible for their sin.

2. THE MEN OF THE FLOOD AND THE RESCUE OF NOAH

The second illustration of the destruction of wickedness which Peter chooses may be said to lead on from the first. The sin introduced into the world by the sinning angels led to that intolerable sin which ended in the destruction by the deluge (*Genesis* 6: 5). In the midst of this destruction God did not forget those who had clung to him. Noah was saved together with seven others, his wife, his sons, Shem, Ham, and Japhet, and their wives. In Jewish tradition Noah acquired a very special place. Not only was he regarded as the one

man who had been saved; but also as the preacher who had
done his best to turn men from the evil of their ways.
Josephus says, "Many angels of God lay with women and
begat sons, who were violent and who despised all good, on
account of their reliance on their own strength. . . . But
Noah displeased and distressed at their behaviour, tried to
induce them to alter their dispositions and conduct for the
better" (*Antiquities* 1.3.1).

Attention in this passage is concentrated not so much on the
people who were destroyed as on the man who was saved.
Noah is offered as the type of man who, amidst the destruction
of the wicked, receives the salvation of God. His outstanding
qualities were two.

(i) In the midst of a sinning generation he remained faithful
to God. Later Paul was to urge his people to be not conformed
to the world but transformed from it (*Romans* 12: 2). It may
well be said that often the most dangerous sin of all is
conformity. To be the same as others is always easy; to be
different is always difficult. But from the days of Noah until
now he who would be the servant of God must be prepared
to be different from the world.

(ii) The later legends pick out another characteristic of
Noah. He was the preacher of righteousness. The word for
preacher used here is *kērux,* which literally means *a herald.*
Epictetus called the philosopher the *kērux* of the gods. The
preacher is the man who brings to men an announcement
from God. Here is something of very considerable significance.
The good man is concerned not only with the saving of his
own soul but just as much with the saving of the souls of
others. He does not, in order to preserve his own purity
live apart from men. He is concerned to bring God's message
to them. A man ought never to keep to himself the grace
which he has received. It is always his duty to bring light
to those who sit in darkness, guidance to the wanderer and
warning to those who are going astray.

3. The Destruction of Sodom and Gomorrah and the Rescue of Lot

THE third example is the destruction of Sodom and Gomorrah and the rescue of Lot.

The terrible and dramatic story is told in *Genesis* 18 and 19. It begins with Abraham's plea that God should not destroy the righteous with the guilty and his request that, if even ten just men are found in these cities, they may be spared (*Genesis* 18: 16–33). Then follows one of the grimmest tales in the Old Testament.

The angelic visitors came to Lot and he persuaded them to stay with him; but his house was surrounded by the men of Sodom demanding that these strangers might be brought out for them to use for their unnatural lust (*Genesis* 19: 1–11). By that terrible deed—at once the abuse of hospitality, the insulting of angels and the raging of unnatural lust—the doom of the cities was sealed. As the destruction of heaven came upon them Lot and his family were saved, except his wife, who lingered and looked back and turned into a pillar of salt (*Genesis* 19: 12–26). "So it was that, when God destroyed the cities of the valley, God remembered Abraham, and sent Lot out of the midst of the overthrow, when he overthrew the cities in which Lot dwelt" (*Genesis* 19: 29). Here again is the story of the destruction of sin and the rescue of righteousness. As in Noah, we see in Lot the characteristics of the righteous man.

(i) Lot lived in the midst of evil, and the very sight of it was a constant distress to him. Moffatt reminds us of the saying of Newman: "Our great security against sin lies in being shocked at it." Here is something very significant. It often happens that, when evils first emerge, people are shocked at them; but, as time goes on, they cease to be shocked at them and accept them as a matter of course. There are many things at which we ought to be shocked. In our own generation there are the problems of prostitution and promiscuity, drunkenness and drugs, the extraordinary gambling fever which has the country in its grip, the breakdown of the marriage bond, violence, vandalism and crime, death upon the roads, still-existing slum conditions and many others. In many cases the tragedy is that these things have ceased to shock and are accepted in a matter-of-fact style as part of the normal order of things. For the good of the world and of our own souls, we must keep alive the sensitiveness which is shocked by sin.

(ii) Lot lived in the midst of evil, and yet he escaped its taint. Amidst the sin of Sodom he remained true to God. If a man will remember it, he has in the grace of God an antiseptic which will preserve him from the infection of sin. No man need be the slave of the environment in which he happens to find himself.

(iii) When the worst came to the worst, Lot was willing to make a clean break with his environment. He was prepared, however much he did not want to do so, to leave it for ever. It was because his wife was not prepared to make the clean break that she perished. There is a strange verse in the Old Testament story. It says that, when Lot lingered, the angelic messengers took hold of his hand (*Genesis* 19: 16). There are times when the influence of heaven tries to force us out of some evil situation. It may come to any man to have to make the choice between security and the new start; and there are times when a man can save his soul only by breaking clean away from his present situation and beginning all over again. It was in doing just this that Lot found his salvation; and it was in failing to do just this that his wife lost hers.

THE PICTURE OF THE EVIL MAN

2 Peter 2: 4–11 (*continued*)

VERSES 9–11 give us a picture of the evil man. Peter with a few swift, vivid strokes of the pen paints the outstanding characteristics of him who may properly be called the bad man.

(i) He is *the desire-dominated man*. His life is dominated by the lusts of the flesh. Such a man is guilty of two sins.

(*a*) Every man has two sides to his nature. He has a physical side; he has instincts, passions and impulses which he shares with the animal creation. These instincts are good—*if they are kept in their proper place*. They are even necessary for the preservation of individual life and the continuation of the race. The word *temperament* literally means a *mixture*. The picture behind it is that human nature consists of a large variety of ingredients all mixed together. It is clear that the efficacy of any mixture depends on each ingredient being there in its proper proportion. Wherever there is either excess or defect the mixture is not what it ought to be. Man has a physical nature and also a spiritual nature; and manhood depends on a correct mixture of the two. The desire-dominated man has allowed his animal nature to usurp a place it should not have; he has allowed the ingredients to get out of proportion and the recipe for manhood has gone wrong.

(*b*) There is a reason for this loss of proportion—*selfishness*. The root evil of the lust-dominated life is that it proceeds on the assumption that nothing matters but the gratification of its own desires and the expression of its own feelings. It has ceased to have any respect or care for others. Selfishness and desire go hand in hand.

The bad man is he who has allowed one side of his nature a far greater place than it ought to have and who has done so because he is essentially selfish.

(ii) He is the *audacious man*. The Greek is *tolmētēs*, from the verb *tolman, to dare*. There are two kinds of daring. There is the daring which is a noble thing, the mark of true courage. There is the daring which is an evil thing, the shameless performance of things which are an affront to decency and right. As the character in Shakespeare had it: "I dare do all becomes a man. Who dares do more is none." The bad man is he who has the audacity to defy the will of God as it is known to him.

(iii) He is the *self-willed man. Self-willed* is not really an adequate translation. The Greek is *authadēs*, derived from *autos, self,* and *hadōn, pleasing,* and used of a man who had no idea of anything other than pleasing himself. In it there is

always the element of obstinacy. If a man is *authadēs*, no
logic, nor common sense, nor appeal, nor sense of decency will
keep him from doing what he wants to do. As R. C. Trench
says, "Thus obstinately maintaining his own opinion, or
asserting his own rights, he is reckless of the rights, opinions
and interests of others." The man who is *authadēs* is
stubbornly and arrogantly and even brutally determined on
his own way. The bad man is he who has no regard for either
human appeal or divine guidance.

(iv) He is *the man who is contemptuous of the angels.* We
have already seen how this goes back to allusions in Hebrew
tradition which are obscure to us. But it has a wider meaning.
The bad man insists on living in one world. To him the
spiritual world does not exist and he never hears the voices
from beyond. He is of the earth earthy. He has forgotten
that there is a heaven and is blind and deaf when the
sights and sounds of heaven break through to him.

DELUDING SELF AND DELUDING OTHERS

2 Peter 2: 12–14

> But these, like brute beasts, knowing no law but their instincts,
> born only for capture and corruption, speak evil of the things
> about which they know nothing; they will be destroyed with their
> own corruption, and, like a man who is cheated, they will even
> lose the reward at which their iniquity aimed. They regard daylight
> debauchery as pleasure. They are spots and blots, revelling in their
> dissipations, carousing in their cliques amongst you. They have
> eyes full of adultery, eyes which can never gaze their fill on sin.
> They entrap souls which are not firmly founded in the faith.
> They have a heart which is trained in unbridled ambition for the
> things they have no right to have. They are accursed.

PETER launches out into a long passage of magnificent
invective. Through it glows the fiery heat of flaming moral
indignation.

The evil men are like brute beasts, slaves of their animal

instincts. But a beast is born only for capture and death, says Peter; it has no other destiny. Even so, there is something self-destroying in fleshly pleasure. To make such pleasure the be-all and the end-all of life is a suicidal policy and in the end even the pleasure is lost. The point Peter is making is this, and it is eternally valid. If a man dedicates himself to these fleshly pleasures, in the end he so ruins himself in bodily health and in spiritual and mental character, that he cannot enjoy even them. The glutton destroys his appetite in the end, the drunkard his health, the sensualist his body, the self-indulgent his character and peace of mind.

These men regard daylight debauchery, dissipated revelling, abandoned carousing as pleasure. They are blots on the Christian fellowship; they are like the blemishes on an animal, which make it unfit to be offered to God. Once again we must note that what Peter is saying is not only religious truth but also sound common sense. The pleasures of the body are demonstrably subject to the law of diminishing returns. In themselves they lose their thrill, so that as time goes on it takes more and more of them to satisfy. The luxury must become ever more luxurious; the wine must flow ever more freely; everything must be done to make the thrill sharper and more intense. Further, a man becomes less and less able to enjoy these pleasures. He has given himself to a life that has no future and to pleasure which ends in pain.

Peter goes on. In verse 14 he uses an extraordinary phrase which, strictly, will not translate into English at all. We have translated it: "They have eyes full of adultery." The Greek literally is: "They have eyes which are full of an adulteress." Most probably the meaning is they see a possible adulteress in every woman, wondering how she can be persuaded to gratify their lusts. "The hand and the eye," said the Jewish teachers, "are the brokers of sin." As Jesus said, such people look in order to lust (*Matthew* 5: 28). They have come to such a stage that they cannot look on anyone without lust's calculation.

As Peter speaks of this, there is a terrible deliberateness about it. They have *hearts trained in unbridled ambition for the things they have no right to have*. We have taken a whole phrase to translate the one word *pleonexia* which means the desire to have more of the things which a man has no right even to desire, let alone have. The picture is a terrible one. The word used for *trained* is used for an athlete exercising himself for the games. These people have actually trained their minds to concentrate on nothing but the forbidden desire. They have deliberately fought with conscience until they have destroyed it; they have deliberately struggled with their finer feelings until they have strangled them.

There remains in this passage one further charge. It would be bad if these people deluded only themselves; it is worse that they delude others. They entrap souls not firmly founded in the faith. The word used for *to entrap* is *deleazein*, which means *to catch with a bait*. A man becomes really bad when he sets out to make others as bad as himself. The hymn has it:

> All the mischief we have wrought,
> All forbidden things we've sought,
> All the sin to others taught:
> Forgive, O Lord, for Jesus' sake.

Every man must bear the responsibility for his own sins, but to add to that the responsibility for the sins of others is to carry an intolerable burden.

ON THE WRONG ROAD

2 *Peter* 2: 15, 16

They have left the straight road and have gone awandering, and have followed the road of Balaam, the son of Beor, who loved the profit which unrighteousness brings and who was convicted of his lawlessness. A dumb ass spoke with a man's voice and checked the prophet's folly.

PETER likens the evil men of his time to the prophet Balaam. In the popular Jewish mind Balaam had come to stand as the type of all false prophets. His story is told in *Numbers* 22 to 24. Balak, King of Moab, was alarmed at the steady and apparently irresistible advance of the Israelites. In an attempt to check it he sent for Balaam to come and curse the Israelites for him, offering him great rewards. To the end of the day Balaam refused to curse the Israelites, but his covetous heart longed after the rich rewards which Balak was offering. At Balak's renewed request Balaam played with fire enough to agree to meet him. On the way his ass stopped, because it saw the angel of the Lord standing in its path, and rebuked Balaam.

It is true that Balaam did not succumb to Balak's bribes, but if ever a man wanted to accept a bribe, that man was he. In *Numbers* 25 there follows another story. It tells how the Israelites were seduced into the worship of Baal and into lustful alliances with Moabite women. Jewish belief was that Balaam was responsible for leading the children of Israel astray; and when the Israelites entered into possession of the land, "Balaam the son of Beor they slew with the sword" (*Numbers* 31 : 8). In view of all this Balaam became increasingly the type of the false prophet. He had two characteristics which were repeated in the evil men of Peter's day.

(i) Balaam was *covetous*. As the *Numbers* story unfolds we can see his fingers itching to get at the gold of Balak. True, he did not take it; but the desire was there. The evil men of Peter's day were covetous; out for what they could get and ready to exploit their membership of the Church for gain.

(ii) Balaam *taught Israel to sin*. He led the people out of the straight and into the crooked way. He persuaded them to forget their promises to God. The evil men of Peter's day were seducing Christians from the Christian way and causing them to break the pledges of loyalty they had given to Jesus Christ.

The man who loves gain and who lures others to evil for ever stands condemned.

THE PERILS OF RELAPSE

2 Peter 2: 17–22

These people are waterless springs, mists driven by a squall of wind; and the gloom of darkness is reserved for them. With talk at once arrogant and futile, they ensnare by appeals to shameless, sensual passions those who are only just escaping from the company of those who live in error, promising them freedom, while they themselves are the slaves of moral corruption; for a man is in a state of slavery to that which has reduced him to helplessness.

If they have escaped the pollution of the world by the knowledge of the Lord and Saviour Jesus Christ, and if they allow themselves again to become involved in these things and to be reduced to moral helplessness by them, the last state is for them worse than the first. It would be better for them not to have known the way of righteousness than to have known it and then to turn back from the holy commandment which was handed down to them. In them the truth of the proverb is plain to see: "A dog returns to his own vomit" and "The sow which has been washed returns to rolling in the mud."

PETER is still rolling out his tremendous denunciation of the evil men.

They flatter only to deceive. They are like wells with no water and like mists blown past by a squall of wind. Think of a traveller in the desert being told that ahead lies a spring where he can quench his thirst and then arriving at that spring to find it dried up and useless. Think of the husbandman praying for rain for his parched crops and then seeing the cloud that promised rain blown uselessly by. As Bigg has it: "A teacher without knowledge is like a well without water." These men are like Milton's shepherds whose "hungry sheep look up and are not fed." They promise a gospel and in the end have nothing to offer the thirsty soul.

Their teaching is a combination of arrogance and futility. Christian liberty always carries danger. Paul tells his people that they have indeed been called to liberty but that they must

not use it for an occasion to the flesh (*Galatians* 5: 13). Peter
tells his people that indeed they are free but they must not use
their freedom as a cloak of maliciousness (1 *Peter* 2: 16). These
false teachers offered freedom, but it was freedom to sin as
much as a man liked. They appealed not to the best but to the
worst in a man. Peter is quite clear that they did this because
they were slaves to their own lusts. Seneca said, "To be
enslaved to oneself is the heaviest of all servitudes." Persius
spoke to the lustful debauchees of his day of "the masters that
grow up within that sickly breast of yours." These teachers
were offering liberty when they themselves were slaves, and the
liberty they were offering was the liberty to become slaves of
lust. Their message was *arrogant* because it was the contradiction of the message of Christ; it was *futile* because he who
followed it would find himself a slave. Here again in the background is the fundamental heresy which makes grace a
justification for sin instead of a power and a summons to
nobility.

If they have once known the real way of Christ and have
relapsed into this, their case is even worse. They are like the
man in the parable whose last state was worse than his first
(*Matthew* 12: 45; *Luke* 11: 26). If a man has never known the
right way, he cannot be condemned for not following it. But, if
he has known it and then deliberately taken the other way, he
sins against the light; and it were better for him that he had
never known the truth, for his knowledge of the truth has
become his condemnation. A man should never forget the
responsibility which knowledge brings.

Peter ends with contempt. These evil men are like dogs who
return to their vomit (*Proverbs* 26: 11) or like a sow which has
been scrubbed and then goes back to rolling in the mud. They
have seen Christ but are so morally degraded by their own
choice that they prefer to wallow in the depths of sin rather
than to climb the heights of virtue. It is a dreadful warning that
a man can make himself such that in the end the tentacles of
sin are inextricably around him and virtue for him has lost
its beauty.

THE PRINCIPLES OF PREACHING

2 *Peter* 3: 1, 2

> Beloved, this is now the second letter that I have written to you,
> and my object in both of them is to rouse by reminder your pure
> mind to remember the words spoken by the prophets in former times,
> and the commandment of the Lord and Saviour which was brought
> to you by your apostles.

IN this passage we see clearly displayed the˙ principles of
preaching which Peter observed.

(i) He believed in the value of *repetition*. He knows that it is
necessary for a thing to be said over and over again if it is to
penetrate the mind. When Paul was writing to the Philippians,
he said that to repeat the same thing over and over again was
not a weariness to him, and for them it was the only safe way
(*Philippians* 3: 1). It is by continued repetition that the
rudiments of knowledge are settled in the mind of the child.
There is something of significance here. It may well be that
often we are too desirous of novelty, too eager to say new
things, when what is needed is a repetition of the eternal truths
which men so quickly forget and whose significance they so
often refuse to see. There are certain foods of which a man
does not get tired; necessary for his daily sustenance, they are
set before him every day. We speak about a man's *daily bread*.
And there are certain great Christian truths which have to be
repeated again and again and which must never be pushed into
the background in the desire for novelty.

(ii) He believed in *the need for reminder*. Again and again
the New Testament makes it clear that preaching and teaching
are so often not the introducing of new truth but the reminding
of a man of what he already knows. Moffatt quotes a saying
of Dr. Johnson: "It is not sufficiently considered that men
more frequently require to be reminded than informed." The
Greeks spoke of "time which wipes all things out," as if the
human mind were a slate and time a sponge which passes across
it with a certain erasing quality. We are so often in the position

of men whose need is not so much to be taught as to be reminded of what we already know.

(iii) He believed in *the value of a compliment*. It is his intention to rouse *their pure mind*. The word he uses for pure is *eilikrinēs*, which may have either of two meanings. It may mean that which is sifted until there is no admixture of chaff left; or it may mean that which is so flawless that it may be held up to the light of the sun. Plato uses this same phrase—*eilikrinēs dianoia*—in the sense of *pure reason*, reason which is unaffected by the seductive influence of the senses. By using this phrase Peter appeals to his people as having minds uncontaminated by heresy. It is as if he said to them: "You really are fine people—if you would only remember it." The approach of the preacher should so often be that his hearers are not wretched creatures who deserve to be damned but splendid creatures who must be saved. They are not so much like rubbish fit to be burned as like jewels to be rescued from the mud into which they have fallen. Donald Hankey tells of "the beloved captain" whose men would follow him anywhere. He looked at them and they looked at him, and they were filled with the determination to be what he believed them to be. We always get further with people when we believe in them than when we despise them.

(iv) He believed in *the unity of Scripture*. As he saw it there was a pattern in Scripture; and the Bible was a book centred in Christ. The Old Testament foretells Christ; the gospels tell of Jesus the Christ; and the apostles bring the message of that Christ to men.

THE DENIAL OF THE SECOND COMING

2 Peter 3: 3, 4

To begin with, you are well aware that in the last days there will come mockers with their mocking, guiding their steps by the law of their own lusts and saying, "What has happened to the promise of his Coming? For, since the day when our fathers fell asleep, everything remains the same as it was from the foundation of the world."

THE characteristic of the heretics which worried Peter most of all was their denial of the Second Coming of Jesus. Literally, their question was: "Where is the promise of his Coming?" That was a form of Hebrew expression which implied that the thing asked about did not exist at all. "Where is the God of justice?" asked the evil men of Malachi's day (*Malachi* 2: 17). "Where is your God?" the heathen demanded of the Psalmist (*Psalm* 42: 3; 79: 10). "Where is the word of the Lord?" his enemies asked Jeremiah (*Jeremiah* 17: 15). In every case the implication of the question is that the thing or the person asked about does not exist. The heretics of Peter's day were denying that Jesus Christ would ever come again. It will be best here at the beginning to summarize their argument and Peter's answer to it.

The argument of Peter's opponents was twofold (verse 4). "What has happened," they demanded, "to the promise of the Second Coming?" Their first argument was that the promise had been so long delayed that it was safe to take it that it would never be fulfilled. Their second assertion was that their fathers had died and the world was going on precisely as it always did. Their argument was that this was characteristically a stable universe and convulsive upheavals like the Second Coming did not happen in such a universe.

Peter's response is also twofold. He deals with the second argument first (verses 5–7). His argument is that, in fact, this is not a stable universe, that once it was destroyed by water in the time of the Flood and that a second destruction, this time by fire, is on the way.

The second part of his reply is in verses 8 and 9. His opponents speak of a delay so long that they can safely assume that the Second Coming is not going to happen at all. Peter's is a double answer. (*a*) We must see time as God sees it. With him a day is as a thousand years and a thousand years as a day. "God does not pay every Friday night." (*b*) In any event God's apparent slowness to act is not dilatoriness. It is, in fact, mercy. He holds his hand in order to give sinning men another chance to repent and find salvation.

Peter goes on to his conclusion (verse 10). The Second Coming is on the way and it will come with a sudden terror and destruction which will dissolve the universe in melting heat.

Finally comes his practical demand in face of all this. If we are living in a universe on which Jesus Christ is going to descend and which is hastening towards the destruction of the wicked, surely it behoves us to live in holiness so that we may be spared when the terrible day does come. The Second Coming is used as a tremendous motive for moral amendment so that a man may prepare himself to meet his God.

Such, then, is the general scheme of this chapter and now we look at it section by section.

DESTRUCTION BY FLOOD

2 *Peter* 3: 5, 6

> What they wilfully fail to see is that long ago the heavens were created and the earth was composed out of water and through water; and through these waters the ancient world perished, when it was overwhelmed in a deluge of water.

PETER's first argument is that the world is not eternally stable. The point he is making is that the ancient world was destroyed by water, just as the present world is going to be destroyed by fire. The detail of this passage is, however, difficult.

He says that the earth was composed out of water and through water. According to the *Genesis* story in the beginning there was a kind of watery chaos. "The Spirit of God moved over the face of the waters. . . . God said, Let there be a firmament in the midst of the waters, and let it separate the waters from the waters" (*Genesis* 1: 2, 6). Out of this watery chaos the world was formed. Further, it is through water that the world is sustained, because life is sustained by the rain which comes down from the skies. What Peter means is that the world was created out of water and is sustained by water;

and it was through this same element that the ancient world was destroyed.

Further to clarify this passage we have to note that the flood legend developed. As so often in *Second Peter* and *Jude* the picture behind this comes not directly from the Old Testament but from the Book of Enoch. In *Enoch* 83: 3–5 Enoch has a vision: "I saw in a vision how the heaven collapsed and fell to the earth, and, where it fell to the earth, I saw how the earth was swallowed up in a great abyss." In the later stories the flood involved not only the obliteration of sinners but the total destruction of heaven and earth. So the warning which Peter is giving may be put like this: "You say that as things are, so they have ever been and so they ever will be. You build your hopes on the idea that this is an unchanging universe. You are wrong, for the ancient world was formed out of water and was sustained by water, and it perished in the flood."

We may say that this is only an old legend more than half-buried in the antiquities of the past. But we cannot say that a passage like this has no significance for us. When we strip away the old Jewish legend and its later development, we are still left with this permanent truth that the man who will read history with open eyes can see within it the moral law at work and God's dealings with men. Froude, the great historian, said that history is a voice sounding across the centuries that in the end it is always ill with the wicked and well with the good. When Oliver Cromwell was arranging his son Richard's education, he said, "I would have him know a little history." In fact, the lesson of history is that there is a moral order in the universe and that he who defies it does so at his peril.

DESTRUCTION BY FIRE

2 *Peter* 3: 7

But by the same word the present heavens and earth are treasured up for fire, reserved for the day of judgment and the destruction of impious men.

IT is Peter's conviction that, as the ancient world was destroyed by water, the present world will be destroyed by fire. He says that that is stated "by the same word." What he means is that the Old Testament tells of the flood in the past and warns of the destruction by fire in the future. There are many passages in the prophets which he would take quite literally and which must have been in his mind. Joel foresaw a time when God would show blood, and fire, and pillars of smoke (*Joel* 2:30). The Psalmist has a picture in which, when God comes, a devouring fire shall precede him (*Psalm* 50:3). Isaiah speaks of a flame of devouring fire (*Isaiah* 29:6; 30:30). The Lord will come with fire; by fire and by his sword will the Lord plead with all flesh (*Isaiah* 66:15, 16). Nahum has it that the hills melt and the earth is burned at his presence; his fury is poured out like fire (*Nahum* 1:5, 6). In the picture of Malachi the day of the Lord shall burn as an oven (*Malachi* 4:1). If the old pictures are taken literally, Peter has plenty of material for his prophecy.

The Stoics also had a doctrine of the destruction of the world by fire; but it was a grim thing. They held that the universe completed a cycle; that it was consumed in flames; and that everything then started all over again, exactly as it was. They had the strange idea that at the end of the cycle the planets were in exactly the same position as when the world began. "This produces the conflagration and destruction of everything which exists," says Chrysippus. He goes on: "Then again the universe is restored anew in a precisely similar arrangement as before . . . Socrates and Plato and each individual man will live again, with the same friends and fellow-citizens. They will go through the same experiences and the same activities. Every city and village and field will be restored, just as it was. And this restoration of the universe takes place, not once, but over and over again—indeed to all eternity without end. . . . For there will never be any new thing other than that which has been before, but everything is repeated down to the minutest detail." History as an eternal tread-mill, the unceasing recurrence of the sins, the sorrows and the mistakes of men—that is one of the grimmest views of history that the mind of man has ever conceived.

It must always be remembered that, as the Jewish prophets saw it, and as Peter saw it, this world will be destroyed with the conflagration of God but the result will not be obliteration and the grim repetition of what has been before; the result will be a new heaven and a new earth. For the biblical view of the world there is something beyond destruction; there is the new creation of God. The worst that the prophet can conceive is not the death agony of the old world so much as the birth pangs of the new.

THE MERCY OF GOD'S DELAY

2 Peter 3: 8, 9

Beloved, you must not shut your eyes to this one fact that with the Lord one day is as a thousand years and a thousand years as one day. It is not that God is dilatory in fulfilling his promise, as some people reckon dilatoriness; but it is that for your sakes he patiently withholds his hand, because he does not wish any to perish, but wishes all to take the way to repentance.

THERE are in this passage three great truths on which to nourish the mind and rest the heart.

(i) Time is not the same to God as it is to man. As the Psalmist had it: "A thousand years in thy sight are but as yesterday when it is past, or as a watch in the night" (*Psalm* 90: 4). When we think of the world's hundreds of thousands of years of existence, it is easy to feel dwarfed into insignificance; when we think of the slowness of human progress, it is easy to become discouraged into pessimism. There is comfort in the thought of a God who has all eternity to work in. It is only against the background of eternity that things appear in their true proportions and assume their real value.

(ii) We can also see from this passage that time is always to be regarded as an opportunity. As Peter saw it, the years God gave the world were a further opportunity for men to repent and turn to him. Every day which comes to us is a gift of mercy. It is an opportunity to develop ourselves; to render some service to our fellow-men; to take one step nearer to God.

(iii) Finally, there is another echo of a truth which so often lies in the background of New Testament thought. God, says Peter, does not wish any to perish. God, says Paul, has shut them all up together in unbelief, that he might have mercy on all (*Romans* 11 : 32). Timothy in a tremendous phrase speaks of God who will have all men to be saved (1 *Timothy* 2: 4). Ezekiel hears God ask: "Have I any pleasure in the death of the wicked, and not rather that he should return from his way and live?" (*Ezekiel* 18: 23).

Ever and again there shines in Scripture the glint of the larger hope. We are not forbidden to believe that somehow and some time the God who loves the world will bring the whole world to himself.

THE DREADFUL DAY

2 *Peter* 3: 10

> But when it does come, the Day of the Lord will come as a thief and in it the heavens will pass away with a crackling roar; the stars will blaze and melt; and the earth and all its works will disappear.

It inevitably happens that a man has to speak and think in the terms which he knows. That is what Peter is doing here. He is speaking of the New Testament doctrine of the Second Coming of Jesus Christ, but he is describing it in terms of the Old Testament doctrine of the Day of the Lord.

The Day of the Lord is a conception which runs all through the prophetic books of the Old Testament. The Jews saw time in terms of two ages—*this present age,* which is wholly bad and past remedy; and *the age to come,* which is the golden age of God. How was the one to turn into the other? The change could not come about by human effort or by a process of

development, for the world was on the way to destruction. As
the Jews saw it, there was only one way in which the change
could happen; it must be by the direct intervention of God.
The time of that intervention they called the Day of the Lord.
It was to come without warning. It was to be a time when the
universe was shaken to its foundations. It was to be a time when
the judgment and obliteration of sinners would come to pass
and, therefore, it would be a time of terror. "Behold the Day
of the Lord comes, cruel with wrath and fierce anger, to make
the earth a desolation and to destroy its sinners from it"
(*Isaiah* 13: 9). "The Day of the Lord is coming, it is near, a
day of darkness and of gloom, a day of clouds and of thick
darkness" (*Joel* 2: 1, 2). "A day of wrath is that day, a day of
distress and anguish, a day of ruin and devastation, a day of
darkness and gloom, a day of clouds and thick darkness"
(*Zephaniah* 1: 14–18). "The sun shall be turned to darkness
and the moon to blood, before the great and terrible day of
the Lord comes" (*Joel* 2: 30, 31). "The stars of the heaven and
their constellations shall not give their light; the sun will be
dark at its rising and the moon will not shed its light. . . .
Therefore I will make the heavens tremble, and the earth will
be shaken out of its place, at the wrath of the Lord of hosts in
the day of his fierce anger" (*Isaiah* 13: 10–13).

What Peter and many of the New Testament writers did was
to identify the Old Testament pictures of the Day of the Lord
with the New Testament conception of the Second Coming of
Jesus Christ. Peter's picture here of the Second Coming of
Jesus is drawn in terms of the Old Testament picture of the
Day of the Lord.

He uses one very vivid phrase. He says that the heavens will
pass away with a crackling roar (*roizēdon*). That word is used
for the whirring of a bird's wings in the air, for the sound a
spear makes as it hurtles through the air, for the crackling of
the flames of a forest fire.

We need not take these pictures with crude literalism. It is
enough to note that Peter sees the Second Coming as a time
of terror for those who are the enemies of Christ.

One thing has to be held in the memory. The whole conception of the Second Coming is full of difficulty. But this is sure—there comes a day when God breaks into every life, for there comes a day when we must die; and for that day we must be prepared. We may say what we will about the Coming of Christ as a future event; we may feel it is a doctrine we have to lay on one side; but we cannot escape from the certainty of the entry of God into our own experience.

THE MORAL DYNAMIC

2 *Peter* 3: 11–14

> Since these things are going to be dissolved like that, what kind of people ought you to be, living a life of constant holiness and true piety, you who are eagerly awaiting and doing your best to hasten on the Day of the Lord, by whose action the heavens will burn and be dissolved and the stars blaze and melt! For it is new heavens and a new earth, as he promised, for which we wait, in which righteousness has its home. So, then, beloved, since these are the things for which you eagerly wait, be eager to be found by him at peace, without spot and blemish.

THE one thing in which Peter is supremely interested is the moral dynamic of the Second Coming. If these things are going to happen and the world is hastening to judgment, obviously a man must live a life of piety and of holiness. If there are to be a new heaven and a new earth and if that heaven and earth are to be the home of righteousness, obviously a man must seek with all his mind and heart and soul and strength to be fit to be a dweller in that new world. To Peter, as Moffatt puts it, "it was impossible to give up the hope of the advent without ethical deterioration." Peter was right. If there is nothing in the nature of a Second Coming, nothing in the nature of a goal to which the whole creation moves, then life is going nowhere. That, in fact, was the heathen position. If there is no goal, either for the world or for the individual life, other than extinction, certain attitudes to life become well-nigh inevitable. These attitudes emerge in heathen epitaphs.

(i) If there is nothing to come, a man may well decide to make what he can of the pleasures of this world. So we come on an epitaph like this: "I was nothing: I am nothing. So thou who art still alive, eat, drink, and be merry."

(ii) If there is nothing to live for, a man may well be utterly indifferent. Nothing matters much if the end of everything is extinction, in which a man will not even be aware that he is extinguished. So we come on such an epitaph as this: "Once I had an existence; now I have none. I am not aware of it. It does not concern me."

(iii) If there is nothing to live for but extinction and the world is going nowhere, there can enter into life a kind of lostness. Man ceases to be in any sense a pilgrim for there is nowhere to which he can make pilgrimage. He must simply drift in a kind of lostness, coming from nowhere and on the way to nowhere. So we come on an epigram like that of Callimachus. "Charidas, what is below?" "Deep darkness." "But what of the paths upward?" "All a lie." "And Pluto?" (The God of the underworld). "Mere talk." "Then we're lost." Even the heathen found a certain almost intolerable quality in a life without a goal.

When we have stripped the doctrine of the Second Coming of all its temporary and local imagery, the tremendous truth it conserves is that life is going somewhere—and without that conviction there is nothing to live for.

HASTENING THE DAY

2 *Peter* 3: 11–14 (*continued*)

THERE is in this passage still another great conception. Peter speaks of the Christian as not only eagerly awaiting the Coming of Christ but as actually hastening it on. The New Testament tells us certain ways in which this may be done.

(i) It may be done by *prayer*. Jesus taught us to pray: "Thy

Kingdom come" (*Matthew* 6: 10). The earnest prayer of the Christian heart hastens the coming of the King. If in no other way, it does so in this—that he who prays opens his own heart for the entry of the King.

(ii) It may be done by *preaching*. Matthew tells us that Jesus said, "And this gospel of the Kingdom will be preached throughout the whole world, as a testimony to all nations; and then the end will come" (*Matthew* 24: 14). All men must be given the chance to know and to love Jesus Christ before the end of creation is reached. The missionary activity of the Church is the hastening of the coming of the King.

(iii) It may be done by *penitence* and *obedience*. Of all things this would be nearest to Peter's mind and heart. The Rabbis had two sayings: "It is the sins of the people which prevent the coming of the Messiah. If the Jews would genuinely repent for one day, the Messiah would come." The other form of the saying means the same: "If Israel would perfectly keep the law for one day, the Messiah would come." In true penitence and in real obedience a man opens his own heart to the coming of the King and brings nearer that coming throughout the world. We do well to remember that our coldness of heart and our disobedience delay the coming of the King.

PERVERTERS OF SCRIPTURE

2 *Peter* 3: 15, 16

Regard the Lord's willingness to wait as an opportunity of salvation, as indeed our beloved brother Paul has written to us, in the wisdom which has been given to him, and as he says in all his letters, when he touches on these subjects, letters which contain some things which are difficult to understand, things which those who lack knowledge and a firm foundation in the faith twist, as they do the rest of the Scriptures, to their own destruction.

PETER here cites Paul as teaching the same things as he himself teaches. It may be that he is citing Paul as agreeing that a pious and a holy life is necessary in view of the approaching Second Coming of the Lord. More likely, he is citing Paul as agreeing that the fact that God withholds his hand is to be regarded not as indifference on God's part but as an opportunity to repent and to accept Jesus Christ. Paul speaks of those who despise the riches of God's goodness and forbearance and patience, forgetting that his kindness is designed to lead a man to repentance (*Romans* 2: 4). More than once Paul stresses the forbearance and the patience of God (*Romans* 3: 25; 9: 22). Both Peter and Paul were agreed that the fact that God withholds his hand is never to be used as an excuse for sinning but always as a means of repentance and an opportunity of amendment.

With its reference to Paul and its tinge of criticism of him, this is one of the most intriguing passages in the New Testament. It was this passage which made John Calvin certain that Peter did not himself write *Second Peter* because, he says, Peter would never have spoken about Paul like this. What do we learn from it?

(i) We learn that Paul's letters by this time were known and used throughout the Church. They are spoken of in such a way as to make it clear that they have been collected and published, and that they are generally available and widely read. We are fairly certain that it was about the year A.D. 90 that Paul's letters were collected and published in Ephesus. This means that *Second Peter* cannot have been written before that and, therefore, cannot be the work of Peter, who was martyred in the middle sixties of the century.

(ii) It tells us that Paul's letters have come to be regarded as Scripture. The misguided men twist them as they do the other Scriptures. This again goes to prove that *Second Peter* must come from a time well on in the history of the early Church, for it would take many generations for the letters of Paul to rank alongside the Scriptures of the Old Testament.

(iii) It is a little difficult to determine just what the attitude to Paul is in this passage. He is writing "in the wisdom which has been given to him." Bigg says neatly that this phrase can be equally a commendation or a caution! The truth is that Paul suffered the fate of all outstanding men. He had his critics. He suffered the fate of all who fearlessly face and fearlessly state the truth. Some regarded him as great but dangerous.

(iv) There are things in Paul's letters which are hard to understand and which ignorant people twist to their own ruin. The word used for *hard to understand* is *dusnoētos,* which is used of the utterance of an oracle. The utterances of Greek oracles were always ambiguous. There is the classic example of the king about to go to war who consulted the oracle at Delphi and was given the answer: "If you go to war, you will destroy a great nation." He took this as a prophecy that he would destroy his enemies; but it happened that he was so utterly defeated that by going to war he destroyed his own country. This was typical of the dangerous ambiguity of the ancient oracles. It is that very word which Peter uses of the writings of Paul. They have things in them which are as difficult to interpret as the ambiguous utterance of an oracle.

Not only, Peter says, are there things in Paul's writings that are hard to understand; there are things which a man may twist to his own destruction. Three things come immediately to mind. Paul's doctrine of *grace* was twisted into an excuse and even a reason for sin (*Romans* 6). Paul's doctrine of Christian *freedom* was twisted into an excuse for unchristian licence (*Galatians* 5: 13). Paul's doctrine of *faith* was twisted into an argument that Christian action was unimportant, as we see in *James* (*James* 2: 14–26).

G. K. Chesterton once said that orthodoxy was like walking along a narrow ridge; one step to either side was a step to disaster. Jesus is God and man; God is love and holiness; Christianity is grace and morality; the Christian lives in this world and lives in the world of eternity. Overstress either side of these great two-sided truths, and at once destructive heresy emerges. One of the most tragic things in life is when a man twists Christian truth and Holy Scripture into an excuse and even a reason for doing what he wants to do instead of taking them as guides for doing what God wants him to do.

A FIRM FOUNDATION
AND A CONTINUAL GROWTH

2 Peter 3: 17, 18

As far as you are concerned, beloved, you have been forewarned. You must, therefore, be on your guard not to be carried away by the error of lawless men and so to fall from your own foundation; rather, you must see to it that you grow in grace and in understanding of our Lord and Saviour Jesus Christ.

To him be glory both now and to the day of eternity.

IN conclusion Peter tells us certain things about the Christian life.

(i) The Christian is a man who is forewarned. That is to say, he cannot plead ignorance. He knows the right way and its rewards; he knows the wrong way and its disasters. He has no right to expect an easy way, for he has been told that Christianity means a cross, and he has been warned that there will always be those who are ready to attack and to pervert the faith. To be forewarned is to be forearmed; but to be forewarned is also a grave responsibility, for he who knows the right and does the wrong is under a double condemnation.

(ii) The Christian is a man with a basis for life. He ought to be rooted and founded in the faith. There are certain things of which he is absolutely certain. James Agate once declared that his mind was not a bed to be made and remade but that on certain things it was finally made up. There is a certain inflexibility in the Christian life; there is a certain basis of belief which never changes. The Christian will never cease to believe that, "Jesus Christ is Lord" (*Philippians* 2: 11); and he will never cease to be aware that there is laid on him the duty of making his life fit his belief.

(iii) The Christian is a man with a developing life. The inflexibility of the Christian life is not the rigidity of death. The Christian must daily experience the wonder of grace, and daily grow in the gifts which grace can bring; and he must daily enter more and more deeply into the wonder which is in Jesus Christ.

It is only on a firm foundation that a great building can tower into the air; and it is only because it has a deep root that a great tree can reach out to the sky with its branches. The Christian life is at once a life with a firm foundation and with an ever outward and upward growth.

And so the letter finishes by giving glory to Christ, both now and to the end of time.

FURTHER READING

James

E. C. Blackman, *The Epistle of St James* (Tch; *E*)
J. B. Mayor, *The Epistle of St James* (MmC; *G*)
C. L. Mitton, *The Epistle of St James*
J. Moffatt, *The General Epistles: James, Peter and Jude* (MC; *E*)
J. H. Ropes, *St James* (ICC; *G*)

1 Peter

F. W. Beare, *The First Epistle of Peter* (*G*)
E. Best, *1 Peter* (NCB; *E*)
C. Bigg, *St Peter and St Jude* (ICC; *G*)
C. E. B. Cranfield, *1 and 2 Peter and Jude* (Tch; *E*)
E. G. Selwyn, *The First Epistle of St Peter* (MmC; *G*)

2 Peter

C. Bigg, *St Peter and St Jude* (ICC; *G*)
C. E. B. Cranfield, *1 and 2 Peter and Jude* (Tch; *E*)
J. B. Mayor, *The Second Epistle of St Peter and the Epistle of St Jude* (MmC; *G*)
J. Moffatt, *The General Epistles: James, Peter and Jude* (MC; *E*)

Abbreviations

ICC : International Critical Commentary
MC : Moffatt Commentary
MmC: Macmillan Commentary
NCB : New Century Bible
Tch : Torch Commentary

E : English Text
G : Greek Text

THE DAILY STUDY BIBLE

Published in 18 Volumes